Our Past and Future Hope

Reintroducing a Traditional Faith-Building Eschatology

Jason Giles

Reforming Eschatology Books

Contents

Introduction

Over a decade ago, I sat down alone in a quiet place to read the Bible yet again as I tried (and often failed) to do faithfully each day. Another day, another devotion. Admittedly, at this point it was primarily out of duty- an obligation I felt committed to ever since I got saved as a kid. Even though I prayed for understanding before I started, the last thing I expected was to be surprised by God's Word. You see, I had read the entire Bible at least twice by now, and growing up in a faithful Christian family that never missed church, I naively felt like I understood it all well enough.

Yet here I was going through the book of Daniel, having just read chapter nine with the 'seventy weeks' prophecy. Frankly, I was sick of it, and I finally had to admit that I had no idea what any of it meant. In desperation, I broke down and decided to do the unthinkable- search for a commentary on the internet. This was a bold move for me, having been conditioned to be wary of commentaries. Why do we need to hear the opinion of some smarmy academic, lording their knowledge over us in their ivory tower, all head and no heart? We have the Holy Spirit to show us what it means, and that's all we really need, right?

This was my 'Ethiopian eunuch' moment:

Now an angel of the Lord said to Philip, "Go south to the road—the desert road—that goes down from Jerusalem to Gaza." So he started out, and on his way he met an Ethiopian eunuch, an important official in charge of all the treasury of the Kandake (which means "queen of the Ethiopians"). This man had gone to Jerusalem to worship, and on his way home was sitting in his chariot reading the Book of Isaiah the prophet. The Spirit told Philip, "Go to that chariot and stay near it."

Then Philip ran up to the chariot and heard the man reading Isaiah the prophet. "Do you understand what you are reading?" Philip asked.

"How can I," he said, "unless someone explains it to me?" So he invited Philip to come up and sit with him. (Acts 8:26-31)

I was finally ready to humbly admit that I did not understand what I was reading, and that I wouldn't be able to unless someone explained it to me.

The commentary I ended up stumbling upon was by a man named Fred Miller. He explained the historical interpretation of the Seventy Week prophecy, and how this astounding prediction was fulfilled with the ministry and death of the Messiah, Jesus Christ.[1] As a matter of fact, the timing in this prophecy is so precise, that the Jewish calendar was inexplicably changed centuries ago by over 150 years from the Biblical dating of the world, and now it points to the failed messianic rebellion of Bar Kokhba in 132 AD.[2] Anything, anyone other than Jesus the Nazarene!

I was floored, and my jaw was literally hanging open. How did I miss this before? Wasn't this just another prophecy that we were waiting on God to fulfill? Like many other prophecies in the Old and New Testaments, I was taught that we were waiting for the Rapture, when Jesus would take us away from this evil world, and then Antichrist would appear. Seven short but devastating years later, we would return with the victorious Son of Man to destroy his enemies and rule with him for 1000 years. How could this passage be fulfilled already?

But it made so much more sense now. The message delivered to Daniel by the angel Gabriel was suddenly cohesive, instead of being split apart as I had been taught before. The beginning and end of the prophecy were clearly and spectacularly marked by historical events, all recorded in other parts of the Bible!

The Messiah came precisely when this passage predicted he would come, and he was killed just as it said he would be. And bittersweetly, Jerusalem and the Second Temple (still future from Daniel) would once again face devastation, even as Daniel was hoping and praying for its restoration (we will go over Daniel chapter nine in more detail later on in the book).

A Dialogue with Tradition

As hesitant as I was to consult a commentary, Miller did not provide some kind of *gnosis* or secret knowledge to unlock the meaning of the text. Instead of continuing to simply have a two-way conversation- just 'me and the Bible'- I had now brought in a third party: the tradition of biblical interpretation. In his book *Reading the Bible with Giants: How 2000 Years of Biblical Interpretation Can Shed New Light on Old Texts*, Dr. Parris puts it this way:

> As members of the church this three-way dialogue is very significant. After all, we claim that God's interactions with humanity are recorded in this book we call the Bible and that our personal faith and Christian community rest on it. We believe that through the illumination of the Holy Spirit, God uses this book to inspire, console, correct, and guide us. If we claim that God speaks to us through the Bible we should be open to what others claim God has revealed to them. Especially if we consider that in the two thousand years since the church was inaugurated there have been countless individuals who had sharper minds, were better readers, and were more devout than we are. We should be grateful to sit at their feet![3]

Just as the Ethiopian eunuch invited Phillip to sit with him and explain how Jesus fulfilled the suffering servant passages in Isaiah, I had invited the history and tradition of biblical interpretation to give me their take on Daniel 9. As it turns out, the view I had been taught from childhood was a relatively new idea, not the uniform understanding I had imagined it to be from time immemorial. About 150 years ago a completely different interpretation was taught, and it had been interpreted that way for centuries before then. How could I have known that, unless someone told me?

Please do not get me wrong- there is nothing wrong with the two-way dialogue many of us have with the Scriptures daily. It is a vital part of our personal devotion, and the Holy Spirit speaks through them to guide us. But there are benefits from engaging with our tradition "in a receptive and critical manner—to bring tradition to the table, so to speak, as an active dialogue partner when we read the Bible."[4] We do not simply accept what tradition tells us whole cloth, but we ask questions and learn from the answers: "What have been some of the best interpretations and applications of this particular story? What mistakes have others made when interpreting this passage? Have the rules changed for what counts as a valid interpretation over time? Have others read the text in the same manner as we do today?"[5] Just as the noble Bereans exhaustively searched the Scriptures to make sure that what Paul was preaching to them was true, we also check to ensure that what we're being taught jibes with the historical and grammatical context of the Bible. Having a three-way dialogue with traditional interpretation is simply another tool in the chest for rigorously engaging with God's Word, along with others like historical studies, background, word studies, grammar, narrative analysis, etc.

Sadly, in modern times, committed evangelical Christians have been conditioned to be deeply distrustful of any outside input, shunning anyone and anything that dares to intrude in our one-on-one conversation with the Bible. We are taught to avoid commentaries and be extremely wary of even conservative Christian universities, which are seen as little more than 'apostate factories' where our faith goes to die. We rigorously adhere to the misnomer of *solo scriptura*- our faith is to be informed by the Scriptures alone- instead of *sola scriptura*, in which the Bible is our top authority on issues of doctrine, with tradition and church authority still playing an important but subservient role.

These opposing views of the role of tradition are defined in Timothy Ward's book *Words of Life* as "'Tradition I'... the view that tradition is a tool to aid in the faithful interpretation of Scripture, with Scripture remaining the only source of infallible divine revelation, to which the tradition is always subject."[6] This was the predominant view of the church during its Early Period, and this was the position taken by the Reformers. In the 12th-15th centuries, a different view of tradition was innovated by the Roman Catholic Church called "'Tradition II'. It asserts that there are two distinct sources of divine revelation, Scripture and church tradition, with the latter being handed down either orally or through customary church practices."[7]

In response to these views of tradition, the Anabaptists of the Radical Reformation held to what has been described as "'Tradition 0'. It exalts the individual's interpretation of Scripture over that of the corporate interpretation of past generations of Christians."[8] This was the view relayed to me in my upbringing in the American Evangelical world. Many modern Christians still mistake *sola scriptura* for this view of altogether rejecting tradition, when in truth, the Reformers "had a very positive understanding of tradition."[9]

A Lack of Understanding

We have denied traditional biblical interpretation from entering our dialog with the Scriptures for so long that it has had devastating effects on our interpretation of many passages. Nowhere is this more evident than in our understanding of prophetic and apocalyptic portions of the Bible. We are typically only nominally aware of the modern popular view mentioned above: a secret rapture of the elect, a seven-year tribulation, the triumphant return of Christ, reigning with him for 1000 years. Most of these beliefs are gleaned from popular culture (novels and movies like the *Left Behind* series) rather than the Bible, so we can hardly recognize their scriptural origins. When we encounter prophetic passages we don't understand, our instinct is to assume they are unfulfilled without so much as taking a glance at history or traditional interpretation. "I don't understand this fully because it's still in the future," we tell ourselves.

Assuming so many promises are yet unfulfilled, our individualistic approach to interpretation causes our imaginations to run wild. Fear-driven speculation is evident by our enormous amount of misguided, crapshoot guesses. Antichrist lurks around every corner, and each popular new leader of the opposing political party is accused of being *the one*. Or maybe it's a foreign leader- is he Islamic, or is he European? Nations entering any sort of pact becomes the harbinger of the New World Order in which the Antichrist will rise to power. What's the latest in Israel- aren't they going to rebuild the Temple soon? One more recent egregious example is the mark of the beast: one moment it's a computer chip implanted into our skin, the next it's nanomachines in a vaccine, or maybe it's the latest mobile phone data standard. We give ear to the wildest conspiracies, our eyes glued to the headlines, eager to discover the next possible fulfillment as we're ushered into the apocalypse.

Worst of all, we've lost sight of what God *has* done, and the promises he has already fulfilled. Going back to the example of the Seventy Weeks prophecy in Daniel 9, which was traditionally interpreted as being fulfilled by Christ's mission on earth, and finished with his death: "to finish disobedience, and to make an end of sins, and to make reconciliation for iniquity, and to bring in everlasting righteousness, and to seal up vision and prophecy, and to anoint the most holy" (Daniel 9:24b). The modern popular interpretation pushes these things far into the future, and severs the continuity of the message. Now 69 of the 'weeks' are said to have passed, with a pause of close to 2000 years, and the 70th still to come. This amazing time prophecy completely loses its precision, utterly draining it of the faith-building wonder God intended it to have. When viewing this prophecy through the modern lens, its once powerful message simply whimpers away, becoming yet another perplexing and incomplete prophecy as it gets thrown into the pile with the others.

Ultimately, the burden of our lost vision becomes almost too much to bear. We continue to read the Bible faithfully, but more from duty than awe. We eagerly await the return of our Savior, yet we might start to wonder what the plan really is. Why did he tell us what would happen so far into the future- what is the deal with this 2000-year holding period? In the past, there was said to be 400 years of silence before the coming of the Messiah, when no prophet spoke; today, we have five times that amount. Perhaps I suppressed many of these thoughts out of fear of being irreverent, but if I were honest, a part of me wondered what God is waiting for. Maybe you feel the same, to some degree at least.

Or maybe you've just given up trying to understand these difficult prophecies in Scripture altogether. It's all too mysterious, there are too many conflicting opinions, so much confusion- what's the point in trying to figure it out? We joke that we're 'pan-millennial: it will all pan out in the end.' Besides, many of us know believers that are fixated on the end times, obsessed with trying to pinpoint the identity of the Antichrist, the mark of the beast, or even the date of the return of Christ. So many have insisted on this date or that, this world event is a sign, the next 'blood moon' is *the one*, even extrabiblical phenomena like the end of the Aztec calendar become proof. Time passes, the dates come and go, the supposed Antichrist does his time on the world stage and then fades into obscurity, and every sign ends up becoming just another blip in the end. Each failed prediction becomes another mark of shame on the body of Christ. Why on Earth would we want to be a part of that madness?

Strength for Today and Bright Hope for Tomorrow

It is not so hopeless of course. When we consult the historical biblical interpretation, giving the giants who came before us a seat at the table, letting them have a chance to speak and entering a three-way dialog with them, we can rediscover the wonder and delight of not only the prophetic passages, but all of God's Holy and Powerful Word. When I humbly realized that men and women much better than myself in so many ways have wrestled with the same passages for centuries and came away with brilliant insights, my burden was much lighter- we share the load of interpretation. I was no longer on my own, using *solo scriptura*. Instead, I was now practicing *sola scriptura* as the Reformers intended, with tradition aiding me in interpretation, while the Bible remains our sole, final authority.

By gazing into the Scriptures with God's people beside me, I started to recognize more and more of God's faithfulness to his people throughout history. Our God is the One who keeps his promises to the letter. In fact, some prophecies are fulfilled so precisely that secular scholars insist that they had to have been written after the fact, due to how closely they mirror actual events in history![10] The more I realized this, the more I began to notice a pattern in how God speaks to his people through prophetic Scripture: he never leaves us without an idea of what he intends to accomplish in the world, especially as it pertains to his people. Remember the 400 years of silence I mentioned earlier? It's true that there were no new Scriptures being written in that time (although Maccabees came close), nor was there a prophet speaking in God's name, yet those years were anything but silent. The prophecies in the Book of Daniel give a clear picture of the empires that would rise and fall, the wars they would wage, the persecution and ultimate victory the Jews would go through. They spoke of the Messiah to come, the fate of Jerusalem and the Temple, and the beginning of God's kingdom on Earth.

When they are understood in this way, these prophecies represent 'a small but exact map' of God's plan and providence for his people.[11] Before the 400 years of silence, God provided this map to his people so that their faith would be strengthened as they watched history unfold as told by the God who sees and knows all things, past, present, and future. As I began to see that not all of these prophecies are to be pushed into the future as is commonly taught today, my own faith and hope grew in leaps and bounds when I understood God's faithfulness to his people in the past.

God is consistent, there is 'no shadow of turning in Thee.' Just as God filled the so-called silent years with clear examples of what he intended to accomplish throughout them, he has not snatched this map from us. "Now as Daniel makes up the hiatus or defect of the history of the Old Testament, so the Revelation of John supplies that of the New, by leading us down from Christ's first to his second coming."[12] Revelation is a map to us in the same way that Daniel was a map to God's people before the first coming of Christ. This contradicts what we are taught about Revelation today, however- the most common refrain is that none of it has happened (futurism/dispensationalism), or less commonly that nearly all of it has been fulfilled (preterism/partial-preterism). There is also the teaching that none of it pertains to historical events (idealism). What good is a map that shows us only the destination, but no clear idea of where we are currently? Likewise, the map that shows us only the starting and ending points is nearly as useless, as is the map that only shows us the type of terrain we might expect to encounter along the way. No, God gave us a useful map just as he gave his people before, and "these two books give us the exact plan of a divine history."[13]

A Traditional Interpretation

This book is an introduction to the traditional interpretation of prophecy in Scripture, most often called historicism. A historicist "sees the book of Revelation as a prewritten record of the course of history from the time of John to the end of the world. Fulfillment is thus considered to be in progress at present and has been unfolding for nearly two thousand years."[14] This classical approach was the majority view among Protestants from the time of the Reformation to about the middle of the 19th century, and it is the oldest of the four major developed views of understanding Revelation.[15] "An abbreviated list of the luminaries of the past who took this view would have to include Huss, Wycliffe, Tyndale, Luther, Calvin, Zwingli, Melanchthon, John Knox, Sir Isaac Newton, John Foxe, John Wesley, Jonathan Edwards, George Whitefield, Charles Finney, C. H. Spurgeon, Matthew Henry, Adam Clarke, Albert Barnes, E. B. Elliott, H. Grattan Guinness, and Bishop Thomas Newton."[16]

Because it is an older view, the best historicist writings are over 100 years old at this point. There are modern authors and commentaries, but they are rare and often not very accessible (more resources for studying the historicist view, old and new, can be found at the end of this book). The purpose of this book is to reintroduce an old but wise understanding of biblical prophecy to the general public in the most accessible way possible. I heartily recommend learning about each of the other views of Revelation- futurism, preterism, and idealism- but there are already plenty of other modern resources available to do this (also found at the end of this book). We will also not be delving too deep into the three different millennial views- premillennialism, postmillennialism, and amillennialism- because the Millennium is only explicitly mentioned in one chapter of the Bible (Revelation 20), and besides, historicism is compatible with all three of them.

It is my hope that you will benefit as much as I have from entering a three-way dialog in your study of the Bible and learn by standing on the shoulders of giants. Using traditional interpretation in this way does not mean we blindly accept what we discover, but we engage with theologians from the past (and present, for that matter) using critical thinking. Some might have been strong in one area, and weak or downright wrong in another. We examine their thoughts and insights in light of the context of other Scriptures; we try to understand their own context in the period and area in which they wrote; we identify any connections to our own context. Whether we end up agreeing with them or not, many times we end up learning more about church history, about the development of our beliefs and those of others, and we end up becoming wiser and more empathetic to those around us.

We cannot afford to ignore prophecy in the Bible. According to Peter,

> And we have the prophetic word more fully confirmed, to which you will do well to pay attention as to a lamp shining in a dark place, until the day dawns and the morning star rises in your hearts, knowing this first of all, that no prophecy of Scripture comes from someone's own interpretation. For no prophecy was ever produced by the will of man, but men spoke from God as they were carried along by the Holy Spirit. (2 Peter 1:19-21 ESV).

The book of Revelation promises a blessing to those who read and hear it (Revelation 1:3). We will not start in Revelation, but in the easiest-to-understand and most agreed-upon parts of Daniel, and other parts of the Old and New Testament. It will become clear that God is faithful to his promises as we focus on fulfilled prophecies, and we will become even more confident in our hope as we look at those yet to be fulfilled. In the end, our faith will be bolstered as we look to Jesus, the very center of our past and future hope.

---

1. Fred Miller, "Revelation: a Panorama of the Gospel Age", 200. Available online at http://moellerhaus.com/70week.htm

2. Floyd Nolan Jones, "The Seder Olam Rabbah- Why Jewish Dating is Different", 42-46.
Available online at https://assets.answersingenesis.org/doc/articles/cm/Divided.pdf

3. David Paul Parris, "Reading the Bible with Giants: How 2000 Years of Biblical Interpretation Can Shed New Light on Old Texts", Kindle location 200.

4. Parris, ibid, Kindle location 173.

5. Parris, ibid, Kindle location 200.

6. Heiko Oberman qtd. in Timothy Ward, "Words of Life - Scripture as the Living and Active Word of God", 144.

7. Oberman qtd. in Ward, ibid, 145.

8. Oberman qtd. in Ward, ibid, 148.

9. Alister McGrath, "Historical Theology - An Introduction to the History of Christian Thought", 165.

10. "Daniel 11:1-35 is either the most precise and accurate prophecy of the future, fully demonstrating its divine inspiration, or as Porphyry claimed, it is a dishonest attempt to present history as if prophesied centuries earlier. Modern critics of Daniel have not gone much beyond the basic premise of Porphyry, namely, that such detailed prophecy is impossible, and, there-

fore, absurd and incredible."

John Walvoord, "Daniel- The Key To Prophetic Revelation", Chapter 11.

Available online at https://walvoord.com/article/252#P1649_705536

11. Robert Fleming, "Apocalyptical Key: A Discourse on the Rise and Fall of the Anti-Christ", 90.

    Available online at https://play.google.com/store/books/details?id=zW EJAQAAMAAJ

12. Fleming, ibid, 91.

13. Fleming, ibid, 91.

14. Steve Gregg, "Revelation - Four Views, Revised and Updated", 13.

15. By 'views' I mean 'frameworks', not sub-views of the Millennium (see chapter 12 of this book).

    On the development of the four major views, see Gregg, ibid, 48-55. "...the western fathers of the Ante-Nicene church whose works have survived took a quasi-literal and eschatological approach to the Book of Revelation. They lived, of course, too early in history for them to take a historicist approach, such as that which later arose and which spread the fulfillments of the prophecies over the space of over 1,800 years. Events, which later historicists would view as ancient history, were, in those days, present and future realities. This means that the fathers would have spoken futuristically, even if they were identifying the prophetic events with the same phenomena that historicists, and some preterists, now associate with past fulfillments" (50). Gregg goes on to cover the development of historicism starting in the 9th century, and later modern futurism and preterism in the 16th century.

16. Gregg, ibid, 56.

This book is dedicated to the memory of

Fred P. Miller (May 8, 1931 - Feb. 9, 2018)

For reintroducing me to the traditional interpretation of Daniel and Revelation,

and leading me to "THE master" of it, Albert Barnes.

Chapter One

The Foundation of Apocalyptic Prophecy

Daniel 2

The State of Biblical Prophecy Today

I looked again, and then I saw in my dream that Christian continued his long journey on the narrow path to Mount Zion. Up ahead, he noticed an older veiled person by the name of Prophecy. As Christian approached, the man said in a clear voice, "You must take a map for the journey ahead, for the road to Mount Zion is still very far from here. There are no more guides ahead, except for the Spirit who lights the path directly before you."

"Gladly, sir. What does it cost?" Christian asked.

Prophecy replied, "The map is given freely, but first let me ask: which type of map would you prefer? There is one here that will show you the last seven miles of the journey clearly."

Christian wondered aloud, "The last seven miles… well, how much farther is there to go?"

"Hundreds, at least," said Prophecy. "I have another map that will reveal the next seven miles from here, but then it is blank, except for a picture of the destination."

"That's not much better!" exclaimed Christian. "What else do you have?"

"This one is more like a guide to the terrain, flora, fauna, and creatures you should expect to encounter along the way," replied Prophecy.

Christian began to despair. "None of these are like the maps I'm used to! Please tell me there is one that will show me where I am now, until I reach the destination," he begged.

"Ah, here is one that was sealed, and no one except the Lamb of God himself was able to break its seals! Now it is opened to you, but know this: you will need to know the Master's words well to understand it, and there are parts that only the wise shall understand. You must also be aware of the Master's works in this land, and his careful provision for his bride. There are monuments along the way, erected by those who have gone before you. Heed them, and the map shall serve you well the entire way."

*G*od never leaves his people without direction. "Surely the Sovereign Lord does nothing without revealing his plan to his servants the prophets" (Amos 3:7). Yet at one point in history, during the exile and postexilic period of the Jews- up to the first coming of Christ- there was said to be a time without prophets.[1] There was no one with the authority to say, "Thus saith the Lord," who encouraged, rebuked, and shared God's future plans for his people for nearly 400 years. These are sometimes called 'the 400 years of silence.'

Even still, *God never leaves his people without direction.* Though there was no prophet in the land, our sovereign God left his people with a grand list of what he intended to accomplish in the world throughout the years of silence and beyond. He showed them the world empires that would come and go, and when to expect the founding of his eternal kingdom on Earth. He revealed the future of Jerusalem and the Temple, their restoration, and their second downfall. He warned them of the troubles they would face at the hands of wicked kings, yet ultimately prevailing. He not only told them about the coming of the Anointed One, the Messiah, but also gave them a clear time of when to expect him. He showed them the future of wars between kingdoms in such detail that secular historians today insist it had to be written after they happened. Such scholars do not know the power of our God, who "reveals deep and hidden things" (Daniel 2:22).

In this way, biblical prophecy is like a map. To the original audience who receives it, it predicts the future. For the Jews before Christ, the Book of Daniel was their map during the years of silence. As time passed and passages were fulfilled, it eventually became a divine history. We are blessed to be able to study this divine history and see God's faithfulness to his promises. We know that we can count on his future promises because of this.

God never leaves his people without direction. Here we are nearly 2000 years after Christ ascended into heaven, and the biblical canon has been closed for centuries. There are no new prophets with the authority to say, "Thus saith the Lord," who confirm their words with power and miracles. These times can be said to be similar to the years of silence that Jews faced for centuries before the coming of Christ. Yet just as before, God has left us with another grand list of what he intends to accomplish in the world throughout the history of his church. He shows us the rise and fall of the final worldly empire, and the church's victory over paganism. He reveals the terrible union of boastful, tyrannical leaders in the church and civil authorities in the state that oppose God's people. He tells us about the rise of an oppressive power in the East and its deadly campaigns over a large part of the world. He shares with us the fate of the church, from its time of protection in the wilderness to its eventual triumph as God punishes her enemies. All of this is done in a similar awe-inspiring fashion as before, so that even secular history books give an eerily parallel account to God's Word.

We have been given a map just as before, yet most Christians in the West have forgotten how their ancestors read it. We are now told that it reveals the distant future, and that none of the events it describes have come to pass these nearly two millennia since it was written for us. Or sometimes it is taught that it was made purely for the use of the original audience, and that nearly all of its promises were fulfilled in the century it was inked. But as careful study reveals, this is not how the map that was given to the Jews before their years of silence functioned at all. To understand the hope that God's people clung to when there were no prophets in the land- to learn how to read our own map- we need to take a hard look at the promises that were fulfilled in the divine history before the first coming of the Messiah.

The best place to start this journey is the first prophecy given to us in Daniel, arguably the easiest to understand and one of most agreed upon in the history of interpretation in the church.[2] We will take a quick look at the context and run through a summary of the narrative, then slow down and take a more detailed look at the actual prophecy. After that, we'll analyze how the traditional interpretation differs from the modern one we are typically taught today. This same format will be used for each passage we will look at in the following chapters of this book.

This book is an introduction to the traditional interpretation of prophetic passages in the Bible, not an exhaustive or academic commentary. Any beginner should be able to follow along! But if you'd like to study more, there are many excellent, accessible, and free resources available listed in the appendix. I rely chiefly on the commentaries by Albert Barnes, considered a 'master' of this traditional interpretation, and Fred Miller, one of the few modern authors who presented it.

Daniel 2: The Beginning of the Eternal Empire

This is the dream God gave to the Babylonian ruler Nebuchadnezzar, the statue that reveals the four world empires, and the beginning of God's eternal empire that grows to fill the whole Earth.

At this point in history, the Kingdom of Israel had already long been laid to waste by the Assyrians. The Kingdom of Judah had just faced the first of three stages of exile (606 B.C.) by the Babylonians under King Nebuchadnezzar, in which Daniel, Hananiah, Mishael, and Azariah (called Belteshazzar, Shadrach, Meshach, and Abednego by the Babylonians) were among those taken to Babylon. Being sent into training to learn to serve in King Nebuchadnezzar's court, Daniel and his companions had already shown their worth and moral fortitude by obeying God's commands while under tremendous pressure to conform to Babylonian norms. They were recognized by Nebuchadnezzar for the surpassing wisdom and understanding God had given them, and entered into the king's service (Daniel 1).

In the second year of King Nebuchadnezzar's reign, he had dreams that greatly troubled him, and he expected his court "magicians, enchanters, sorcerers and astrologers" (Daniel 2:2) to tell him what the dream was about, as well as its interpretation. Either King Nebuchadnezzar remembered the dream and gave his court the impossible task of telling him what it was to prove themselves, or he could not recall the dream. Either way, when his court explained that "There is no one on earth who can do what the king asks! No king, however great and mighty, has ever asked such a thing of any magician or enchanter or astrologer. What the king asks is too difficult. No one can reveal it to the king except the gods, and they do not live among humans" (Daniel 2:10-11), the king flew into a rage and ordered their deaths.

The commander of the king's guard came to Daniel and his companions to fulfill the king's order and put them to death as well. This was the first they had heard about the king's ordeal, so Daniel asked the king for time to interpret the dream. Daniel and his friends prayed to God for mercy about this mysterious dream, so that they wouldn't be put to death with the rest of the wise men. God reveals the mystery to Daniel, and he praises the God of heaven:

> Praise be to the name of God for ever and ever;
> wisdom and power are his.
> He changes times and seasons;
> he deposes kings and raises up others.
> He gives wisdom to the wise
> and knowledge to the discerning.
> He reveals deep and hidden things;
> he knows what lies in darkness,
> and light dwells with him.
> I thank and praise you, God of my ancestors:
> You have given me wisdom and power,
> you have made known to me what we asked of you,
> you have made known to us the dream of the king. (Daniel 2:20-23)

What a beautiful prayer! God is sovereign, and the fate of kings and nations is under his control. Additionally, our God does not leave us in the dark, but graciously reveals his plans for the human race, even to pagan kings. Daniel tells him, "No wise man, enchanter, magician or diviner can explain to the king the mystery he has asked about, but there is a God in heaven who reveals mysteries. He has shown King Nebuchadnezzar what will happen in days to come" (Daniel 2:27-28).

History Looks Like a Statue

Daniel tells Nebuchadnezzar his dream:

> "Your Majesty looked, and there before you stood a large statue—an enormous, dazzling statue, awesome in appearance. The head of the statue was made of pure gold, its chest and arms of silver, its belly and thighs of bronze, its legs of iron, its feet partly of iron and partly of baked clay. While you were watching, a rock was cut out, but not by human hands. It struck the statue on its feet of iron and clay and smashed them. Then the iron, the clay, the bronze, the silver and the gold were all broken to pieces and became like chaff on a threshing floor in the summer. The wind swept them away without leaving a trace. But the rock that struck the statue became a huge mountain and filled the whole earth." (Daniel 2:31-35)

This is the vision without interpretation. Thankfully it is interpreted for us by Daniel in the next part of the chapter. But before we move onto that, a few notes about the vision that might not be apparent at first:

- *The rock was cut out of a mountain* - The description says the rock was cut out, but out of what? Later in verse 45, Daniel says, "This is the meaning of the vision of the rock cut out of a mountain...". Albert Barnes notes that this is also expressed in the Latin and Greek translations of this passage. "The vision appears to have been that of a colossal image 'standing on a plain' in the vicinity of a mountain, standing firm, until, by some unseen agency, and in an unaccountable manner, a stone became detached from the mountain, and was made to impinge against it."[3]

- *The size and meaning of 'the rock cut out, but not by human hands' -* The word translated as rock does not tell us the size of it, but it seems to be implied that it was surprisingly small for how much damage it did to the statue, especially in that it ground the statue down to 'chaff.' As for not being cut out by human hands, it moved on its own. It was detached from the mountain and projected at the statue, but not by anything that could be seen.[4]

- *It struck the statue -* The statue was likely struck once in the feet and fell into pieces, but then repeatedly struck until it became like chaff or fine dust that blew away. It was a longer process of continual striking that ground the pieces to powder. The reason for this is that the word 'struck' used here is nearly identical to the Hebrew term (Daniel 2 is primarily written in Aramaic) for clapping hands, as in Psalms 98:8, Isaiah 55:12, and Ezekiel 25:6. The word for pieces is also not just fragments, but 'ground to powder,' like the golden calf idol in Exodus 32:20.[5]

And now for the interpretation by Daniel:

"This was the dream, and now we will interpret it to the king. Your Majesty, you are the king of kings. The God of heaven has given you dominion and power and might and glory; in your hands he has placed all mankind and the beasts of the field and the birds in the sky. Wherever they live, he has made you ruler over them all. You are that head of gold.

"After you, another kingdom will arise, inferior to yours. Next, a third kingdom, one of bronze, will rule over the whole earth. Finally, there will be a fourth kingdom, strong as iron—for iron breaks and smashes everything—and as iron breaks things to pieces, so it will crush and break all the others. Just as you saw that the feet and toes were partly of baked clay and partly of iron, so this will be a divided kingdom; yet it will have some of the strength of iron in it, even as you saw iron mixed with clay. As the toes were partly iron and partly clay, so this kingdom will be partly strong and partly brittle. And just as you saw the iron mixed with baked clay, so the people will be a mixture and will not remain united, any more than iron mixes with clay.

"In the time of those kings, the God of heaven will set up a kingdom that will never be destroyed, nor will it be left to another people. It will crush all those kingdoms and bring them to an end, but it will itself endure forever. This is the meaning of the vision of the rock cut out of a mountain, but not by human hands—a rock that broke the iron, the bronze, the clay, the silver and the gold to pieces.

"The great God has shown the king what will take place in the future. The dream is true and its interpretation is trustworthy." (Daniel 2:36-45)

God gave the pagan king Nebuchadnezzar a vision of the successive empires that would come after his own. The vision gives a picture of the history of world empires that looks like a statue. The majority of interpreters throughout history have agreed on the identity of these empires: The head of gold is Babylon, as told to us by Daniel himself. The chest and arms of silver are Medo-Persia, which succeeds Babylon even in Daniel's time and is mentioned in Daniel 8. The belly and thighs of bronze are Greece, as hinted at in Daniel chapter 10 and also mentioned by name in Daniel 8. The legs of iron and feet mixed with clay is Rome, at first united, later weakened and divided.

The rock is the kingdom of the Messiah, arriving in the time of the Roman Empire, and growing to fill the whole earth. The question is, has this happened yet, or is it still future? There are three reasons we can be confident that this occurred in the time when the Roman empire still existed: (1) it is in harmony with the image given to us in the vision; (2) Jesus preached that the kingdom of God was 'at hand'; (3) the church starts small but is growing to fill the earth.

Harmony with the Vision

The image of the rock hitting the statue around the time of Christ's first advent is the interpretation that harmonizes best with the vision. We see this in how the proportions of the different parts of the statue match the length of time each world empire existed, as Fred Miller demonstrates:

> For the head [Babylon] was barely 69 years (unless you date it from Nebuchadnezzar's first taking of Babylon, which would add a few more years) before the portion of chest and shoulders allotted to the Medo Persians, came and went, consuming some 214 years, from Cyrus to Alexander. If we date the beginning of the Roman Empire at the Battle of Actium, as many do, then the Greek period of the loins stretches 290 years. From that point the legs, and feet, representing the Roman Empire are 511 years long. That would make the upper torso and head be 504 years long and the rest of the body 511 years long. If you will use those proportions you will find that not only did Daniel predict the coming four empires but gave an accurate prediction of their proportionate rules.

> If you used this proportion allowing seven inches for the head, twenty one for the chest, twenty nine from diaphragm to hips, and fifty one from hip joints to feet, you will find that history indeed does match the proportions of a statue. And the church starting in the days of the Roman Empire, with its consequent struggle that saw the old pagan system pass away and Christianity take its place, fits the vision exactly, by the little stone striking the image, chronologically as well as physically in the spot, at or

toward the latter times of that Empire, but before it was divided into ten kingdoms.[6]

On the other hand, if the rock hitting the statue is not yet fulfilled- if the Kingdom of God is interpreted to begin with the Millennium after Christ's second coming- the harmony of the picture given in the vision is shattered. The first four kingdoms are well past gone, so we would be living in the time of 'the toes' now for over 1500 years. The toes of the statue would be over twice as long as the statue is tall! The image below shows just such a grotesque statue from Clarence Larkin, who earnestly tried to illustrate such a timeline (except in truth, the toes would be even longer). [7]

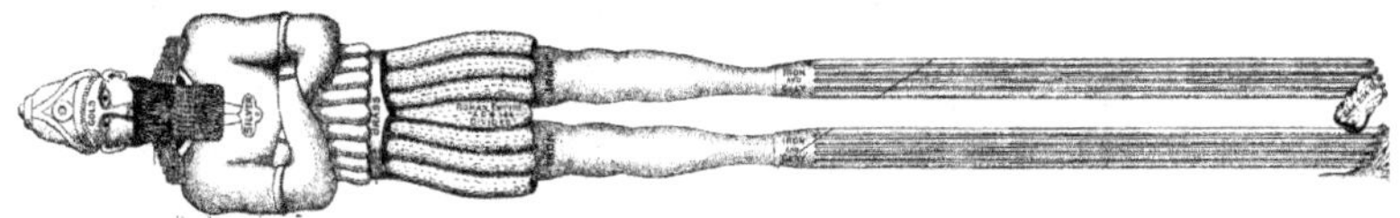

This is not the picture God gives us in the vision. It has obviously been distorted to try to make it fit an interpretation that does not match the vision of history God gave Daniel.

The Kingdom of God is at Hand

Not only does the timing of Christ's establishment of the Church match the rock striking the statue, but he himself proclaimed the beginning of the Kingdom of God with his first coming: "The time is fulfilled, and the kingdom of God is at hand; repent and believe in the gospel" (Mark 1:15, ESV). He also said, "The kingdom of God is not coming in ways that can be observed, nor will they say, 'Look, here it is!' or 'There!' for behold, the kingdom of God is in the midst of you" (Luke 17:20-21, ESV). Barnes says about this verse, "The Messiah has come. John has ushered in the kingdom of God, and you are not to expect the appearance of the Messiah with great pomp and splendor, for he is now among you."[8] In another passage, Jesus says, "But if it is by the Spirit of God that I drive out demons, then the kingdom of God has come upon you" (Matthew 12:28). Jesus is the King of the Kingdom of God, and he had arrived. John the Baptist heralded the Kingdom of God, and Jesus inaugurated it.

Maybe you're thinking that if God's kingdom is here today, it sure doesn't look like much- ruthless tyrants oppress their subjects, nation wars against nation, and in many countries God's own people are still martyred every day. This is due to the 'already, but not yet' aspect of the Kingdom of God you have probably heard of. The *already* aspect is that Jesus has inaugurated, or begun the Kingdom. The *not yet* aspect is the consummation, or finalizing of the Kingdom. Before leaving Earth, Jesus said that "All authority in heaven and on earth has been given to me. Therefore go and make disciples of all nations..." (Matthew 28:18-19). He has not lost his authority; he is still king. Speaking of himself from Psalm 110, Jesus quoted: "'The Lord said to my Lord: sit at my right hand until I put your enemies under your feet'" (Matthew 22:44). In Psalm 2 it says, "He said to me, "You are my son; today I have become your father. Ask me, and I will make the nations your inheritance, the ends of the earth your possession. You will break them with a rod of iron; you will dash them to pieces like pottery" (Psalm 2:7-9). The time is coming when Jesus returns as the conquering Son of Man, under whom every knee shall bow, and every tongue will confess as Lord.

In the meantime, the Kingdom has begun with the coming of the meek and lowly Lamb of God, just as he said it would. It is the perfect picture of a little stone striking a huge and imposing statue, breaking it to pieces, and grinding it to powder. The Kingdom has been inaugurated- it is here, now- and we are citizens of it. We eagerly await the consummation of the Kingdom, the day when all people will declare Jesus is Lord. While we wait, we obey the King's command, making disciples, and watching God's Kingdom grow to fill the whole Earth.

The Mountain that Fills the Earth

The rock that hits the statue is not a large one- the vision is astonishing in that such a little stone can bring down a giant statue, grinding it down to chaff that blows away with the wind. This stone grows and becomes a huge mountain that fills the whole Earth. Daniel says that this image symbolizes the Kingdom that God sets up "that will never be destroyed, nor will it be left to another people. It will crush all those kingdoms and bring them to an end, but it will itself endure forever" (Daniel 2:44). The world empires are not immediately destroyed, but in the end they are nowhere to be found, replaced by the Eternal Kingdom.

As we have seen, the vision of the statue foretold God's Kingdom beginning in the time of the Roman Empire, when Christ came to Earth. We also know that in the Gospels, Christ preached that the Kingdom had come with him and all authority was his. The vision is also accurate in the way that it shows God's Kingdom growing from a little rock to a mountain that will eventually take over the whole world.

Jesus was not the warrior King that the Jews had anticipated. They expected the conquering Son of Man who would throw off Roman oppression and set up an earthly kingdom. When the Pharisees asked Jesus when they could expect this earthly Messianic kingdom, Jesus replied, "The kingdom of God is not coming in ways that can be observed, nor will they say, 'Look, here it is!' or 'There!' for behold, the kingdom of God is in the midst of you" (Luke 17:20-21, ESV). They would not see the earthly kingdom they expected, yet the King was standing right there before them. Even John the Baptist began to wonder, sending his disciples to ask Jesus, "'Are you the one who is to come, or should we expect someone else?'" (Luke 7:20). Standing broken and bloody before Pilate, Jesus said "'My kingdom is not of this world. If it were, my servants would fight to prevent my arrest by the Jewish leaders. But now my kingdom is from another place" (John 18:36). Just as the little rock was cut from the mountain without human agency, God's kingdom had arrived 'from another place.' Instead of coming as the vengeful conquering king, he tried to explain to his disciples that he had to suffer and die, just as Isaiah and other prophets had foretold. The Kingdom of God was beginning in a way no one expected it to.

The Kingdom of God also grew in a way that no one expected. Christians did not form armies and bear weapons against the Roman Empire, taking power by force. Theirs was a counter-cultural revolution, "a radical change in the way human society thought of the individual, the family, work, religion, community, attitudes toward life and death, and even government."[9] The growth was slow but sure over centuries:

> Beginning with the precedent set by Nero in Rome in the midsixties of the first century, Roman law increasingly targeted Christians, and especially the leaders of the Church. By the end of the first century, Christians were tortured and executed simply for admitting to being followers of Christ... In spite of the persecution, the Church grew steadily throughout its first three centuries, until there were some urban areas with a Christian majority, and Christians could be found among the ranks of the poor and the rich, even in the imperial court. By the end of the fourth century, Christianity had become the official religion of the Roman Empire.[10]

No amount of persecution or human effort could stop God's Kingdom from expanding. It grows to this day, to the point where there are now more Christians in the global South than in the West. The growth continues in Africa, Asia, Latin America, and Oceania.[11] One day, The Kingdom of God will be like a vast mountain filling the entire world, and every nation, tribe, people, and language will worship the conquering King.

Traditional Vs. Modern Interpretation

Throughout this chapter, we've seen that the most cohesive understanding of the vision of the rock breaking the statue fits with the first advent of Christ-the timing of the world empires fits the proportions of the statue; the Gospels are full of Christ declaring that the Kingdom of God had arrived with him; Christians collectively further the Kingdom as the Church, which has steadily grown and continues to grow.

Alternatively, the modern understanding pushes the idea that the statue still stands, even if the toes are getting kind of long. But ignoring that unsightly part of the picture, Jesus is still the rock that will strike them, but with his second coming, not the first. The modern futurist interpretation is that the Kingdom of God begins when Christ reigns personally on Earth, during the Millennium mentioned in Revelation 20. The empire he is said to strike will be a future alliance of many nations, or a new world order of some sort. This interpretation is unnecessarily forced onto prophecies like this one in order to bolster a similar interpretation of Revelation.

What is gained, and what is lost by doing violence to the vision of the statue, pushing it into the future? It becomes another piece of evidence of the future glory of Jesus' consummation of the Kingdom, at the cost of de-emphasizing his first advent and the inauguration of the Kingdom. Take the *already, but not yet* principle- the *already* is lost, and the *not yet* aspect of the Kingdom is all that's left. There's not much to do other than wait patiently for the fulfillment of the strange and mysterious vision, hoping for the Kingdom of God to start soon.

But what if the traditional understanding of this prophecy is true? First off, the harmony of the vision is restored- the picture and interpretation God gave Daniel make perfect sense! God's Eternal Empire began in such an other-worldly, unassuming manner, breaking onto the scene right on time in the midst of the pompous and imposing Roman Empire. The vision becomes an amazing testimony of the importance of Christ's first advent, and how the Kingdom of God truly was in our midst, just as he testified. The rule of the King of Kings has begun, and all authority in heaven and on earth has been given to him.

Secondly, we as citizens of the Kingdom have important work to do in helping God's kingdom to grow. The King left us with commands before he left: to go and make disciples of all nations. We do not stand by merely hoping and waiting for God's Kingdom to start- it began long ago, and it has grown so much already. In the preface of Dynamic Diversity, author Bruce Milne describes a 'wave of worship' that travels across the globe every Sunday, starting at the South Pacific islands and ending at the South Sea islands, passing through every continent and nation in between.[12] Between one and two billion Christians are united in this international celebration each week, representing a vast diversity of forms, styles, shapes, colors, and ages, all focused on the King of Kings, Jesus Christ: "What ranges of generation and gender, language and culture, customs and worship styles, social status and wealth indices, educational levels and forms of employment; what degrees of freedom, involving in some places intrusive restrictions and even persecution; what varieties of personal faith stories, and levels of comprehension and commitment!"[13] The King is alive, and there is much to celebrate as well as work to be done as we await his return and the consummation of the Kingdom.

---

1. J. Julius Scott Jr., "Jewish Backgrounds of the New Testament", 111.

2. Fred Miller, "Revelation: A Panorama of the Gospel Age", 27. Available online at http://moellerhaus.com/rev666.htm

3. Albert Barnes, "Notes, Critical, Illustrative, and Practical", Daniel 2:34. Available online at https://www.studylight.org/commentaries/eng/bnb/daniel-2.html

4. Barnes, ibid, Daniel 2:34.

5. Barnes, ibid, Daniel 2:34.

6. Miller, ibid, 29.

7. Clarence Larkin, "Daniel and Revelation Compared". Available online at https://www.blueletterbible.org/assets-v3/images/bibleMedia/larkin/c74.jpg
Fred Miller writes that "if the proper proportions were used it would take at least another page to draw the toes, even if the artist's view of history were used!" (ibid, 280).
Available online at http://moellerhaus.com/statue.htm

8. Barnes, ibid, Luke 17:21.

9. Mike Aquilina and James Papandrea, "Seven Revolutions, How Christianity Changed the World and Can Change It Again", 11.

10. Aquilina and Papandrea, ibid, 16.

11. Gina Zurlo, Todd Johnson, and Peter Crossing, "World Christianity and Mission 2020: Ongoing Shift to the Global South", 10.
Available online at https://journals.sagepub.com/doi/full/10.1177/2396939319880074

12. Bruce Milne, "Dynamic Diversity, The New Humanity Church for Today and Tomorrow", 9

13. Milne, ibid, 11.

Chapter Two

Evidence of God's Past Faithfulness

Daniel 8 and 11

Our God is sovereign, the author of the past, present, and future. He knows what will happen before it comes to pass. As Daniel testified, "he changes times and seasons; he deposes kings and raises up others" (Daniel 2:21). He also shares this knowledge with us, to prove his great power and strengthen our faith. As we saw in the last chapter, God gave his people a vision of the world empires that would rise and fall, and foretold the beginning of his Eternal Empire that would grow to fill the whole earth, replacing those empires and enduring forever. This began with the head of gold- Babylon- who had brought the Jews into captivity. After that were the chest and arms of silver- the Medes and Persians- who sent the Jews home to rebuild Jerusalem. Next was the belly and thighs of bronze- Greece. God gave Daniel visions of what would happen to the Jews in the time of the Grecian Kingdom and of a specific king who would persecute the faithful. But God assured his people that they would endure, giving them a play-by-play story of the events that would eventually lead to their restoration.

We are blessed to have these events recorded, now a divine history, so that our faith might be built up. The time prophecy in Daniel chapter 8 and the events recorded in chapter 11 are so precise that secular scholars in centuries past and to the present day insist that they had to have been written after they happened. "One of two things, indeed, is certain - either that this was written after the events here referred to occurred, or that Daniel was inspired. No man by any natural sagacity could have predicted these events with so much accuracy and particularity."[1]

But there are many proofs that Daniel was written and accepted by the post-exilic Jewish community (who carefully scrutinized and guarded inspired writings) well before these events happened. Fred Miller notes the following evidence:[2]

- The Mishnah, the first major written collection of Jewish oral traditions, references the existence and acceptance of the book of Daniel as Scripture before and at the time of Christ.

- Jesus mentions Daniel and quotes from the book of Daniel in Matthew and Mark.

- "The fact that surviving large portions of manuscripts of the book of Daniel were found among the Dead Sea Scrolls is empirical evidence of the existence of the book over 100 years before Christ, which is the time of the writing of the scrolls."[3] This is evidence you can touch with your hands.

- The Septuagint, called the LXX, is the Greek translation of the Hebrew from the Old Testament. "The Hebrew text of Daniel was translated at the time of the translation of the Septuagint Version,-- 285 B.C. This is another empirical evidence of the existence of the book of Daniel, pushing it back to 285 B.C."[4]

- A book was only considered canonical and included in the Old Testament if it was added before the Great Synagogue (in Ezra's time), which met before 400 B.C.

"There was not a time, as we have noted, that Daniel has not been accepted as a part of Jewish Scripture."[5] God gave Daniel very specific visions of what would happen in the future, and they were written down well before their fulfillment. In this chapter, we will look at the divine history of what the Jewish people would face in the time of the Grecian Kingdom.

The Ram and the Goat

Fortunately, the prophecy in Daniel 8 is interpreted for us once again, just like the statue in Daniel 2. Barnes writes, "This is one of the few prophecies in the Scriptures that are explained to the prophets themselves, and it becomes, therefore, important as a key to explain other prophecies of a similar character."[6] It begins right away with the vision:

> 1 In the third year of King Belshazzar's reign, I, Daniel, had a vision, after the one that had already appeared to me. 2 In my vision I saw myself in the citadel of Susa in the province of Elam; in the vision I was beside the Ulai Canal. 3 I looked up, and there before me was a ram with two horns, standing beside the canal, and the horns were long. One of the horns was longer than the other but grew up later. 4 I watched the ram as it charged toward the west and the north and the south. No animal could stand against it, and none could rescue from its power. It did as it pleased and became great.
>
> 5 As I was thinking about this, suddenly a goat with a prominent horn between its eyes came from the west, crossing the whole earth without touching the ground. 6 It came toward the two-horned ram I had seen standing beside the canal and charged at it in great rage. 7 I saw it attack the ram furiously, striking the ram and shattering its two horns. The ram was powerless to stand against it; the goat knocked it to the ground

and trampled on it, and none could rescue the ram from its power. 8 The goat became very great, but at the height of its power the large horn was broken off, and in its place four prominent horns grew up toward the four winds of heaven.

9 Out of one of them came another horn, which started small but grew in power to the south and to the east and toward the Beautiful Land. 10 It grew until it reached the host of the heavens, and it threw some of the starry host down to the earth and trampled on them. 11 It set itself up to be as great as the commander of the army of the Lord; it took away the daily sacrifice from the Lord, and his sanctuary was thrown down. 12 Because of rebellion, the Lord's people and the daily sacrifice were given over to it. It prospered in everything it did, and truth was thrown to the ground.

13 Then I heard a holy one speaking, and another holy one said to him, "How long will it take for the vision to be fulfilled—the vision concerning the daily sacrifice, the rebellion that causes desolation, the surrender of the sanctuary and the trampling underfoot of the Lord's people?"

14 He said to me, "It will take 2,300 evenings and mornings; then the sanctuary will be reconsecrated." (Daniel 8:1-14)

- *Historical context*: Daniel is still in the service of the King of Babylon, now King Belshazzar (see the story of his end and the end of Babylon in Daniel chapter 5). Daniel is likely physically in Susa on government business, but this is not stated explicitly- only that the vision is set there. Susa became the capital of the next empire that was predicted to come after Babylon, namely Persia.

- *"Evenings and mornings":* Some older translations like the King James Version used the word 'days' in verse 14, and so this has been called the 2,300 days prophecy in the past. But the Hebrew word for days (*yôm*) is not in the passage; instead, it is the singular 'evening-morning' (*'ereb-bōqer*). So the New International Version above translates it as evenings and mornings, as well as the ESV, NASB, NLT, and others. This is what connects it to the 'daily sacrifice' in verse 13, which happened twice a day at the Temple- once in the evening, and once in the morning. Rather than being 2,300 days, it is 2,300 sacrifices over 1,150 days.

On to the interpretation by Gabriel:

15 When I, Daniel, had seen the vision, I sought to understand it. And behold, there stood before me one having the appearance of a man. 16 And I heard a man's voice between the banks of the Ulai, and it called, "Gabriel, make this man understand the vision." 17 So he came near where I stood. And when he came, I was frightened and fell on my face. But he said to me, "Understand, O son of man, that the vision is for the time of the end."

18 And when he had spoken to me, I fell into a deep sleep with my face to the ground. But he touched me and made me stand up. 19 He said, "Behold, I will make known to you what shall be at the latter end of the indignation, for it refers to the appointed time of the end. 20 As for the ram that you saw with the two horns, these are the kings of Media and Persia. 21 And the goat is the king of Greece. And the great horn between his eyes is the first king. 22 As for the horn that was broken, in place of which four others arose, four kingdoms shall arise from his nation, but not with his power. 23 And at the latter end of their

kingdom, when the transgressors have reached their limit, a king of bold face, one who understands riddles, shall arise. 24 His power shall be great—but not by his own power; and he shall cause fearful destruction and shall succeed in what he does, and destroy mighty men and the people who are the saints. 25 By his cunning he shall make deceit prosper under his hand, and in his own mind he shall become great. Without warning he shall destroy many. And he shall even rise up against the Prince of princes, and he shall be broken—but by no human hand. 26 The vision of the evenings and the mornings that has been told is true, but seal up the vision, for it refers to many days from now."

27 And I, Daniel, was overcome and lay sick for some days. Then I rose and went about the king's business, but I was appalled by the vision and did not understand it. (Daniel 8:15-27, ESV)

Again, because an interpretation is given to us, the meaning of the vision is clear. Even modern futurist interpreters admit that it has been fulfilled in history, except they write that it *also* has a double 'prophetic' future fulfillment.[7]

As it was explained by the angel Gabriel, the ram symbolizes the united Medo-Persian Empire. The Medes came first, and then Persia came and grew mightier, "so that the name Media became finally almost dropped, and the united kingdom was known in Grecian history as the Persian."[8] So the Medes are represented by the shorter horn, and the Persians by the longer one.

Just as the ram "charged toward the west and the north and the south" (Daniel 8:4), the conquests of the Medo-Persian Empire were in the same directions: "On the west the conquests embraced Babylonia, Mesopotamia, Syria, and Asia Minor; on the north, Colchis, Armenia, Iberia, and the regions around the Caspian Sea; and on the south, Palestine, Ethiopia, Egypt, and Lybia."[9] They were very successful and subdued a large part of the known world. At one point their army was said to be over 2.5 million warriors strong, and "by 480 BCE, the empire accounted for approximately 49.4 million of the world's 112.4 million people – equivalent to 44% of the world's entire population."[10]

Then comes the goat, symbolizing the Kingdom of Greece. Alexander the Great is symbolized by the single horn the goat has at first. Interestingly, Greece has used the emblem of a goat (at times with one horn!) at different points in its history:

- Caranus was the first king of the ancient Greek kingdom of Macedonia. According to Greek myth, Caranus was told by an oracle to follow the lead of goats in his quest for an empire. He discovered a valley with many goats and built a city there. He established that city as his capital and kept goats on his army standards to commemorate it.

- There have been archaeological finds of bronze one-horned goats in Macedon.

- There is a monument of a pilaster in Persepolis "where a goat is depicted with one immense horn on his forehead, and a Persian holding the horn, by which is intended the subjection of Macedon by Persia" before it was conquered.[11]

- There are many Greek coins with goats on them, and "in the reign of Archelaus of Macedon, 413 B.C., there occurs on the reverse of a coin of that king the head of a goat having only one horn."[12]

- There is "An engraving from an ancient gem, representing the appropriate symbols of Persia and Macedonia, under the figures of a ram, and a goat with one horn. This gem was probably engraved in the time of Alexander the Great, and denotes the union of Persia and Macedonia under the same empire."[13]

How appropriate the symbols of a ram and a goat are in this prophecy!

The goat comes from the west and seems to almost fly across the whole earth (Daniel 8:5). Greece is to the west of Persia. Alexander the Great conquered Persia and the rest of the known world quickly, within 12 years of becoming the commander of the Greeks. After his conquests, he was said to have wept that there were no more worlds to conquer.

But when Greece was at its strongest, Alexander died at the young age of 32- and so "the great horn was broken" (Daniel 8:8, ESV). Four horns rose in its place, symbolizing the division of the Kingdom of Greece into "four kingdoms that would fill up about the same space in the world, occupy about the same territory, and have about the same characteristics - so that they might be regarded as the succession to the one dynasty."[14] As history shows, after a short period of wars and rivalries for the throne after Alexander's death, Greece was divided into four stable kingdoms: Ptolemaic Egypt, Seleucid Mesopotamia and Central Asia, Attalid Anatolia, and Antigonid Macedon.

A little horn is said to grow out of one of these four horns and move toward the south, the east, and "the glorious land" (Daniel 8:9, ESV). A few generations after the formation of the four kingdoms, a ruler of the Seleucid kingdom took power and set his sights on Egypt, Persia, and the land of the Israelites- Antiochus Epiphanes. The books of Maccabees described his acts of infamy, and how on his return from sacking Egypt, he "turned aside and invaded Judea, and ultimately robbed the temple, destroyed Jerusalem, and spread desolation through the land."[15] Another of his primary aims was to spread Greek culture, and he imposed Greek laws and customs on the Jews. After a few years he stopped the daily sacrifice in the Temple, setting up an idol and sacrificing pigs on it. "The temple fell into disuse, weeds and brush grew up in its courtyards. This was the root cause of the rebellion of the Maccabean family, who after three years of fighting, defeated the Greek forces, cleansed the temple, and reinstituted the daily sacrifice. Antiochus, upon hearing of this and other setbacks, took to his bed and in a fever died shortly thereafter."[16] The majority of both secular and Christian scholars agree that these events are what is symbolized in this chapter, so closely does it follow history. But it gets even wilder- the timeline for stopping and reinstituting the daily Temple sacrifices is fulfilled *to the very day!*

The 2300 Evenings and Mornings

As stated previously, the King James Version of the Bible interpreted the "evenings and mornings" in Daniel 8:14 as days, and so commentators in the past used to look for a fulfillment in that timeframe. 2,300 days would be a little over six years, which is remarkably close to how long the entire struggle was between the Jews and the Seleucid kingdom. One way this could be calculated is starting from when Antiochus desecrated the Temple by erecting a statue of the Greek god Zeus on the altar of burnt offering, thus stopping the daily sacrifice. The end of 2,300 days from that point goes past the time of the death of Antiochus and the reinstating of the daily sacrifice, to the Jewish victory over the Seleucid general Nicanor. Another way could be when Antiochus installed his own candidate Menelaus as the Temple high priest, and ending when Antiochus died. Either way, it is difficult to pinpoint the exact beginning and end of a 2,300-day period when applied to this prophecy.

Nearly all modern translations of the Bible now use the precise interpretation of the original language of "evenings and mornings", which shows a clear connection to the daily evening and morning sacrifice in the Temple. Gabriel also calls this prophecy "the vision of the evenings and mornings" in verse 26. The number of 2,300 evening and morning Temple sacrifices would take place over the course of 1,150 days.

The starting point of these 1,150 days according to the passage could be a few things, as this vision is said to be "concerning the daily sacrifice, the rebellion that causes desolation, the surrender of the sanctuary and the trampling underfoot of the Lord's people" (Daniel 8:13). The end of it is clearer, though: "it will take 2,300 evenings and mornings; *then the sanctuary will be reconsecrated*" (Daniel 8:14, emphasis mine). The ending of the time period given is when the Temple is cleansed and the daily sacrifice can be continued.

While the precise dates of different events in this period of history are not always certain, the dates for the desecration and reconsecration of the Temple are exact. The daily sacrifice was stopped when the Temple was desecrated by Antiochus, as recorded in 1 Maccabees 1:54: "Now on the fifteenth day of Chislev, in the one hundred forty-fifth year, they erected a desolating sacrilege on the altar of burnt offering" (RSVA). This same book also records the exact date the daily sacrifices began again: "Early in the morning on the twenty-fifth day of the ninth month, which is the month of Chislev, in the one hundred forty-eighth year, they rose and offered sacrifice, as the law directs, on the new altar of burnt offering that they had built" (1 Maccabees 4:52-53, RSVA).

According to our modern calendar, calculating the days between these dates looks as simple as adding three years and ten days, which would only be 1,105. The modern Gregorian calendar was introduced in the 16th century; before that, most of the Western world used the similar Julian calendar, introduced by Julius Caesar in 46 B.C. Before that, the Greek calendar was in use. The most ancient Greek calendar year was 354 days, and every other year an intercalary or 'leap' month was added (like our leap year with 366 days instead of 365). The Hebrew calendar had a 360-day year, also using a leap month at the discretion of the high priest. Using the Greek calendar of 354 days, two leap months of 30 days, and the extra ten days brings us to 1,132 days- not quite up to the 1,150 days we're looking at.

Yet the Greek historian Herodotus- referred to as "the Father of History"- wrote in about the year 445 B.C. about how the Greeks in his day calculated time:

Take seventy years as the span of a man's life: those seventy years contain 25,200 days, without counting intercalary months. Add a month every other year to make the seasons come round with proper regularity, and you will have thirty-five additional months, which will make 1050 additional days. Thus the total of days for your seventy years is 26, 250, and not a single one of them is like the next in what it brings.[17]

I'll leave the math to an endnote,[18] but this means that they considered a year to be 360 days, with a leap month of 30 days added every other year. This is likely how the years would have been calculated by Antiochus and the Maccabees.[19] If the leap month occurred in the years 145 and 148 in the dates above, the total would be exactly 1,150 days. This is the 2300 "evenings and mornings," the precise number of daily sacrifices that would be missed!

Fred Miller, who championed this calculation in his commentary, says the following:

Using the Greek calendar is obviously the correct way to compute the number of days between the dates in Maccabees. Using that method arrives at the correct computation. Do not lose sight of the fact that Daniel wrote this prophecy years before it was fulfilled. The angel who spoke knew the future. The divine nature of the book of Daniel is validated by this prophecy. God's messenger told Daniel there would be a period when a king, who would rise up out of one of four divisions of the coming Greek Empire, who would attack the Holy Land and stop the daily sacrifice for 2,300 times. The future came round, centuries later, and validated the prophecy. Certainly the Bible is a living miracle![20]

Daniel 11: Playbook of History

The prophecy in Daniel chapter 8 gave a sweeping description of the empires to come, the four kingdoms that would replace a unified Greece, and a king that would come from one of these kingdoms who would dreadfully persecute God's people. This king would even cause the daily sacrifices in the Temple to cease, but only for a very specific amount of time before relief came and the sacrifices were reinstated. Daniel chapter 11 goes into even more detail about the rise and fall of the wicked ruler Antioch Epiphanes, and the prophecy reads like a play-by-play summary of the events in this period of history. This chapter fits right next to Daniel 8 as such an impossibly clear understanding of these times, that it can only be inspired by God, or written after the fact: "Daniel 11:1-35 is either the most precise and accurate prophecy of the future, fully demonstrating its divine inspiration, or as Porphyry claimed, it is a dishonest attempt to present history as if prophesied centuries earlier."[21]

This vision is introduced in chapter 10 and continues to the end of Daniel in chapter 12. Daniel is given this vision during the third year of Cyrus, king of Persia (Daniel 10:1), who let the Jews return home from captivity to rebuild the Temple. This event is another amazing story of the faith-building truth of God's Word, as Cyrus is mentioned by name in Isaiah 45:1, written over 200 years before he came to power! Cyrus had been prophesied in many chapters of Isaiah as the one who would let the Jews return to Jerusalem, and this happened precisely as Isaiah said.

Below are the verses of the prophecy in Daniel 11 and their fulfillment in history:

> "Now then, I tell you the truth: Three more kings will arise
> in Persia, and then a fourth, who will be far richer than all the
> others. When he has gained power by his wealth, he will stir up
> everyone against the kingdom of Greece. (Daniel 11:2)

The three Persian kings after Cyrus were Cambyses (530-522 B.C.), Smerdis (pseudo-Smerdis or Gaumata; 522 B.C.), and Darius I Hystaspes (522-486 B.C.). The fourth was Xerxes I (486-465 B.C.), who did attack Greece (like in the movie *300*).

> Then a mighty king will arise, who will rule with great power
> and do as he pleases. (Daniel 11:3)

Alexander the Great, symbolized by the one horn on the goat in Daniel 8:5.

> After he has arisen, his empire will be broken up and parceled
> out toward the four winds of heaven. It will not go to his de-
> scendants, nor will it have the power he exercised, because his
> empire will be uprooted and given to others. (Daniel 11:4)

Alexander's empire did not stay with his sons but was split into four kingdoms, symbolized by the four horns in the place of the one in Daniel 8:8.

> "The king of the South will become strong, but one of his
> commanders will become even stronger than he and will rule
> his own kingdom with great power. (Daniel 11:5)

Now we come to a section that recounts the wars between two of the four Grecian kingdoms: the king of the South, or Ptolemaic Egypt, and the king of the North, or Seleucid Mesopotamia. These took place from the death of Alexander (323 B.C.) to the reign of Antiochus Epiphanes (175-163 B.C.). The first king of the South is one of Alexander's four generals, Ptolemy I Soter (323-285 B.C.). The first king of the North (in this verse, the commander that becomes even stronger) is another of Alexander's generals, Seleucus I Nicator (312/11-280 B.C.).

The following verses span the wars between these two kingdoms for about six generations, up to the time of Antiochus Epiphanes (the fourth with the name Antiochus), who is introduced in verse 21. Needless to say, there is a great deal of politics, intrigue, and war, sometimes involving Jews who joined the king of the North on his campaigns (verse 14). Barnes says about this section of Scripture that "these kingdoms are particularly referred to, probably because their conflicts would affect the holy land, and pertain ultimately to the history of religion, and its establishment and triumph in the world. In the notice of these two sovereignties, there is considerable detail - so much so that the principal events could have been readily anticipated by those who were in possession of the writings of Daniel."[22] Barnes is a great resource (whose full commentary can be found for free online) for details on this chapter, showing that "the leading events are traced as accurately as would be a summary of the history made out after the transactions had occurred."[23]

> "He will be succeeded by a contemptible person who has not
> been given the honor of royalty. He will invade the kingdom
> when its people feel secure, and he will seize it through intrigue.
> (Daniel 11:21)

This verse introduces Antiochus Epiphanes, and the chapter up to verse 36 details his wars with the king of the South, his designs for the holy land, and the persecution of the Jews. The historical narrative of God's faithfulness to his people in this time can be read about in detail in I and II Maccabees, an epic tale of Judas Maccabeus' (called "The Hammer") revolt against Antiochus. If you had a typical evangelical Christian upbringing like myself, you might have been taught to avoid the Books of the Maccabees, due to their deuterocanonical association of being a part of the Catholic and Orthodox Bible. I would like to recommend reading them, maybe not as Scripture, but as a helpful history lesson and great background to the prophecies here in Daniel 8 and 11.

"His armed forces will rise up to desecrate the temple fortress
and will abolish the daily sacrifice. Then they will set up the
abomination that causes desolation. (Daniel 11:31)

This verse is about the desecration of the Temple by Antiochus, and how
he set up an idol of Zeus and sacrificed pigs there, marking the beginning of
the 2300 evenings and mornings without the daily sacrifices in Daniel 8. This
is one of three instances where 'abomination' and 'desolation' are mentioned
together in Daniel, the others being in chapters 9 and 12. This instance here
in chapter 11 is related to 12, and chapter 9 (which Jesus quotes in Matthew
24) is a completely different event that we will look at in more detail in the next
chapter of this book.

Verses 36-45 (the end of the chapter) are said by many today to refer to
someone other than Antiochus- a future Antichrist, thousands of years after the
other events recorded in this chapter. There are four problems with this view
that Barnes' observes:

(a) that the allusion in the previous verses is undoubtedly to
Antiochus Epiphanes.

(b) There is no indication of any "change," for the prophetic
narrative seems to proceed as if the allusion to the same person
continued.

(c) The word "king" is not a word to be applied to Antichrist,
it being nowhere used of him.

(d) Such a transition, without anymore decided marks of it,
would not be in accordance with the usual method in the
prophetic writings, leaving a plain prediction in the very midst
of the description, and passing on at once to a representation

of one who would arise after many hundreds of years, and of whom the former could be considered as in no way the type.[24]

Storms says of this section that "it must be admitted that there is no indication of a break or a change of subject. Vv. 36-45 appear to flow in continuation with the preceding paragraph. There is reference to the 'king' and to the 'king of the South' and 'king of the North' without the slightest indication that the three are any different from those in the 4th-2nd centuries B.C. who are described by the same names in the preceding verses."[25]

Barnes sees this section "as containing a recapitulation, or a summing up of the series of events, with a statement of the manner in which they would close."[26] This prophecy beginning in chapter 10 spans some 350 years, while the whole reign of Antiochus was only 11 years at the very end of that large period of time, and was the most dangerous part for the Jews. It is proper to end the events with a synopsis of the main villain, Antiochus Epiphanes, and an assurance of his demise.

Traditional Vs. Modern Interpretation

Daniel 8 and 11 are evidence of God's faithfulness and sovereignty over world events. He knew which empires were to come, and the kings and kingdoms that would arise within them. He gave us symbols that were spot on, and actually used by the kingdoms they represented. He saw the struggle his people would face, but he assured them they would prevail, and gave an exact timeline that they could expect the interrupted daily sacrifices to start again. All of these things were told to Daniel centuries before they came to pass, and they were fulfilled so precisely that secular historians can only insist they were written afterward.

If secular scholars look at these passages and dismiss them as being written after the fact because they follow history too closely, how can Christians insist that they are still unfulfilled? Nearly all Christian interpreters concede that Daniel 8 and 11 refer to historical events, yet many still succumb to the obsession with seeking the future in every prophecy. Such interpreters will say that they point to Antiochus in part, and to another future Antichrist as well. This is a major stretch when it comes to Daniel 8, but it is true that Daniel 12 (the end of the exchange with the angel that started in chapter 10) does mention the future resurrection. The end of Daniel 11 (verses 36-45) can be confusing if not understood as a synopsis, even though the setting or language does not change- it distorts the harmony of the passage when we insist that it suddenly speaks about events thousands of years in the future.

When we rip these passages from their historical context and fulfillment, we lose sight of just how faithful God is to his promises. Because the focus is put on the future element of any given prophecy, the actual historical fulfillment becomes a mere footnote. Some allow their minds to go wild with speculation about who the future Antichrist will be, others become overwhelmed at the sheer amount of promises there are in the Bible that are said to be unfulfilled. It was the latter in my case- I would read chapters like Daniel 8 or 11, and then come to a verse that I had always heard was unfulfilled (even though I had very little knowledge of the historical context to verify that). From there, I would assume the whole chapter was unfulfilled, and then just file it in the 'future stuff - do not speculate' part of my brain. On to the next chapter, and repeat. With the current popular interpretation of prophecy pushing everything into the future, all of God's promises end up in the 'still not fulfilled' bin.

This futurist cycle of interpretation gives us little incentive to further investigate the historical context of the prophecies. Why bother looking into the past, when I need to keep my eyes glued to the evening news to look for clues? It also completely impairs our ability to understand how prophecies in different chapters and books relate to one another. We start to lose all sense of our place in God's timeline- everything is 'not yet, but soon.' Instead, we should be amazed at what he has done, and excited for what's ahead. If he fulfilled his promises so precisely back then, all the way up to the current date, nothing can stop his amazing Word! As Miller said, the Bible is truly *a living miracle.*

1. Albert Barnes, "Notes, Critical, Illustrative, and Practical", Daniel 8 intro. Available online at https://www.sacred-texts.com/bib/cmt/barnes/dan0 08.htm

2. Fred Miller, "Revelation: A Panorama of the Gospel Age", 21-26. Available online at http://moellerhaus.com/rev666.htm

3. Miller, ibid, 23.

4. Miller, ibid, 24.

5. Miller, ibid, 25.

6. Barnes, ibid, Daniel 8 intro.

7. See John Darby on Daniel 8 for an example of this kind of interpretation. Available online at https://www.christianity.com/bible/commentary/dr by/daniel/8

8. Barnes, ibid, Daniel 8:3.

9. Barnes, ibid, Daniel 8:4.

10. Michelle Chua, "The Strength and Structure of the Ancient Persian Army", Introduction. Available online at https://brewminate.com/the-strength-and-structure -of-the-ancient-persian-army/

11. James Strong and John McClintock, "The Cyclopedia of Biblical, Theological, and Ecclesiastical Literature", Macedonia. Available online at https://www.biblicalcyclopedia.com/M/macedonia. html

12. Barnes, ibid, Daniel 8:5.

13. Thomas Smiley, "Scripture Geography", 246. Available online at https://archive.org/details/scripturegeograp00smil

14. Barnes, ibid, Daniel 8:8.

15. Barnes, ibid, Daniel 8:9.

16. Miller, ibid, 217.

17. Herodotus (trans. De Selincourt and Marincola), "Histories", 1.32.

18. Fred Miller writes: "Using the Greek calendar according to Herodotus and assuming that the years 146 and 148 were intercalary years, we come up with the following calculation: 9-15-145 to 9-25-148, the dates given in Maccabees from the desecration to the cleansing, is three years and ten days. Thus, the math sentence following the Greek calendar which was in use at the time the prophecy was fulfilled would be: (3 X 360) + (2 X 30) + 10. Let's diagram it.

    3 x 360 equals ******************1080 days
    2 x 30 (2 intercalary months) ******60 days
    From 15th to 25th equals *********10 days
    ____
    Total ****************************1150 days" (Miller, ibid, 223-224)

19. Miller, ibid, 223.

20. Miller, ibid, 224.

21. John Walvoord, "Daniel- The Key To Prophetic Revelation", Chapter 11. Available online at https://walvoord.com/article/252#P1649_705536

22. Barnes, ibid, Daniel 11 intro.

23. Barnes, ibid, Daniel 11 intro.
    Available online at https://biblehub.com/commentaries/barnes/daniel/11.htm

24. Barnes, ibid, Daniel 11:36.

25. Sam Storms, "Daniel 11:2-12:13", 11:36.
Available online at https://www.samstorms.org/all-articles/post/daniel
-11:2-12:13

26. Barnes, ibid, Daniel 11:40.

Chapter Three

Messiah and the Fate of Jerusalem

Daniel 9

> In the first year of Darius son of Xerxes (a Mede by descent),
> who was made ruler over the Babylonian kingdom— in the
> first year of his reign, I, Daniel, understood from the Scrip-
> tures, according to the word of the Lord given to Jeremiah the
> prophet, that the desolation of Jerusalem would last seventy
> years. (Daniel 9:1-2)

Daniel was likely a teenager when he was taken from his home in
Jerusalem, and into captivity in Babylon. He had served the kings of
two different empires faithfully. Now an older man, he wondered when God's
promises to restore Jerusalem would be fulfilled. He knew the prophet Jeremiah
had foretold that the desolation of Jerusalem would last 70 years:

> This whole country will become a desolate wasteland, and these
> nations will serve the king of Babylon seventy years. (Jeremiah

25:11)

> This is what the Lord says: "When seventy years are completed
> for Babylon, I will come to you and fulfill my good promise to
> bring you back to this place. For I know the plans I have for
> you," declares the Lord, "plans to prosper you and not to harm
> you, plans to give you hope and a future. (Jeremiah 29:10-11)

Now the time was nearer than ever- or quite possibly, Cyrus had already decreed that the Jews may go and rebuild the city and the Temple- but the Temple was still not built, and the city was in shambles.

So Daniel pleads with God, acknowledging His faithfulness and love, admitting that his people have sinned and are covered in shame. Long ago, Moses warned them that they would be taken into captivity if they refused to obey, and it came to pass exactly as he said. But just as God delivered his people from Egypt, he was certainly able to deliver them from Babylon and restore Jerusalem. He begs God to act for his own glory: "We do not make requests of you because we are righteous, but because of your great mercy. Lord, listen! Lord, forgive! Lord, hear and act! For your sake, my God, do not delay, because your city and your people bear your Name" (Daniel 9:18b-19). I suggest taking the time to read the whole prayer- Miller calls it "the most insistent and pleading prayer in the whole Bible outside of Gethsemane."[1]

Have you ever felt the way Daniel did here? You know that God has promised to restore all creation, that Jesus is returning to consummate his Kingdom, and that he has made a place for us to be with him- but things look so bleak in the world around us. We have a feeling that it should be soon, but where are we in God's plan right now? Wouldn't it be comforting to have some kind of word from him, some idea of what he has been doing throughout the last 2000 years to the current day? Maybe it feels like too much to ask for... but we're not asking to know 'the day or hour.' Perhaps we can acknowledge the same longing in our hearts that Daniel has here- to better understand God's plan.

Seventy 'Sevens'

While Daniel was still praying, the angel Gabriel came with an answer: "Daniel, I have now come to give you insight and understanding. As soon as you began to pray, a word went out, which I have come to tell you, for you are highly esteemed. Therefore, consider the word and understand the vision: Seventy 'sevens' are decreed for your people and your holy city..." (Daniel 9:22b-24a). God's answer to Daniel is one of the most amazing time prophecies in the Bible. Daniel asked for a word regarding the end of the 70 years of the desolation of Jerusalem, and the prophecy he is given is seven times that amount, or 'seventy times seven.'

Older translations of the Bible, including the King James Version, translated this as seventy 'weeks', or 490 days, but modern translations like the NIV quoted above give the more literal seventy 'sevens' instead. This is done for a few reasons: 'sevens' does not necessarily mean a week of days, but also of years as in Genesis 29:27; Daniel is asking about a prophecy concerning 'years' and is answered with the same unit; interpreters have universally understood this prophecy to mean seventy 'sevens' of years, or 490 years. This passage is one of the clearest examples of a day symbolizing a year in biblical prophecy. Others include Numbers 14:34, where the Israelites were sentenced to wander in the wilderness for 40 years, "one year for each of the forty days you explored the land." Also Ezekiel 4:4-5, where the prophet is told to lie on his left side and put the sin of Israel on himself "the same number of days as the years of their sin. So for 390 days you will bear the sin of the people of Israel."

Six Wondrous Events

Gabriel explains what the prophecy is about: "Seventy 'sevens' are decreed for your people and your holy city to finish transgression, to put an end to sin, to atone for wickedness, to bring in everlasting righteousness, to seal up vision and prophecy and to anoint the Most Holy Place" (Daniel 9:24). Christians might be familiar with a few of these concepts, because it is how the New Testament describes what Jesus Christ has done. This prophecy concerns not only Jerusalem and the Temple, but the long awaited Messiah! The following are examples of how he has fulfilled these six things:

1. *To finish transgression:* The more natural reading of the Hebrew here is to restrain transgression.[2] Jesus has broken the power of sin over our lives: "For we know that our old self was crucified with him so that the body ruled by sin might be done away with, that we should no longer be slaves to sin— because anyone who has died has been set free from sin" (Romans 6:6-7).

2. *To put an end to sin:* Before Christ, animal sacrifices were required at the Temple year after year to take away sin. But "Christ was sacrificed once to take away the sins of many" (Hebrews 9:28), "we have been made holy through the sacrifice of the body of Jesus Christ once for all" (Hebrews 10:10), "for by one sacrifice he has made perfect forever those who are being made holy" (Hebrews 10:14).

3. *To atone for wickedness:* The often quoted verse begins: "For all have sinned and fall short of the glory of God, and all are justified freely by his grace through the redemption that came by Christ Jesus" (Romans 3:23-24). It goes on to say that "God presented Christ as a sacrifice of atonement, through the shedding of his blood—to be received by faith" (Romans 3:25).

4. *To bring in everlasting righteousness:* Paul writes that "now apart from the law the righteousness of God has been made known, to which the Law and the Prophets testify. This righteousness is given through faith in Jesus Christ to all who believe" (Romans 3:21-22a). It is an everlasting righteousness "because the benefit of it is to endure to everlasting life."[3]

5. *To seal up vision and prophecy:* As just stated, Jesus is the One "to which

the Law and the Prophets testify" (Romans 3:21). Barnes writes, "All the prophecies, and all the visions, had a reference more or less direct to the coming of the Messiah, and when he should appear they might be regarded as complete. The spirit of prophecy would cease, and the facts would confirm and seal all that had been written."[4] Jesus himself read from the prophet Isaiah and confirmed that he is the fulfillment: "'The Spirit of the Lord is on me, because he has anointed me to proclaim good news to the poor. He has sent me to proclaim freedom for the prisoners and recovery of sight for the blind, to set the oppressed free, to proclaim the year of the Lord's favor.' Then he rolled up the scroll, gave it back to the attendant and sat down. The eyes of everyone in the synagogue were fastened on him. He began by saying to them, 'Today this scripture is fulfilled in your hearing'" (Luke 4:18-21).

6. *To anoint the Most Holy Place:* The NIV version we quoted has a footnote that the Hebrew can also mean 'the most holy One.' Jesus is the Anointed One, the meaning of Messiah, or Christ. He is also the new Temple according to the New Testament: when asked by the Jews for a sign to prove his authority to turn tables in the Temple, he answered them, "Destroy this temple, and I will raise it again in three days" (John 2:19). Also, in Ephesians it says: "Consequently, you are no longer foreigners and strangers, but fellow citizens with God's people and also members of his household, built on the foundation of the apostles and prophets, *with Christ Jesus himself as the chief cornerstone.* In him the whole building is joined together and rises to become *a holy temple in the Lord.* And in him you too are being built together to become a dwelling in which God lives by his Spirit" (Ephesians 2:19-22, emphasis mine).

Together with Christ as the chief cornerstone, we are the new Temple. Jesus is the Most Holy One, who proclaims he is anointed in Luke 4:18.

But even if we insist on keeping the translation of Most Holy Place, Jesus fulfills this as well. Hebrew 9:11-12 tells us that Christ entered the Most Holy Place in Heaven by his own blood: "But when Christ came as high priest of the good things that are now already here, he went through the greater and more perfect tabernacle that is not made with human hands, that is to say, is not a part of this creation. He did not enter by means of the blood of goats and calves; but he entered the Most Holy Place once for all by his own blood, thus obtaining eternal redemption" (Hebrews 9:11-12).

All of these events are said to be accomplished within the seventy sevens, or 490 years.

The Beginning of the 490 Years

Gabriel goes on to explain when these 490 years will start: "Know and understand this: From the time the word goes out to restore and rebuild Jerusalem... It will be rebuilt with streets and a trench, but in times of trouble." (Daniel 9:25a...b). They begin with the command to restore and rebuild Jerusalem, and not just the Temple, but the streets and a trench (likely a defensive moat outside of a wall. The KJV says 'wall' instead of trench). Which command was this, and when did it happen?

As mentioned in the previous chapter of this book, Cyrus allowed the Jews to return to Jerusalem to rebuild the Temple. This is recorded in Ezra 1: "This is what Cyrus king of Persia says: 'The Lord, the God of heaven, has given me all the kingdoms of the earth and he has appointed me to build a temple for him at Jerusalem in Judah. Any of his people among you may go up to Jerusalem in Judah and build the temple of the Lord, the God of Israel, the God who is in Jerusalem, and may their God be with them" (Ezra 1:2-3). Barnes writes, "in this order there is nothing said of the restoration of the city, and that in fact occurred at a different time, and under the direction of different leaders."[5]

The next event to look at is a command given by a later Persian king, Darius Hystaspis. This is recorded in Ezra chapters 5 and 6. It is a command to finish the rebuilding of the Temple which started years earlier, but was delayed after only finishing the foundation. Another command is recorded in Ezra 7, given by Xerxes I (called Artaxerxes in Ezra 7), to use funds and authority given to Ezra to restore public worship in the newly completed Temple. But still, nothing regarding the rest of the city of Jerusalem.

Finally, Nehemiah is granted the authority by Artaxerxes I, king of Persia, to rebuild the city and walls of Jerusalem as written in the book of Nehemiah 2:1-10. It is recorded there that the rebuilding was successful, "but in times of trouble" (Daniel 9:25), just as the prophecy says. Their neighbors in Samaria opposed the city's construction, so Nehemiah and his helpers "did their work with one hand and held a weapon in the other" (Nehemiah 4:17).

It is difficult to determine the exact date this command was given, but Barnes and other scholars suppose it was in 454 B.C. With this, we now have the event and the date that marks the beginning of the seventy 'sevens,' or 490 years.

Until the Anointed One Comes

Looking at the vision again, it says: "Know and understand this: From the time the word goes out to restore and rebuild Jerusalem until the Anointed One, the ruler, comes, there will be seven 'sevens,' and sixty-two 'sevens.' It will be rebuilt with streets and a trench, but in times of trouble" (Daniel 9:25). The Messiah comes after seven 'sevens' (or 49 years), and sixty-two 'sevens' (or 434 years). Together, these equal 483 years from the command to restore and rebuild Jerusalem until the Messiah comes. The years are consecutive, but why are they separated? Is there anything that happens 49 years after the command that distinguishes it?

As stated previously, Nehemiah secured the king's decree to rebuild Jerusalem. The wall was rebuilt after some time, but he also enacted other reforms, such as enforcing the Sabbath, tithes to the priest, and separation from foreigners. It so happens that the final reforms of Nehemiah in the last chapter of that book can be dated to around 408 B.C., which is 46 years after the beginning of the seventy 'sevens' in 454 B.C. It could actually be closer, but we can arrive at that date at least because of Nehemiah 13:28, which says that Joiada was the high priest, which was around 408 B.C. Barnes writes that "the time, then, if this be the event referred to, is sufficiently accurate to make it coincide with the prophecy- sufficiently so to divide the previous period from what succeeded it."[6] Jerusalem was finally rebuilt and restored to its previous condition before it became desolate, seven 'sevens' after it was decreed to happen.

After this period there are sixty-two more 'sevens,' or 434 years, "until the Anointed One, the ruler, comes" (Daniel 9:25). This brings us to 29 A.D., right around the time of Jesus' baptism and the beginning of his public ministry. Even if we stopped looking at this prophecy right here, this is an amazing fulfillment of the vision. The Anointed one, the Messiah, Jesus Christ, came at exactly the time it was foretold he would come! Remember, we have empirical evidence that Daniel was written centuries before this happened.

If this prophecy points right to Jesus as the Messiah, why don't Jews recognize him? It turns out that traditional Jewish teachers cut off 164 years from the Persian period of their calendar so that it points to the failed messianic rebellion of Bar Kokhba in 132 A.D.[7] Jewish Torah historian Rav Shimon Schwab speculates on the reason they did this:

> How could it have been that our forebears had no knowledge of a historic period, otherwise widely known and amply documented, which lasted over a span of at least 165 years and which was less than 600 years before the days of the Sages who recorded our traditional chronology in Seder Olam? ...it seems possible that our Sages, for some unknown reason, "covered up" a certain historic period and purposely eliminated and suppressed all records and other material pertaining thereto... Had it not been for the fact that important parts of those prophecies had been left out or were purposely obscured, the clues for the Messianic date found in Daniel might have yielded the desired results. This

was rendered impossible through the hiding of certain data and chronological material.[8]

The Last 'Seven'

The prophecy so far has been about the coming of the Anointed One, sixty-nine 'sevens' from the command to restore and rebuild Jerusalem. Now the vision shifts to what the Messiah will accomplish in the last 'seven.' Daniel will also be shown the fate of Jerusalem and the Temple, the matter he so earnestly prayed to God about at the beginning of the chapter.

Gabriel continues: "After the sixty-two 'sevens,' the Anointed One will be put to death and will have nothing" (Daniel 9:26a). This is not to happen immediately at the start of the last 'seven,' because the prophecy goes on to tell us what the Messiah will do for the rest of the week. But it is the next major event.

This is another prophecy from the Old Testament that reveals that the Messiah would be put to death. The phrase 'and will have nothing' can also be interpreted as 'but not for himself'- that is, he died for others- a view of the atonement for our sins. But it can also mean that he died without ruling his kingdom in the manner many Jews expected- that is, not as the conquering 'Son of Man' we will see in Daniel chapter 7. He set up his kingdom when he came, but he said, "My kingdom is not of this world. If it were, my servants would fight to prevent my arrest by the Jewish leaders. But now my kingdom is from another place" (John 18:36). The Kingdom of God came in an unexpected manner.

The vision continues by stating what will happen at some point after the death of the Messiah: "The people of the ruler who will come will destroy the city and the sanctuary. The end will come like a flood: War will continue until the end, and desolations have been decreed" (Daniel 9:26b). Jerusalem and the Temple were to become desolate again. Jesus predicted that this would happen within 40 years from when he said it (Matthew 24:34), and it occurred in 70

A.D. just as he foretold- the Temple was utterly destroyed, and the city was a bloodbath. We will look at this event more in the next chapter. Again, this was not to happen right after the sixty-two 'sevens,' or even in the last week. The scope of the seventy 'sevens' is the six things that Jesus accomplished with his death and resurrection: "to finish transgression, to put an end to sin, to atone for wickedness, to bring in everlasting righteousness, to seal up vision and prophecy and to anoint the Most Holy Place" (Daniel 9:24). The primary focus of this prophecy is not on "the people of the ruler," but on the Anointed One. However, just as the prophecy begins with the command to restore and rebuild Jerusalem, the desolation of the city after the Messiah is in sight.

In the last verse of the vision, we turn again to what the Messiah does in the last seven years: "He will confirm a covenant with many for one 'seven.' In the middle of the 'seven' he will put an end to sacrifice and offering" (Daniel 9:27a). Jesus confirmed the new covenant that was foretold by the prophets Jeremiah and Ezekiel:

> "The days are coming," declares the Lord, "when I will make a new covenant with the people of Israel and with the people of Judah... This is the covenant I will make with the people of Israel after that time," declares the Lord. "I will put my law in their minds and write it on their hearts. I will be their God, and they will be my people." (Jeremiah 31:31,33)

> I will give you a new heart and put a new spirit in you; I will remove from you your heart of stone and give you a heart of flesh. And I will put my Spirit in you and move you to follow my decrees and be careful to keep my laws. (Ezekiel 36:26-27)

Jesus told the disciples at the Last Supper, "This cup is the new covenant in my blood, which is poured out for you" (Luke 22:20). Jesus' ministry was chiefly among the Jews, and it wasn't until about three years after his death that Gentiles became a part of the church (with Peter going to Cornelius, and Paul being converted). As the vision told to Daniel is "for your people and your holy city" (Daniel 9:24), it could be said to be fulfilled with the Messiah (and his apostles) confirming the covenant among many of the Jews for seven years. After this, the church was flooded with Gentile converts, as other Jews began to reject Christ.

"In the middle of the 'seven' he will put an end to sacrifice and offering" (Daniel 9:27a). After only three years of public ministry since his baptism, the Messiah is suddenly 'cut off,' or put to death. This happens in the middle of the last 'seven.' Upon his death, the Temple curtain is torn in two (Matthew 27:51), as the final sacrifice had been made:

> We have been made holy through the sacrifice of the body of Jesus Christ once for all. Day after day every priest stands and performs his religious duties; again and again he offers the same sacrifices, which can never take away sins. But when this priest had offered for all time one sacrifice for sins, he sat down at the right hand of God, and since that time he waits for his enemies to be made his footstool. For by one sacrifice he has made perfect forever those who are being made holy. (Hebrews 10:10b-14)

Sacrifices were only a shadow of what was to be fulfilled in Jesus: "The law is only a shadow of the good things that are coming—not the realities themselves. For this reason it can never, by the same sacrifices repeated endlessly year after year, make perfect those who draw near to worship" (Hebrews 10:1). After Jesus' death, there is no use for any more animal sacrifices.

There is an interesting example of this truth from Jewish sources. On the Hebrew holiday called Yom Kippur- the Day of Atonement- two male goats were chosen by lot. One was to be killed as a sin offering, and the other to be a scapegoat, the goat that would carry the sins of Israel into the wilderness (Leviticus 16). Rabbi Tovia Singer admits the following:

In Tractate Yoma 39b, the Talmud...discusses numerous re-markable phenomena that occurred in the Temple during the Yom Kippur service...There was a strip of scarlet-dyed wool tied to the head of the scapegoat which would turn white in the presence of the large crowd gathered at the Temple on the Day of Atonement. The Jewish people perceived this miraculous transformation as a heavenly sign that their sins were forgiven. The Talmud relates, however, that 40 years before the destruc-tion of the second Temple [approximately AD 30] the scarlet colored strip of wool did not turn white.[9]

The miraculous sign of the scarlet cloth tied to the scapegoat turning white no longer appeared after the death of Christ. Animal sacrifices were no longer effective for taking away sin. Jesus fulfills the Day of Atonement, the ultimate and final sacrifice for sin.

With the events of the seventieth 'seven' now revealed, the vision turns again to the desolation of Jerusalem and the Temple. "And at the temple he will set up an abomination that causes desolation, until the end that is decreed is poured out on him (Daniel 9:27b). The NIV has a footnote with a varied translation of this part: "And one who causes desolation will come upon the wing of the abominable temple, until the end that is decreed is poured out on the desolated city." In fact, translators have a very difficult time with this part of the verse, due to the sources having variations: "The Latin Vulgate is, 'And there shall be in the temple the abomination of desolation.' The Greek, 'And upon the temple shall be an abomination of desolations.' The Syriac. 'And upon the extremities of the abomination shall rest desolation.' The Arabic, 'And over the sanctuary shall there be the abomination of ruin.'"[10] If you look up any of the English translations, you will notice the same kind of variety.

One way to understand this last verse better is to see it in parallel with the previous one. That is,

In verse 26:

A. The Anointed One is cut off.

B. In the second part of the verse, the people of the prince destroy the city and sanctuary.

In verse 27:

A. The Anointed One makes a covenant with many for one week and puts an end to sacrifice in the middle of the week.

B. In the second part, the people of the prince set up an abomination in the Temple.

Another way to understand it is that Jesus himself quotes this verse: "So when you see standing in the holy place 'the abomination that causes desolation,' spoken of through the prophet Daniel—let the reader understand—then let those who are in Judea flee to the mountains" (Matthew 24:15-16). The parallel account of this passage is in Luke: "When you see Jerusalem being surrounded by armies, you will know that its desolation is near. Then let those who are in Judea flee to the mountains, let those in the city get out, and let those in the country not enter the city" (Luke 21:20-21). So this 'abomination that causes desolation' has to do with the armies surrounding the city and entering the Temple, ravaging both. Not only was the Temple desecrated, but it was torn apart brick by brick. This was fulfilled in 70 A.D.- within one generation, or about 40 years after Jesus said it would happen. We will look into this more in the next chapter of this book.

In this way, the vision ends on a somewhat bleak note. It was undoubtedly comforting to Daniel that the Temple would be restored, and astounding in its timeline for the appearance and work of the Messiah... but its chief purpose is fulfilled in Christ, and so it becomes desolate once again.

Traditional Vs. Modern Interpretation

Growing up in a Christian home, I had read this chapter many times. I never paid much attention to it, because once again, surely this was all 'future stuff.' It was drilled into my head repeatedly that the 'abomination of desolation' (whatever that was supposed to be) would someday appear in a rebuilt Third Temple, sometime soon. All focus was put on the apparently unfulfilled last two verses of this prophecy. The rest of the chapter? Footnotes we rush past to get to the 'good stuff'', the part we can speculate on, the titillating unknown but fast-approaching future. All incentive to study the historical context of this chapter was lost on me. Why bother even checking a commentary (besides Scofield, of course)? We can't trust those!

Dutifully reading through the Bible again as an older adult, I finally caved when I got to this chapter. I was ready to admit that I had no idea what it really meant. I was even brave (or desperate) enough to check a commentary after praying for protection. Little did I realize that my mind was about to be blown... this prophecy is fulfilled by Jesus?! I always thought the spotlight was on Antichrist, the anti-hero of this chapter. The story is so compelling, I was never more motivated to learn history. And the timing of it all! I was absolutely astonished at what God had done. "What remarkable coincidence in this wonderful 70 week prophecy. No human could have devised this before the events transpired. It is a faith-building prophecy."[11]

Yes, it is faith-building, as I have witnessed in my own life. Encountering the traditional interpretation of this chapter sent me on a renewed journey of wonder in God's Living Word, and every beautiful book in it was chock-full of fresh and inspiring surprises. God keeps his promises, it can be verified, it's all recorded there- we just need to pay attention to it.

But it's difficult to see the evidence when we are so fixated on the future. The modern way of interpreting prophecy in the Bible trains us to do this- it's called *futurism* for a reason. Every passage of Scripture we've looked at so far (and those we will study in the rest of the book) are said to be unfulfilled in major ways; all of them are pushed into the future. The stone in Daniel 2 is yet to hit the statue, so the kingdom of God is yet to come. Sure, the little horn in Daniel 8 is partly about Antiochus Epiphanes, but it's *really* about the future Antichrist. Maybe the sixty-nine 'sevens' have passed, but the last 'seven' is still to come- 2000 years later? Yes, there is said to be an unmentioned 'gap' in this prophecy- less a gap and more a vast chasm- as if the vision was put on pause. What violence has been done to this vision! Why mention dates at all if this was the case? It would have been better to leave the time portion out of it, if that was the correct interpretation. Author Steve Gregg likens it to asking a friend for a ride:

> It's as if I asked you to take me to the airport this Saturday, and you said, "well, how far is the airport from here?" I said, "well, I think it's about 40 miles from here... it's 40 miles from here." Now you said, "yeah, I can do that." So we get in your car and we drive towards Seattle, and we go 35 miles, 36 miles, 37 miles, 38 miles, 39 miles. You're expecting the airport in the next mile or so. Well we go 45 miles, 50 miles, 100 miles! 200 miles! You say, "I thought you said the airport is 40 miles from here?" I say "oh, you didn't understand. Between the 39th and the 40th mile there's a gap of 200 miles." So the real distance is really 240 miles. Well, you would probably think I had lied to you, rather than had given you any information.[12]

Historical events confirm that the vision is fulfilled: the city and walls were rebuilt in a time of trouble; Messiah brings the new covenant but is cut off; the city and the Temple become desolate once again. Scripture confirms that the six works Messiah was to do are wonderfully fulfilled in him, all within the timeline of 490 consecutive years as told to Daniel. The vision is breathtaking in its scope and accuracy when understood this way.

Please don't get me wrong- I'm not going to go through every prophecy in the Bible and tell you they're all fulfilled (that's called preterism). There are prophecies we will look at that are still waiting for fulfillment. But what the modern interpretation has done is taken obviously fulfilled prophecies and pushed them inexplicably into the future, wreaking havoc on the picture of God's faithfulness they give us, and causing us to lose all sense of reference for where we are now or how to understand other prophecies.

But if you get nothing else from this book and disagree with its conclusions, at least stand next to me and gaze in wonder at the fulfillments we can agree on: Jesus came to earth at precisely the appointed time. A time recorded centuries before it happened- what an incredible miracle! Only our God knows and guides the future. And even though our Savior was 'cut off', he accomplished all he came to do. I wish I had understood at least this much of the prophecy decades ago.

---

1. Fred Miller, "Revelation: a Panorama of the Gospel Age", 205.
   Available online at http://moellerhaus.com/70week.htm

2. Albert Barnes, "Notes, Critical, Illustrative, and Practical", Daniel 9:24.
   Available online at https://biblehub.com/commentaries/barnes/daniel/9.htm

3. George Whitefield, "The Righteousness of Christ, an Everlasting Right-eousness", fourthly.
   Available online at https://www.biblebb.com/files/whitefield/gw015.htm

4. Barnes, ibid, Daniel 9:24.

5. Barnes, ibid, Daniel 9:25.

6. Barnes, ibid, Daniel 9:25.

7. Floyd Nolan Jones, "The Seder Olam Rabbah- Why Jewish Dating is Different", 42-46.
   Available online at https://assets.answersingenesis.org/doc/articles/cm/Divided.pdf

8. Rav Shimon Schwab qtd. in Rafael Cowan, "History vs □□□in the Purim Story: Can both be correct?"
   Available online at https://www.sefaria.org/sheets/389476.19?lang=bi&with=all&lang2=en

9. Tovia Singer qtd. in Daniel Mann, "Witnessing to the Messianic Fulfillment of the Day of Atonement", 1.
   Available online at https://www.equip.org/PDF/JAE383.pdf

10. Barnes, ibid, Daniel 9:27.

11. Miller, ibid, 209.

12. Steve Gregg, "Daniel 9:24-27 - 70 WEEKS PROPHECY", 55:23.
    Available online at https://youtu.be/QbTmTEVk8WE

Chapter Four

Three Questions, Two Events, One Answer

Matthew 24

I t cannot be overstated just how influential Jesus' words in Matthew 24 are to our view of the end times today. Also known as the Little Apocalypse or the Olivet Discourse, it is where we get our idea of the rapture, the tribulation, and the Antichrist in the Temple, all wrapped up in one place in the Gospels. Jesus hasn't returned yet, so we're still waiting for it all to happen. It seems pretty cut-and-dried, right?

The Most Embarrassing Verse

The problem is that Jesus said these events would happen within 'this generation,' i.e., the people standing there listening to him say it: "Truly I tell you, this generation will certainly not pass away until all these things have happened" (Matthew 24:34). A biblical generation is usually 40 years, which is the length of time the Israelites were made to wander in the wilderness: "The LORD's anger burned against Israel and he made them wander in the wilderness forty years, until the whole generation of those who had done evil in his sight was gone" (Numbers 32:13). So was Jesus really saying that it wouldn't be more than 40 years before the apocalypse happens?

C.S. Lewis believed as much, and so he called Matthew 24:34 "the most embarrassing verse in the Bible."[1] Others try to explain it by interpreting the Greek word for 'generation' as 'race' or 'ethnic group,' meaning that Jews would still be around when the events Jesus mentions will happen. But there is another way to explain this passage that takes Christ's words seriously, and harmonizes with events both past and future.

Three Questions

We often miss one little detail in Matthew 24 that makes a huge difference: Jesus is asked three questions, and gives each one an answer. The problem is that it's not nicely formatted and categorized for us to recognize at a glance which question is being answered where, so we treat it as if one question was asked- "Hey Jesus, what happens in the end times?"

It turns out that *is* one of the questions the disciples asked! But again, there are three. Here is the beginning of the passage:

> Jesus left the temple area and was going on His way when His disciples came up to point out the temple buildings to Him. But He responded and said to them, "Do you not see all *these things*? Truly I say to you, not one stone here will be left upon another, which will not be torn down."

> And as He was sitting on the Mount of Olives, the disciples came to Him privately, saying, "Tell us, when will *these things* happen, and what will be the sign of Your coming, and of the end of the age?" (Matthew 24:1-3, NASB, emphasis mine)

The setting is the view of the Second Temple from the Mount of Olives, newly remodeled by Herod the Builder. The disciples proudly point out the beautiful buildings, when Jesus gives them the shocking news that they will be completely destroyed. The Jewish center of worship, the Temple of the God of the Universe, the place Daniel earnestly prayed would be restored, desolate again? Upon hearing this shocking news, the disciples must know 1.) when will *these things* happen, 2.) what is the sign of your coming, 3.) and of the end of the age?

Right away we can say with all confidence that *these things*- the main subject of the entire discussion- did happen. The Temple was indeed completely destroyed, with not one stone left on another. It remains so to this day, nearly 2000 years later. However, we can also say that Jesus has not yet returned to judge all the people of the earth, nor has 'the end of the age' happened. Is there any way to sort through the rest of the passage?

In a prophetic sense, Jesus is answering all three questions with the same description. Barnes writes:

> To these questions He replies in this and the following chapters. This He does, not by noticing them distinctly, but by intermingling the descriptions of the destruction of Jerusalem and of the end of the world, so that it is sometimes difficult to tell to what particular subject his remarks apply. The principle on which this combined description of two events was spoken appears to be, that "they could be described in the same words," and therefore the accounts are intermingled.[2]

This is the same kind of prophetic language used often in Isaiah, where at many points a more *immediate* future event is foretold along with a *distant* future event. For example, Isaiah 11 foretells the deliverance that Messiah will bring to Israel: "In that day the Root of Jesse will stand as a banner for the peoples; the nations will rally to him, and his resting place will be glorious" (Isaiah 11:10). In the very next verses, it foretells the Lord rescuing his people from captivity: "In that day the Lord will reach out his hand a second time to reclaim the surviving remnant of his people from Assyria, from Lower Egypt, from Upper Egypt, from Cush, from Elam, from Babylonia, from Hamath and from the islands of the Mediterranean. He will raise a banner for the nations and gather the exiles of Israel; he will assemble the scattered people of Judah from the four quarters of the earth" (Isaiah 11:11-12). The two events are centuries apart, but the distant and then immediate futures are intermingled in the same prophecy. "And in the same manner Isaiah, Hosea, Amos, and Micah very often connect the deliverance under the Messiah with that which was to be effected from the captivity at Babylon, without noticing the long train of intermediate events."[3] Commentator Craig Keener also remarks on this:

> Old Testament prophets often grouped events together by their topic rather than their chronology, and in this discourse Jesus does the same. He addresses what in Matthew are grammatically two separate questions: the time of the temple's destruction and the time of the end. The disciples may have viewed these questions as integrally related, but Jesus will distinguish them: when will the temple be destroyed (within a generation)? What will be the sign of his coming (at an hour known to no one)?[4]

Jesus gives an answer to all three questions, which are really two different events, all in one 'discourse.' There are clues in some of the verses in Matthew 24 that help us distinguish which event Jesus is referring to, whether the more immediate future destruction of the Temple, or his distant future return and 'the end of the age.'

'These Things'

Again, the main topic of discussion is the destruction of the Temple, Jesus' shocking words that spurred the first question the disciples asked: when will these things happen? The first section of his answer, verses 4-28, largely concern this more immediate event, but with language of "such an amplitude of meaning as also to express" the more distant event: the coming of Jesus in the last days to judge all the people of the earth.

Jesus begins his answer with a description of what would happen in those days:

> Jesus answered: "Watch out that no one deceives you. For many will come in my name, claiming, 'I am the Messiah,' and will deceive many. You will hear of wars and rumors of wars, but see to it that you are not alarmed. Such things must happen, but the end is still to come. Nation will rise against nation, and kingdom against kingdom. There will be famines and earthquakes in various places. All these are the beginning of birth pains. (Matthew 24:4-8)

All of these events did happen in the disciples' times, especially false messiahs. In the Jewish Wars that ended with the destruction of the Temple in 70 A.D., there was a civil war in Jerusalem between at least three factions, each led by men claiming to be the Messiah.[5] The Jews of this time were expecting the Messiah to rise up and free them from Roman rule, and Jesus did not live up to their expectations in this regard. So false messiahs arose to take up this banner, bringing many to their cause, but failing miserably.

There were also many wars and rumors of wars in the Roman Empire in the time before the destruction of the Temple. When Jesus spoke this prophecy, the Empire was at peace. But 69 A.D. was known as the "Year of the Four Emperors" when civil war engulfed the Empire and four emperors suffered violent deaths in the space of eighteen months. According to the Jewish historian Josephus, other wars were rumored and threatened against Palestine at this time, but they were not carried out.

As for famines and earthquakes, the Scriptures record how Agabus prophesied "that a severe famine would spread over the entire Roman world. (This happened during the reign of Claudius)" (Acts 11:28). According to Josephus, this famine was so severe in Jerusalem that "many people died for want of what was necessary to procure food."[6] Barnes write that "four times in the reign of Claudius (41-54 A.D.) famine prevailed in Rome, Palestine, and Greece."[7] The Roman historian Tacitus also recorded many earthquakes, some of which destroyed entire cities in the Empire.[8] These events were signs that the judgment against Jerusalem was coming.

Jesus continues:

> 9 Then you will be handed over to be persecuted and put to death, and you will be hated by all nations because of me. 10 At that time many will turn away from the faith and will betray and hate each other, 11 and many false prophets will appear and deceive many people. 12 Because of the increase of wickedness, the love of most will grow cold, 13 but the one who stands firm to the end will be saved. 14 And this gospel of the kingdom will be preached in the whole world as a testimony to all nations, and then the end will come. (Matthew 24:9-14)

The disciples certainly saw the fulfillment of persecution as seen in the Scriptures. They were beaten, imprisoned, and brought to trial before the leaders of the synagogues as well as rulers and kings. "Stephen was stoned (Acts 7:59); James was killed by Herod (Acts 12:2)... Most of the apostles, it is believed, died by persecution."[9] Christians were hated throughout the Roman Empire-according to Tacitus, Emperor Nero blamed them for the Great Fire of Rome in 64 A.D., and they were fiercely persecuted:

> Mockery of every sort was added to their deaths. Covered with the skins of beasts, they were torn by dogs and perished, or were nailed to crosses, or were doomed to the flames and burnt, to serve as a nightly illumination, when daylight had expired. Nero offered his gardens for the spectacle...[10]

Just as there were false Messiahs, there were also false prophets. According to Josephus, an Egyptian false prophet gathered 30,000 followers in the wilderness around Jerusalem. He led them to the very site of this prophecy, the Mount of Olives, and attempted to force his way into the city and conquer the Roman garrison. The Roman Procurator Felix prevented the attempt, however, killing or arresting the majority of the mob.[11] Josephus tells us about another false prophet who led thousands to their death by proclaiming that God commanded them to rush to the Temple, where "they should receive miraculous signs of their deliverance," on the very day Roman soldiers overran the Temple.[12] False prophets were common in Jerusalem, because they were bribed to speak a message of God's deliverance in order to keep the people from deserting the city.[13]

It can certainly be said that the events in the verses above were fulfilled in a remarkable way, but how can it be said that the gospel was preached in the whole world (Matthew 24:14)? Because Paul tells us it was: "In the same way, the gospel is bearing fruit and growing throughout the whole world—just as it has been doing among you since the day you heard it and truly understood God's grace... This is the gospel that you heard and that has been proclaimed *to every creature under heaven*, and of which I, Paul, have become a servant" (Colossians 1:6b...23b, emphasis mine). The Greek word for world in Matthew 24:14 is *oikoumenē*, often defined as "the portion of the earth inhabited by the Greeks, in distinction from the lands of the barbarians," or "the Roman empire, all the subjects of the empire."[14] Paul preached the gospel throughout the Roman Empire, and said of the church in Rome in particular that "your faith is being reported all over the world" (Romans 1:8).

Well, if the gospel has been preached in the whole 'world,' how can it be said the end has come (Matthew 24:14)? In a very real way, the destruction of Jerusalem and the Temple was an end to the Jewish system of civic and religious life. But remember, these words are spoken with a gravity that applies to their immediate fulfillment, yet also extends to the final 'end'- the second return of Christ and the judgment of all the people of the Earth. In the same way, the gospel continues to be preached to the whole world, and will truly reach every tribe and tongue and nation (as seen in Revelation 7:9). Both events could be described in the same words.

The Great Tribulation

Jesus then moves on to the main event of 'these things': the razing of Jerusalem and the destruction of the Temple:

> 15 "So when you see standing in the holy place 'the abomination that causes desolation,' spoken of through the prophet Daniel—let the reader understand— 16 then let those who are in Judea flee to the mountains. 17 Let no one on the housetop go down to take anything out of the house. 18 Let no one in the field go back to get their cloak. 19 How dreadful it will be in those days for pregnant women and nursing mothers! 20 Pray that your flight will not take place in winter or on the Sabbath. 21 For then there will be great distress, unequaled from the beginning of the world until now—and never to be equaled again.

> 22 If those days had not been cut short, no one would survive, but for the sake of the elect those days will be shortened. 23 At that time if anyone says to you, 'Look, here is the Messiah!' or, 'There he is!' do not believe it. 24 For false messiahs and false prophets will appear and perform great signs and wonders to deceive, if possible, even the elect. 25 See, I have told you ahead of time.

> 26 "So if anyone tells you, 'There he is, out in the wilderness,' do not go out; or, 'Here he is, in the inner rooms,' do not believe it. 27 For as lightning that comes from the east is visible even in the west, so will be the coming of the Son of Man.

28 Wherever there is a carcass, there the vultures will gather.
(Matthew 24:15-28)

When Jesus mentions 'the abomination that causes desolation,' he is quoting the seventy 'sevens' prophecy in Daniel 9, which we looked at in the previous chapter of this book. That prophecy is about the coming of the Messiah, now fulfilled by Jesus himself! But Daniel earnestly wondered about the fate of Jerusalem and the Temple, and so the last line of that prophecy (verse 27) mentions its final destruction after the Messiah is 'cut off,' or killed suddenly. Jesus was now talking specifically about the terrible judgment to come against the city and Temple. He was warning them to flee Judea quickly when they saw this final sign of its destruction.

What was the nature of this sign? We get a clue from the parallel passage to Matthew 24 in Luke 21:20-21: "'When you see Jerusalem being surrounded by armies, you will know that its desolation is near. 21 Then let those who are in Judea flee to the mountains, let those in the city get out, and let those in the country not enter the city." These were the Roman armies who eventually surrounded the city and laid siege to it. Being Gentiles, their presence in the Holy City and Temple was 'abominable,' as were their army standards with images of the emperor and eagles, which they worshiped as divine. At one point during the siege, the Roman army broke into the city and set up their standards right next to the Temple. After attempting to break into the Temple and nearly succeeding, the Romans pulled back for seemingly no reason whatsoever. Jewish fighters pursued them as they retreated, allowing some to flee the doomed city for a space of about three days.[15] This was their last chance to heed the warning Jesus gave them.

So began the "great tribulation" (verse 21 as it is translated in the KJV), as this is where we get the phrase from. This truth is hard for us to accept for a couple of reasons: 1.) We are often unaware of just how devastating the destruction of Jerusalem and the Temple were, and 2.) We have always been taught that the great tribulation in this passage is a future event.

Never to be Equaled Again

We are rarely taught the gruesome facts of history surrounding the destruction of Jerusalem and the Temple in 70 A.D. The historian Josephus, who gives the most exhaustive account of it, writes, "It appears to me that the misfortunes of all men, from the beginning of the world, if they be compared to these of the Jews are not so considerable as they were."[16]

During this time, Judea was plagued by war in their revolt against Rome. Due to refugees flooding Jerusalem and the celebration of the Passover, the city was estimated to be packed with 3 million people. "Now this vast multitude is indeed collected out of remote places. But the entire nation was now shut up by fate, as in prison; and the Roman army encompassed the city when it was crowded with inhabitants. Accordingly the multitude of those that therein perished exceeded all the destructions that either men or God ever brought upon the world."[17]

The Romans laid siege to the city, and famine came soon after. "Now of those that perished by famine in the city, the number was prodigious; and the miseries they underwent were unspeakable. For if so much as the shadow of any kind of food did any where appear, a war was commenced presently; and the dearest friends fell a fighting one with another about it: snatching from each other the most miserable supports of life."[18] In desperation, they chewed on any leather, fibers, or hay they could find. Josephus relates the tragic story of one woman who had been robbed multiple times, and in hunger and rage she killed, roasted, and ate half of her infant son before being discovered.[19]

Many who attempted to leave the city to forage for food were caught and killed by the Jews as deserters. Those that did make it out were caught by the hundreds daily, and to make an example out of them, the Roman commander Titus had them crucified. So many hundreds died in this way that Josephus says the hills were covered in crosses, and they ran out of both places and wood to put up any more.[20]

Eventually, the Roman armies broke into the city. They killed many whom they found alive, but many more were found already dead by civil war, disease, and famine. Thousands of corpses were found sealed in subterranean chambers under the city where they had attempted to hide. In all, Josephus put the total number of those who died during the whole siege at one million, one hundred thousand. Ninety-seven thousand people were taken into captivity, whether sold into slavery, kept for wild beasts in arenas, or sent to work as slaves in the Egyptian mines.[21] Miller writes:

> There has not been from the foundation of Babylon of old to this day a more horrible destruction. No other city has ever lost over one million people, dead in a single siege! Dio says over 540,000 Jews died directly from battle and the people who died as a result of famine and disease and internal disorder were uncountable. Eusebius gives the same number as Josephus, or 1,100,000 total dead in the siege. Thus are fulfilled the words of Jesus that there would be great tribulation of these proportions associated with the destruction of Jerusalem as well as nations rising against nation.[22]

Jesus the Prophet

Jesus foretold this destruction of the city and the Temple, and the events that would precede it, warning them that 'these things' would happen within 40 years. As the Messiah, he came to fulfill the roles of prophet, priest, and king, and here he was prophesying the judgment to come within the generation of those listening. Moses foretold that this prophet would come long ago: "The Lord your God will raise up for you a prophet like me from among you, from your fellow Israelites. You must listen to him" (Deuteronomy 18:15). He also told them, "You may say to yourselves, "How can we know when a message has not been spoken by the Lord?" If what a prophet proclaims in the name of the Lord does not take place or come true, that is a message the Lord has not spoken. That prophet has spoken presumptuously, so do not be alarmed" (Deuteronomy 18:21-22).

We know that Jesus has spoken the truth, and his prediction came to pass precisely when and how he said it would. Jesus' disciples and the Christians living in Jerusalem took his warnings seriously and were spared because of it:

> Jerusalem was taken in the autumn of 70 A.D. Before its fall the Christians had left the doomed city. While the greater part retired beyond the Jordan and founded Christian colonies at Pella and the neighborhood, the principle leaders of the church -- the surviving apostles and other personal disciples of the Lord -- sought a new home in proconsular Asia. Henceforward we find the headquarters of Christendom no more at Jerusalem, nor even at Antioch but, (for the time at least) in Ephesus. Here John fixed his abode after his temporary banishment in Patmos.[23]

The believers understood and recognized the warning signs Jesus had given them and were spared from calamity! The Greek historian Eusebius tells us the same: "But the people of the church in Jerusalem had been commanded by a revelation, vouchsafed to approved men there before the war, to leave the city and to dwell in a certain town of Perea called Pella."[24] Jesus warned them against false prophets and messiahs, and there were many of both at that time, according to historical records. He rightly said, "See, I have told you ahead of time" (Matthew 24:25).

Why should we be embarrassed of Christ's predictions, as if he were a failed prophet? Or why distort the interpretation of Jesus' words 'this generation' to fit our supposed timeline of the future? When the historical fulfillment is understood, we should be full of joy and wonder that Jesus is *the* Prophet, and his words are vindicated.

The Coming of the Son of Man

As we have just seen by using hindsight and facts of history, verses 4-28 are easily applied to the first topic the disciples asked about: the destruction of the Temple and razing of Jerusalem. In the rest of the chapter, Jesus goes on to answer the questions of his coming and the end of the age, again using the principle that 'both events could be described in the same words.' Yet we must wait for the later fulfillment to completely understand them, because only that event will clear these verses up.

Using our earlier example from Isaiah, when the exiles from Babylon and the other nations they were scattered to had returned to Jerusalem, they could read Isaiah 11:11-12 and understand their fulfillment: "In that day the Lord will reach out his hand a second time to reclaim the surviving remnant of his people from Assyria, from Lower Egypt, from Upper Egypt, from Cush, from Elam, from Babylonia, from Hamath and from the islands of the Mediterranean. He will raise a banner for the nations and gather the exiles of Israel; he will assemble the scattered people of Judah from the four quarters of the earth." Yet they might not quite grasp the verses that came before these: "In that day the Root of Jesse will stand as a banner for the peoples; the nations will rally to him, and his resting place will be glorious" (Isaiah 11:10), because this verse and the ones before it apply to a Messiah that had not yet come. Somehow both are still considered to be "in that day"! This is the nature of prophecy: we must focus on what has been fulfilled, and seeing God's faithfulness to his promises, we look forward in faith to what is sure to come.

The rest of the chapter is below:

29 "Immediately after the distress of those days

"'the sun will be darkened,
and the moon will not give its light;
the stars will fall from the sky,

and the heavenly bodies will be shaken.'

30 "Then will appear the sign of the Son of Man in heaven. And then all the peoples of the earth will mourn when they see the Son of Man coming on the clouds of heaven, with power and great glory. 31 And he will send his angels with a loud trumpet call, and they will gather his elect from the four winds, from one end of the heavens to the other.

32 "Now learn this lesson from the fig tree: As soon as its twigs get tender and its leaves come out, you know that summer is near. 33 Even so, when you see all these things, you know that it is near, right at the door. 34 Truly I tell you, this generation will certainly not pass away until all these things have happened. 35 Heaven and earth will pass away, but my words will never pass away.

36 "But about that day or hour no one knows, not even the angels in heaven, nor the Son, but only the Father. 37 As it was in the days of Noah, so it will be at the coming of the Son of Man. 38 For in the days before the flood, people were eating and drinking, marrying and giving in marriage, up to the day Noah entered the ark; 39 and they knew nothing about what would happen until the flood came and took them all away. That is how it will be at the coming of the Son of Man. 40 Two men will be in the field; one will be taken and the other left. 41 Two women will be grinding with a hand mill; one will be taken and the other left.

42 "Therefore keep watch, because you do not know on what day your Lord will come. 43 But understand this: If the owner of the house had known at what time of night the thief was

coming, he would have kept watch and would not have let his house be broken into. 44 So you also must be ready, because the Son of Man will come at an hour when you do not expect him.

45 "Who then is the faithful and wise servant, whom the master has put in charge of the servants in his household to give them their food at the proper time? 46 It will be good for that servant whose master finds him doing so when he returns. 47 Truly I tell you, he will put him in charge of all his possessions. 48 But suppose that servant is wicked and says to himself, 'My master is staying away a long time,' 49 and he then begins to beat his fellow servants and to eat and drink with drunkards. 50 The master of that servant will come on a day when he does not expect him and at an hour he is not aware of. 51 He will cut him to pieces and assign him a place with the hypocrites, where there will be weeping and gnashing of teeth. (Matthew 24:29-51)

The Day and Hour Unknown

One principle from the previous verses that seems to bear repeating in every generation is that *no one knows the day or the hour* of Christ's return (verse 36). How often this word from Christ is violated, each and every time to our shame and the discrediting of the gospel. Whether it's blood moons, Y2K, the Mayan calendar, the Prophecy of the Popes, or *88 reasons Why The Rapture Will Be in 1988*, each and every one is flawed from the outset. There is good reason to believe that the traditional understanding of prophecy that is being shared in this book, namely *historicism*, fell into decline in part due to this kind of abuse.

Historicism was the most common understanding of prophecy in Scripture from the Reformation until the middle of the 19th century. In that latter time there was a Baptist preacher named William Miller who taught a bastardized version of historicism, and additionally set a date for the return of Christ by

1844. This started a fervor among 'Millerites,' many of whom had given away all their possessions and left their work in anticipation of the three different dates that ended up being set when the previous one failed. When the last precise set date of October 22, 1844, came and went, the event was called *the Great Disappointment*, and they were left disillusioned. The Seventh Day Adventists were born from the leftovers of this movement, still teaching the unorthodox version of historicism that Miller invented. Repeat after me: *no one knows the day or the hour.*

Taken Away

The verses that follow this warning are frequently brought up when teaching about the rapture:

> 37 As it was in the days of Noah, so it will be at the coming of the Son of Man. 38 For in the days before the flood, people were eating and drinking, marrying and giving in marriage, up to the day Noah entered the ark; 39 and they knew nothing about what would happen until the flood came and took them all away. That is how it will be at the coming of the Son of Man. 40 Two men will be in the field; one will be taken and the other left. 41 Two women will be grinding with a hand mill; one will be taken and the other left. (Matthew 24:37-41)

The rapture is a biblical concept where believers will meet Jesus in the air when he returns, based chiefly on 1 Thessalonians 4:16-17: "For the Lord himself will come down from heaven, with a loud command, with the voice of the archangel and with the trumpet call of God, and the dead in Christ will rise first. After that, we who are still alive and are left will be caught up together with them in the clouds to meet the Lord in the air. And so we will be with the Lord forever."

On the other hand, the 'secret' rapture taught today is the popular interpretation that Jesus will come on two separate occasions- once to meet believers in the air secretly, in a way that only they will hear and see him; and again a few years later, alongside the believers, to judge all people and claim his kingdom. There are two problems with using Matthew 24 to support this idea: 1.) all people will see him when he comes, and 2.) being 'taken' in the context of these verses is not necessarily a good thing.

1. *All people will see him*: Matthew 24:27 says, "For as lightning that comes from the east is visible even in the west, so will be the coming of the Son of Man." His coming will be seen by all, and announced with a loud voice and trumpet call: "Then will appear the sign of the Son of Man in heaven. And then all the peoples of the earth will mourn when they see the Son of Man coming on the clouds of heaven, with power and great glory. And he will send his angels with a loud trumpet call, and they will gather his elect from the four winds, from one end of the heavens to the other" (Matthew 24:30-31). The shout and trumpet call are also stated in the verses in 1 Thessalonians 4 about the rapture, quoted above. Revelation 1:7 says, "'Look, he is coming with the clouds,' and 'every eye will see him, even those who pierced him'; and all peoples on earth 'will mourn because of him.' So shall it be! Amen."

2. *Being 'taken' by the flood*: A close look at verses 37-41 reveals that the allusion to being taken is a reference to the 'days of Noah,' when "the flood came and *took them all away*" (verse 39, emphasis mine). So it would be more desirable to be the one 'left behind' rather than *taken* by the flood, or by death.

The biblical idea of the rapture is that Jesus comes once, both to gather the elect, and then judge all people. Christians meet him in the air like a welcoming party, and join him in his triumphant return to Earth.[25] The main idea expressed in this chapter is that the Son of Man came to judge Jerusalem, and he will come again to judge all people. Both events can be described using the same words.

Traditional Vs. Modern Interpretation

Because the immediate and future events in this passage are seemingly all mixed together, it can be difficult to determine what has been fulfilled and what has not. The modern futurist view bypasses this difficulty by pushing everything into the 'unfulfilled' category, except maybe 'the beginning of the birth pains'- wars, famines, earthquakes, false messiahs- things that have undeniably happened these nearly two thousand years later. Yes, the Temple is currently utterly destroyed, but this view insists it must be built again so that a deceitful world leader can stand in it and call himself God. Before this happens, however, the elect are 'taken away'; everyone else is *Left Behind*. The difficulty of 'these things' happening within a generation is resolved by interpreting the word 'generation' as 'race' or 'ethnic group,' so Jews will still be a recognizable group.

Yet the traditional interpretation offers a solution that is much less forced- Jesus answers the disciples' questions about two different events, much like the prophets of old did: by grouping them together according to their topic rather than their chronology. A quick review of history confirms those things that were in the immediate future: never were false prophets and messiahs more prevalent and dangerous than in the times surrounding the destruction of the Temple. There were terrible wars, famines, and earthquakes that destroyed entire cities before that event. The disciples were persecuted severely, nearly all of them ended up as martyrs, and the gospel was preached throughout the Roman Empire. The Roman standards were set up on the Temple grounds, yet the troops 'inexplicably' retreated, allowing those who were previously warned to escape. The destruction and death in Jerusalem were apocalyptic in nature. And, of course, the Temple was destroyed brick by brick- because it had been set on fire, the Roman Army completely dismantled it to retrieve the gold that had melted in the cracks. The city walls were dug up to the foundations, and

Jerusalem was made so desolate that "there was left nothing to make those that came thither believe it had ever been inhabited."[26]

To top it all off, all these things happened within a generation- that is, biblically, 40 years. And because the believers were warned ahead of time, according to the historical record, they were spared that tribulation. All of this put together is absolutely remarkable! There is no reason to be embarrassed by this prophecy. The 'most embarrassing verse' becomes a faith-building prediction, and because he was so accurate, we know that the Son of Man will come again.

---

1. C.S. Lewis, "The World's Last Night and Other Essays", 60.

2. Albert Barnes, "Notes, Critical, Illustrative, and Practical", Matthew 24:3. Available online at https://www.sacred-texts.com/bib/cmt/barnes/mat0 24.htm

3. Barnes, ibid, Introduction to Isaiah.

4. Craig Keener, "The IVP Bible Background Commentary: New Testament", 106.

5. Fred Miller, "Revelation: A Panorama of the Gospel Age", 191. Available online at http://moellerhaus.com/matt24.htm

6. Flavius Josephus, "Antiquities of the Jews", 20:2:5. Available online at http://penelope.uchicago.edu/josephus/ant-20.html

7. Barnes, ibid, Matthew 24:7.

8. Mentioned in Barnes, ibid, Matthew 24:7. For a detailed resource on earthquakes in this period mentioned by Tacitus and others, see "Catalogue of ancient earthquakes in the Mediterranean area up to the 10th century" by Emanuela Guidoboni, available online at https://deadseaquake.info/pdfs/Catg1.pdf

9. Barnes, ibid, Matthew 24:9.

10. Publius Cornelius Tacitus, "The Annals", 15:44
Available online at https://en.wikisource.org/wiki/The_Annals_(Tacitus)/Book_15

11. Josephus, "The Jewish War", 2:13:5.
Available online at https://penelope.uchicago.edu/josephus/war-2.html

12. Josephus, "War", 6:5:2.

13. Josephus, "War", 6:5:2.

14. James Strong, "Strong's Greek Lexicon (kjv)", G3625 - oikoumenē.
Available online at https://www.blueletterbible.org/lexicon/g3625/kjv/tr/0-1/

15. Josephus, "War", 2:19.

16. Josephus, "War", Preface, section 4.

17. Josephus, "War", 6:9:4.

18. Josephus, "War", 6:3:3.

19. Josephus, "War", 6:3:4.

20. Josephus, "War", 5:11:1.

21. Josephus, "War", 6:9:3-4.

22. Miller, ibid, 198.

23. Quoted from Miller, ibid, 193.
J.B. Lightfoot, "Apostolic Fathers: Clement, Ignatius, Polycarp", Vol. 1 pg. 438.

24. Eusebius, "Church History", 3:5:3.
Available online at
https://en.wikisource.org/wiki/Nicene_and_Post-Nicene_Fathers:_Serie
s_II/Volume_I/Church_History_of_Eusebius/Book_III/Chapter_5

25. See Shiao Chong, "What's Wrong with the Rapture?"
Available online at https://www.thebanner.org/columns/2022/09/what
s-wrong-with-the-rapture

26. Josephus, "War", 7:1:1.

Chapter Five

The Coming of the Son of Man

Daniel 7

In the last chapter we jumped from the Old Testament to the New Testament. We went from the Seventy 'Sevens' prophecy in Daniel 9 to look at the related passage in Matthew 24, Jesus' prophecy about the destruction of Jerusalem and the Temple, as well as the future coming of the Son of Man. Now we go back to the Old Testament in Daniel 7, which is where the reference to a messianic 'son of man' comes from. This vision is about the Son of Man- Jesus Christ, the Messiah- coming in glory and receiving his kingdom to rule with the saints.

Again, Daniel 7 is the only place in the Old Testament where the title 'son of man' is clearly linked to the Messiah. When Jesus referred to himself as the Son of Man, this is the passage that the Jews who heard him would recall. The events described by this vision are why the Jews expected the Messiah to be a conquering king who saved them from the Roman Empire and set up his earthly kingdom.

The first chapter of this book goes over Daniel 2, where the 'little stone' strikes down the great statue and grows to fill the whole earth. We looked at how Christ inaugurated the kingdom of God, and how it has been growing larger and larger to this day. The kingdom of God *did* come with the Son of Man, but not in a way that the Jews in his day expected. So Daniel 7 looks forward to a still future event, when the Son of Man comes to *consummate* his Kingdom, and when "'the sovereignty, power and greatness of all the kingdoms under heaven will be handed over to the holy people of the Most High. His kingdom will be an everlasting kingdom, and all rulers will worship and obey him'" (Daniel 7:27).

In Daniel 2, we were also introduced to the four world empires that would arise, one after another, until the little stone broke in to replace them. These world empires are shown to us again here in Daniel 7, this time under the symbol of 'beasts.' Christians largely agree on the identity of these beasts, and it isn't until the details of the fourth beast that interpretations start to diverge.

The Four Beasts

1 In the first year of Belshazzar king of Babylon, Daniel had a dream, and visions passed through his mind as he was lying in bed. He wrote down the substance of his dream.

2 Daniel said: "In my vision at night I looked, and there before me were the four winds of heaven churning up the great sea. 3 Four great beasts, each different from the others, came up out of the sea. (Daniel 7:1-3)

Daniel received this vision during the reign of Belshazzar, the last of the kings of the Babylonian Empire. It is a dream filled with symbols, but thankfully it is interpreted for us in the latter part of the chapter. The use of symbols in the visions of Daniel teaches and prepares us for how to interpret the likewise heavy use of symbols in Revelation. In fact, the very symbols in this chapter of Daniel are used again in Revelation.

God doesn't leave us in the dark when it comes to using symbols in visions and prophecy. They are often interpreted for us in the immediate context, or there are other places in the Bible that give us clues- Scripture interprets Scripture. In this case, we're told later in the chapter that the 'beasts' are kingdoms (verses 17, 23). Of course, these kingdoms do not literally 'come up out the sea,' so what does the great sea stand for? "Among the sacred poets and the prophets, hosts of armies invading a land are compared to overflowing waters, and mighty changes among the nations to the heaving billows of the ocean in a storm. Compare Jeremiah 46:7-8; Jeremiah 47:2; Isaiah 8:7-8; Isaiah 17:12; Isaiah 59:19; Daniel 11:40; Revelation 13:1."[1] The example of Isaiah 17:12 reads, "Woe to the many nations that rage— they rage like the raging sea! Woe to the peoples who roar— they roar like the roaring of great waters!" These kingdoms are formed amidst great turmoil among the nations.

> 4 "The first was like a lion, and it had the wings of an eagle. I watched until its wings were torn off and it was lifted from the ground so that it stood on two feet like a human being, and the mind of a human was given to it. (Daniel 7:4)

The lion is 'the king of beasts,' a symbol of strength, courage, and sovereignty in the Scriptures.[2] Eagles represent swiftness and far-reaching flight.[3] Therefore, these symbols point to a strong and sovereign kingdom that would arise out of the turmoil of the nations, conquering widely and swiftly. But its wings are torn off- its conquests are eventually cut short- and it stands on two feet like a man, with the mind of man given to it. To sum up the symbols, "this mighty empire, carrying its arms with the rapidity of an eagle, and the fierceness of a lion, through the world, would be checked in its career; its ferocity would be tamed, and it would be characterized by comparative moderation and humanity."[4]

Christian interpreters throughout history have agreed that this kingdom is the same 'head on gold' of the statue of Daniel 2: the Babylonian Empire. "All, or nearly all, agree that it refers to the kingdom of Babylon, of which Nebuchadnezzar was the head, and to the gradual diminution of the ferocity of conquest under a succession of comparatively weak princes."[5]

5 "And there before me was a second beast, which looked like a bear. It was raised up on one of its sides, and it had three ribs in its mouth between its teeth. It was told, 'Get up and eat your fill of flesh!' (Daniel 7:5)

The bear is less noble than the lion, but known for its ferocity, especially when 'robbed of her cubs' as it is written in Scripture (Hosea 13:8). It was raised up on one of its sides, possibly a pose of getting ready to attack. It had three ribs in its mouth, suggesting "a kingdom or people of a fierce and rough character having already subdued some, and then, after reposing, rising up with the trophies of its former conquests to go forth to new victories, or to overcome others."[6] It was also told to "'Get up and eat your fill of flesh!'", symbolizing a command from God to go on to further conquests.

If the first kingdom is Babylon, then this would naturally apply to the Medo-Persian Empire, the chest and arms of silver from the statue in Daniel 2. Just as silver is inferior to gold, Medo-Persia was inferior to Babylon (Daniel 2:39), and the bear is less noble than the lion. The bear was raised up on one side- the Persians were raised up over the Medes- or they were poised to strike other kingdoms after their initial conquests. Three ribs were in its mouth- just as Cyrus had conquered Persia, Media, and Lydia- readying himself for about a year before attacking Babylon. God gave the command that Cyrus would go forth and conquer Babylon, mentioning him by name in Isaiah 45:1, centuries before he was born.

6 "After that, I looked, and there before me was another beast, one that looked like a leopard. And on its back it had four wings like those of a bird. This beast had four heads, and it was given authority to rule. (Daniel 7:6)

Scripture characterizes leopards as fast, fierce, and next in dignity to a lion.[7] Having four wings, this kingdom moves even more quickly in its conquests than the lion. It also has four heads, symbolizing one kingdom composed of four separate powers. The Macedonian (or Grecian) Empire comes after the Medo-Persian Empire, and these symbols fit it perfectly. As we saw in Daniel 8, Alexander the Great made his conquests in an extremely short period of time. In Daniel 8, the large horn was broken "at the height of its power," and "in its place four prominent horns grew up toward the four winds of heaven" (Daniel 8:8). The four heads of the leopard are these same four kingdoms that ruled in Alexander's place (Daniel 8:22).

> 7 "After that, in my vision at night I looked, and there before me was a fourth beast—terrifying and frightening and very powerful. It had large iron teeth; it crushed and devoured its victims and trampled underfoot whatever was left. It was different from all the former beasts, and it had ten horns. (Daniel 7:7)

At last, we come to the terrifying fourth beast. It is no problem to identify it, and with near unanimity, it is recognized as the Roman Empire, which came after the Grecian one. "The fourth beast - so mighty, so terrific, so powerful, so unlike all the others, armed with iron teeth, and with claws of brass, trampling down and stamping on all the earth - well represents the Roman dominion."[8]

This is where the unity of interpretations ends. The modern futurist interpretation pushes the rest of the vision into the future, and the preterist view keeps it in the past. But the traditional historicist view looks at how similar symbols have been interpreted in other passages of Scripture, and sees how they align with a historical fulfillment in the Church age, to the present day and beyond.

Ten Horns

The Roman Empire is long gone of course- Ancient Rome, or the Western Roman Empire, dissolved over 1500 years ago. How do we interpret the ten horns of the fourth beast? Daniel wanted to know the same, and the rest of the vision focuses on the fate of the fourth beast, until all kingdoms are handed over to the Son of Man and the holy people of the Most High (Daniel 7:27):

8 "While I was thinking about the horns, there before me was another horn, a little one, which came up among them; and three of the first horns were uprooted before it. This horn had eyes like the eyes of a human being and a mouth that spoke boastfully.

9 "As I looked,

"thrones were set in place,
and the Ancient of Days took his seat.
His clothing was as white as snow;
the hair of his head was white like wool.
His throne was flaming with fire,
and its wheels were all ablaze.
10 A river of fire was flowing,
coming out from before him.
Thousands upon thousands attended him;
ten thousand times ten thousand stood before him.
The court was seated,
and the books were opened.

11 "Then I continued to watch because of the boastful words the horn was speaking. I kept looking until the beast was slain

and its body destroyed and thrown into the blazing fire. 12 (The other beasts had been stripped of their authority, but were allowed to live for a period of time.)

13 "In my vision at night I looked, and there before me was one like a son of man, coming with the clouds of heaven. He approached the Ancient of Days and was led into his presence. 14 He was given authority, glory and sovereign power; all nations and peoples of every language worshiped him. His dominion is an everlasting dominion that will not pass away, and his kingdom is one that will never be destroyed. (Daniel 7:8-14)

The dream is interpreted for Daniel in the next part of the chapter. Concerning the fourth beast and the ten horns: "He gave me this explanation: 'The fourth beast is a fourth kingdom that will appear on earth. It will be different from all the other kingdoms and will devour the whole earth, trampling it down and crushing it. The ten horns are ten kings who will come from this kingdom" (Daniel 7:23-24a). One thing to note in this chapter is that 'kings' and 'kingdoms' are used interchangeably. For instance, "The four great beasts are four *kings* that will rise from the earth" (Daniel 7:17, *emphasis mine*), yet these same are referred to as 'kingdoms' in verse 23 above. So, the ten horns could be ten kings, or ten kingdoms.

There is another place in Daniel that gives us more insight into symbols of animals and horns. In chapter 2 of this book, we looked at the vision of the ram and the goat of Daniel 8. In it, we are told by the angel Gabriel that the ram symbolizes the Medo-Persian Empire, and the one-horned goat is Greece. It is agreed that the one horn of the goat symbolizes Alexander the Great, and after it is broken, "the four horns that replaced the one that was broken off represent four kingdoms that will emerge from his nation but will not have the same power" (Daniel 8:22). The symbols in Daniel 7 are very similar, and it would be natural to look for ten kingdoms to emerge from the Roman Empire, not having the same power.

It turns out that when the Roman Empire fell, ten kingdoms were formed from its ruins. Historians make different lists, but they typically contain ten kingdoms, and are similar to this one by Isaac Newton:

1. The kingdom of the Vandals and Alans in Spain and Africa;

2. the kingdom of the Suevians in Spain;

3. the kingdom of the Visigoths;

4. the kingdom of the Alans in Gallia;

5. the kingdom of the Burgundians;

6. the kingdom of the Franks;

7. the kingdom of the Britons;

8. the kingdom of the Huns;

9. the kingdom of the Lombards;

10. the kingdom of Ravenna.[9]

These historical events are uncanny, and a testament to the divine origin of this prophecy. "One thing is certain, that there never has been a case in which an empire of vast power has been broken up into small sovereignties, to which this description would so well apply as to the rise of the numerous dynasties in the breaking up of the vast Roman power."[10] So far, the biblical use of these symbols and their historical fulfillment are in alignment. The fourth beast is identified as the Roman Empire, and in 476 A.D., that empire fell and was carved up into ten kingdoms.

The Little Horn

So who or what is the 'little horn' that came up among the ten kingdoms, three being uprooted before it, with eyes like a human being, and a mouth that speaks boastfully?

20 I also wanted to know about the ten horns on its head and about the other horn that came up, before which three of them fell—the horn that looked more imposing than the others and that had eyes and a mouth that spoke boastfully. 21 As I watched, this horn was waging war against the holy people and defeating them, 22 until the Ancient of Days came and pronounced judgment in favor of the holy people of the Most High, and the time came when they possessed the kingdom.

23 "He gave me this explanation: 'The fourth beast is a fourth kingdom that will appear on earth. It will be different from all the other kingdoms and will devour the whole earth, trampling it down and crushing it. 24 The ten horns are ten kings who will come from this kingdom. After them another king will arise, different from the earlier ones; he will subdue three kings. 25 He will speak against the Most High and oppress his holy people and try to change the set times and the laws. The holy people will be delivered into his hands for a time, times and half a time.

26 "'But the court will sit, and his power will be taken away and completely destroyed forever. (Daniel 7:20-26)

What follows is a summary from Barnes of what we know about the little horn from this chapter, and what it would fairly symbolize:

- *The little horn came up among the other horns, and stood among them -* It would share the divided power of the Roman Empire with the other kingdoms.

- *The little horn came after the other horns were already there -* It would rise up after the other ten kingdoms were established.

- *It started small, but grew in power and displaced three other horns -* This king or kingdom would start small, but grow large enough to take control over three of the ten kingdoms that were formed after the fall of the Roman Empire.

- *It had a mouth that spoke boastfully, speaking words "against the Most High"* (Daniel 7:25) - This king or kingdom would be proud and arrogant, blaspheming God. If this is the same power as 'the man of lawlessness' in 2 Thessalonians, "He will oppose and will exalt himself over everything that is called God or is worshiped, so that he sets himself up in God's temple, proclaiming himself to be God" (2 Thessalonians 2:4).

- *It would persecute God's people -* This king or kingdom would oppress and wage war against 'the holy people of the Most High' (Daniel 7:21, 25). It would succeed in this for "a time, times, and half a time" (Daniel 7:25), which is three and a half years.

- *It would claim legislative power -* This king or kingdom would "try to change the set times and laws" (Daniel 7:25), especially regarding God's people.[11]

The modern popular interpretation insists that these things are still in the future- the ten horns are ten nations that will be united, and the little horn is a ruler who will take over three of them, tricking Israel into following him. After Christians are secretly raptured, or taken into heaven, the little horn will stand in a newly built Temple and proclaim himself to be God, terrorizing them for three and a half years.

One major problem with this interpretation is the fact that the fourth beast- the Roman Empire- has been long gone, for over 1,500 years now. Once again, an inexplicable, unmentioned 'pause' is introduced to the vision. This is the same type of problem that plagues the interpretation of each prophecy that is forced into the mold of a future fulfillment: the toes of the statue in Daniel 2 are longer than the height of the rest of the statue; instead of being a precise 490-year prophecy, the seventy 'sevens' of Daniel 9 are now 2,480 years and counting; the destruction of the Temple prophesied by Jesus in Matthew 24 is now a future Temple instead of the one that was actually destroyed within the generation he spoke to. All of these, despite the glaring accuracy of a verifiable historical fulfillment for each one, that when recognized, leaves us in awe of a God who knows the future and tells us about it beforehand in order to build our faith.

A Historical Fulfillment

If we were to ask a historian of any faith (or lack thereof), "After the fall of the Roman Empire, was there ever a king, kingdom, or authority figure who started small, but grew in power to the point where they had control of other kingdoms that came from ruins of that Empire?" what would their answer be? We could ask further: "did this king ever boast in his power and authority, equating himself with God? Did he have the authority to change laws, especially for believers? Did they ever declare war against believers who would not obey his commands?" Their answer would be crystal clear, beyond a shadow of a doubt: the Bishop of Rome, the office of the Papacy, the power behind the Holy Roman Empire, the Pope- this is the only authority that fulfills all of the signs of the little horn.

But not many of us are historians. We look at the Pope today and think, "What harm has that old sweet man ever done? In fact, he says many wonderful things and is an inspiration to millions!" It's true, and while the Pope is still a major influence on many, the power of the office of the Papacy today is a shadow of what it once was. We have a hard time grasping the massive authority they held until just a few centuries ago. Perhaps we get little hints of its previous might once in awhile; small glimpses of the power that gripped Europe. For instance, I used to play a computer game called *Medieval II: Total War*, where the player is a ruler of a historical kingdom warring with other kingdoms. In it, the Pope was a faction to be reckoned with, the ruler of the Papal States who could excommunicate you and call crusades against your kingdom if you didn't stay on his good side! Every kingdom in the game had to be careful not to cross the Papacy. Things like this give us an idea of what kind of power the Popes held in the past.

A cursory glance at the history of post-Roman Empire Europe shows a remarkable fulfillment of the prophecy in Daniel 7. We have already mentioned how the Roman Empire's fall left ten kingdoms in its place. In the power vacuum that occurred in Rome, the Papacy served as a source of authority and continuity. The Popes were recognized by the Byzantine Emperors as the head of the church in 533 A.D., and given the title of 'Universal Bishop' in 606 A.D. Not too long after consolidating this spiritual authority, the Papacy secured much greater political power in the form of kingdoms:

> The Papal states were accumulated in pieces between the years 755 and 800. The Exarchate of Ravenna was conferred on the Papacy under Pope Stephen II by Pepin, father of Charlemagne, in the year 755. The kingdom of the Lombards was conquered by Charlemagne, son of Pepin; he conferred that kingdom on the Papacy, laying the documents on the altar of St. Peter in Rome in the year 774, and the Roman senate itself was taken over by the Papacy by degrees. Shortly after 800 the three principalities were included in the Papal states which were held by the Papacy until 1870,- over 1000 years. These states were accumulated with no small amount of intrigue, war, bloodshed and other adjuncts of political turnovers.[12]

Malachi Martin, a high-ranking Jesuit scholar in the Roman Catholic Church, confirms this consolidation of power by 800:

> By the end of the eighth century the pope was, in fact and practice, a temporal ruler of gigantic proportions. The Papal States had been established. As time went on, in addition to the Papal States which were ruled directly by the popes as their own possessions, the Roman pope gained feudal power over other states: they were obligated to pay yearly tribute and to contribute to the defensive and offensive policies of the popes. The Roman pontiffs also acquired political control in still other lands: the rulers were appointed with papal approval, and they were bound by offensive-defensive alliances with the papacy.[13]

Here is the little horn: not just a single man, but a line of 'kings' that quickly grew mighty in the midst of the ten horns of the beast. Three of these horns were felled before the little horn, and their power was given to him.

The Papacy did not stop there. The ultimate form of their political power was in the resuscitation of the Roman Empire, now called the 'Holy Roman Empire.' The fourth beast was given new life! It began just as soon as the three horns were uprooted before the little horn in 800 A.D., when Pope Leo III crowned Charlemagne 'emperor of the Romans.' This is a perfect fulfillment of the events described in Revelation 13, when "The second beast was given power to give breath to the image of the first beast, so that the image could speak and cause all who refused to worship the image to be killed" (Revelation 13:15). The Holy Roman Empire was an image of the Roman Empire that had fallen, becoming the most powerful monarchy in Europe.

Just as the little horn was boastful and blasphemous, the Papacy reveled in the titles it gave itself:

"Our Lord God the Pope; another God upon earth; king of kings and lord of lords. The same is the dominion of God and the Pope. To believe that our Lord God the Pope might not decree as he decreed is heresy. The power of the Pope is greater than all created power, and extends itself to things celestial, terrestrial, and infernal. The Pope doeth whatsoever he listeth, even things unlawful, and is more than God."[14]

With these, "the Pope has claimed, or allowed to be conferred on him, names and prerogatives which can belong only to God."[15] Martin also quotes the Papacy in their belief that all powers in heaven and earth are theirs:

On November 18, 1302, Boniface VIII could issue a famous statement of papal claims which stands as the ultimate expression of the Christian heartland and profound Roman claims on it. "The Church," declared Boniface, "has one body and one head, Christ and Christ's Vicar, Peter and Peter's successor... In his power there are two swords, a spiritual and a temporal sword... Both kinds of power are in the hands of the Roman P ontiff... And furthermore we declare and define it to be believed as a necessary condition for salvation that everything created in the human universe is subject to the Roman Pontiff."[16]

The Papacy used its power to wage war against God's people, and their victims are in the millions:[17]

In the year 1208, a crusade was proclaimed by Pope Innocent III against the Waldenses and Albigenses, in which a million of men perished. From the beginning of the order of the Jesuits, in the year 1540 to 1580, nine hundred thousand were destroyed. One hundred and fifty thousand perished by the Inquisition in thirty years. In the Low Countries fifty thousand persons were hanged, beheaded, burned, or buried alive, for the crime of heresy, within the space of thirty-eight years from the edict of Charles V, against the Protestants, to the peace of Chateau Cambresis in 1559. Eighteen thousand suffered by the hands of the executioner, in the space of five years and a half, during the administration of the Duke of Alva. Indeed, the slightest acquaintance with the history of the Papacy, will convince anyone that what is here said of "making war with the saints" Daniel 7:21, and "wearing out the saints of the Most High" Daniel 7:25, is strictly applicable to that power, and will accurately describe its history.[18]

Finally, the Papacy claimed total legislative power, both civil and spiritual. In the civil realm, they claimed "the right of deposing and setting up kings; of fixing the boundaries of nations; of giving away crowns and scepters; and of exercising dominion over the sacred seasons, the customs, the amusements of nations."[19] As for spiritual authority, "the Pope has claimed to be the head of the church, and has asserted and exercised the right of appointing sacred seasons; of abolishing ancient institutions; of introducing numberless new festival occasions, practically abrogating the laws of God on a great variety of subjects."[20] As an example of this, we can list the claim of infallibility, image worship, the celibacy of the clergy, the doctrines of purgatory and transubstantiation, mandatory holidays for feasting and fasting- "in general to the absolute control claimed by the Papacy over the whole subject of religion."[21]

The sheer amount of historical evidence points clearly to the Papacy as the fulfillment of the little horn of Daniel 7. One thing remains- doesn't the little horn only have power for time, times, and half a time- namely, three and a half years?

The Day-Year Principle

In chapter three of this book, we looked at Daniel 9 and the Seventy 'Sevens' prophecy. In a regular narrative passage, those 'sevens' would have been interpreted as weeks, so the whole period of seventy weeks would be 490 days. Yet the unanimous conclusion among interpreters from all times and backgrounds (futurists, preterists, historicists, Catholics and Protestants) has been that those 490 days are actually a symbol for 490 years. This is the natural conclusion due to the sheer number of events that were prophesied in that chapter, and also because of how wonderfully they coincide with the actual coming of the Messiah. It turns out that in prophecies full of symbols, even the time given might be a symbol.

This is seen a couple of other times in the Old Testament. The first is in Numbers 14:34, where the Israelites were sentenced to wander in the wilderness for 40 years, "one year for each of the forty days you explored the land." Also Ezekiel 4:4-5, where the prophet is told to lie on his left side and put the sin of Israel on himself "the same number of days as the years of their sin. So for 390 days you will bear the sin of the people of Israel." So it is not unnatural in the Scriptures, particularly in symbolic prophecy, for a day to equal a year. Among historicists, this is often called the *day-year principle*, and for hundreds of years, it was the most common way to understand the prophecy in this chapter, as well as the parallel times given in Revelation.

The 'time, times, and half a time,' or three and a half years, are the same amount of days as forty-two months (Revelation 11:2, 13:5) and 1,260 days (Revelation 11:3, 12:6). If a day equals a year in this prophecy, then the Papacy as both a civil and spiritual authority is to have control for 1,260 years.

As mentioned earlier in this chapter, the Papacy consolidated spiritual authority in the years 533 and 606 (with some interesting events happening 1,260 years after those dates that we'll look at in a later chapter). It did not gain civil authority until starting about 752, fully receiving power over three of the ten kingdoms in 800. Even though the Papacy has already faced some judgment, losing much (but not all) of its civil authority, it still has a few decades of the 1,260 years left if these dates are correct.

The Depths of Depravity

Perhaps it's still hard to believe that the Papacy is the same persecuting 'little horn' of Daniel 7. Again, we look at Rome today and see a pope who seems to be humbly refusing the trappings of power and luxury that those before him were lavished with. He's not calling for war or lording his power over kingdoms and nations. Yet when we look at the past, even Catholic scholars admit the dark history of the Papacy. Describing two of the worst periods of Papal depravity called the first and second 'pornacracy', one such Catholic author writes:

> The First Pornocracy (882-964) - Since *porneia* means forni-cation and idolatry, then a *pornocracy* refers to *government* by *corruption* in the worst way. It means sexual corruption, fi-nancial corruption, and most importantly spiritual corruption afflicting the Papacy and the Vatican. There has always been corruption in the Church since Judas and before in Israel. Yet new lows were reached in the tenth century papacy. The sexual and financial corruption of the Papacy by powerful families vy-ing for power were exactly like the modern day Vatican Mafia... Murder, adultery, idolatry, greed and darkness reigned in the Papacy in the tenth century...

> The Second Pornocracy (1471-1563) - This period was worse than the first. This was the Renaissance Papacy. There was not only sexual and financial corruption, but these popes had armies and sought to fight other Christian nation states on the Italian peninsula. Julius II, for instance, was nicknamed "the warrior pope" who named himself after Julius Caesar... The worst pope of this period may have been Alexander VI

(1492-1503). He fathered nine children, seven while a cardinal with two different women, and when he was pope, in his sixties, he convinced nineteen-year-old Giulia Farnese to become his concubine. He had Annius of Viterbo produce an elaborate forgery for him "as part of a Vatican campaign to legitimize and bolster papal claims to parts of Italy" allowing the pope's armies to invade. These forgeries also included the racist ideology of the "curse of Ham" which would be used for centuries to justify the expansion of the old Muhammadan trans-Saharan slave trade into the "Christian" trans-Atlantic slave trade.[22]

Entire books have been written about the obscene deeds of popes like these and others, and I will not delve into them here- they are confirmed in hundreds of other accounts. Many of us just aren't aware of how corrupt and depraved many of the Popes throughout history were.

But even if some were not morally bankrupt according to their personal deeds, the Papacy has never repented of their blasphemous titles- claiming to be God on earth- nor have they ever willingly forsaken temporal power. Catholic scholar Martin writes:

> History also reveals that various popes had opportunities to rid the church of its temporal power and wealth, to stand naked of all human and secular protection, to rely only on the promise made by Jesus that his church would never fail, and to employ the only power Jesus authorized them—the power of the spirit. Usually, such opportunities arose as a disastrous result of pontiffs playing power politics just like secular leaders. On each such occasion, however, we find that the Roman leaders refused the invitation, retreating in horror and confusion from the edge of the precipice. The worst of them fought—and to a large extent succeeded—in reacquiring whatever power they had lost. The best of them—a Pius IX or a Pius XII, for instance— never

wholly surrendered the use of power. And the general practice of popes over the centuries has been to try to regain whatever lost power they could.[23]

Even the best popes held onto the power of the 'little horn', the illicit union of the claim to supreme spiritual and civil authority.

This is in addition to the total spiritual authority they still claim as the head of the Church in all matters of faith, doctrine, and interpretation of the Bible. They've added statements of belief to the Apostle's Creed including: the supremacy of the Roman Catholic Church; total agreement with their interpretation of Scripture; belief in purgatory, transubstantiation, indulgences, and that "the saints reigning with Christ are to be worshipped and prayed unto;"[24] among other things, the Pope is to be given obedience in all things. During their counter-Reformation, they completely rejected the five *solas*- Scripture alone, Christ alone, grace alone, faith alone, to the glory of God alone- and declared anyone who believes them to be *anathema*, or excommunicated.

The Papacy remains unchanged in all that is fundamental. Author Tim Challies sums it up:

> The Roman Catholic Church remains committed to a false gospel, a gospel of salvation by grace plus works. The core doctrinal issues that divided Protestantism from Catholicism remain. The core doctrinal issues that compelled Rome to issue her *anathemas* against Protestantism are unchanged. Rome remains fully committed to a gospel that cannot and will not save a single soul. Those within the Roman Catholic Church who have experienced salvation (and certainly there are those who have!) have done so *despite* the church's official teaching, not through it.[25]

When the Man Comes Around

Daniel 7 ends with the judgment of the little horn and the consummation of the kingdom when the Son of Man comes:

> 26 "'But the court will sit, and his power will be taken away and completely destroyed forever. 27 Then the sovereignty, power and greatness of all the kingdoms under heaven will be handed over to the holy people of the Most High. His kingdom will be an everlasting kingdom, and all rulers will worship and obey him.'
>
> 28 "This is the end of the matter. I, Daniel, was deeply troubled by my thoughts, and my face turned pale, but I kept the matter to myself." (Daniel 7:26-28)

There are not many details given here about the second coming of Christ, other than that when he comes, the little horn will be destroyed entirely, and God's people shall rule with him. This prophecy is expanded upon in Revelation, where the same symbols for the fourth beast are given, except the little horn is portrayed as 'the beast out of the earth' in Revelation 13, and the prostitute in Revelation 17. We will look at these prophecies in more detail later on in this book. The Millennium is also mentioned in Revelation 20, which I believe this period of the saints ruling with Christ is related to. We will also look at this in greater detail in the last chapter of this book.

According to the traditional interpretation of Daniel 7, the Papacy as the little horn will likely meet its end soon. The best historicist commentators in centuries past were careful in their speculation, noting that they would probably not live to see it happen. They guessed that the Papacy became the little horn when it added civil power to its spiritual authority. Because this was anywhere from 752 to 800, its end could be anytime now, to 2060 and beyond. Time will tell if they were correct, but I will not add to their speculation here. They were not obsessed with such times and dates as many of us are tempted to be, and we should follow their example. To clarify- no one who follows Scripture carefully will dare speculate on the timing of the return of Christ, and that is not what these men have done. I will say more about our current time in a later chapter of this book on Revelation 16.

What we can assume based on the fair interpretation of the symbols in this chapter is that the little horn will face absolute destruction- "the beast was slain and its body destroyed and thrown into the blazing fire" (Daniel 7:11b), "his power will be taken away and completely destroyed forever" (Daniel 7:26). Barnes writes, "If applied to the power represented by the 'little horn' - the Papacy - it means that that power which sprang up amidst the others, and which became so mighty - embodying so much of the power of the beast, would wholly pass away as an ecclesiastico-civil power. It would cease its dominion, and as one of the ruling powers of the earth would disappear."[26] It will be destroyed because of its pride and arrogance, and the source will be apparent as coming from God- "the court will sit" (Daniel 7:26a), as though it were a formal court decision of divine judgment.

Finally, the Son of Man comes:

> 13 "In my vision at night I looked, and there before me was one like a son of man, coming with the clouds of heaven. He approached the Ancient of Days and was led into his presence. 14 He was given authority, glory and sovereign power; all nations and peoples of every language worshiped him. His dominion is an everlasting dominion that will not pass away, and his kingdom is one that will never be destroyed...
>
> 27 Then the sovereignty, power and greatness of all the kingdoms under heaven will be handed over to the holy people of the Most High. His kingdom will be an everlasting kingdom, and all rulers will worship and obey him.' (Daniel 7:13-14, 27)

Initially, it is not mentioned in verse 14 that the saints will rule as the Son of Man consummates his kingdom (having already established it with his first coming), but in the interpretation of verse 27 it is expressly stated. This is likely related to the Millennium of Revelation 20. There are three main views of the Millennium that we will look at later. I will not be advocating for any particular view, and each one is compatible with the traditional interpretation given in this book.

In any case, this is the time of triumph and glory we share with the Son of Man, when he claims all power and authority. We desperately look forward to this time of peace, when all nations will obey the law of Christ, when people who fear God will rule. This prophecy promises just such a future, and we can look forward to it with faith and hope- knowing that God has shown us what to expect, and that he has followed through on all of his promises thus far.

Traditional Vs. Modern Interpretation

What the traditional interpretation of apocalyptic prophecies in Daniel makes clear is that God gave Daniel and his people a summary of what he intended to accomplish in the centuries to come. He showed them the world empires they should expect to rise and fall, and the beginning of the Messiah's kingdom. He warned them that a kingdom would arise from the Greeks, with a king who would persecute them fiercely- even revealing the exact amount of days that the Temple would be defiled! He comforted them by assuring Daniel that Jerusalem and the Temple would be rebuilt, and gave a precise timeline of when they should expect the Messiah to come. The prophecies in Daniel give us insight into the truth that *God never leaves his people without direction*. Even when the prophets are seemingly silent, Scripture cries out loud and clear.

In this chapter of Daniel, he showed them what to expect not just in their own day, but in our times as well. With the fourth beast in this chapter having clear parallels to the beasts in Revelation, now we have context from the Old Testament on how to interpret apocalyptic prophecy in the New Testament. And the same principle applies- *God never leaves his people without direction*. In these nearly 2,000 years with no new scriptures being written, with no prophets able to say 'thus saith the LORD,' the prophecies of the New Testament speak loud and clear. God has given us an idea of what he intends to accomplish in these centuries before the second coming of the Son of Man, a divine history of events. As they are fulfilled over time, we can look back with hindsight and recognize God's faithfulness to his promises, knowing with certainty that he will accomplish everything he has decreed shall yet happen.

As we have also seen, nearly all of this wonder is lost with the modern futurist interpretation. Prophecy after prophecy is unnaturally shoved into the future, thrown into a heaping pile with a large sign reading 'UNFULFILLED'. The principle followed is that God only meant to reveal the last seven years out of thousands. We have no reference point to understand what he is doing in the world- only a pat on the head with the promise that all shall be well in the end, and the command to just wait and see. This is not how God's people in Daniel's day understood them, nor did the early church understand it this way, as we shall see in the next chapter.

---

1. Albert Barnes, "Notes, Critical, Illustrative, and Practical", Daniel 7:2. Available online at https://www.sacred-texts.com/bib/cmt/barnes/dan0 07.htm

2. Barnes lists numerous examples: Gen 49:9; Eze 19:2-3; Sa2 23:20; Psa 7:2; Psa 22:21; Psa 57:4; Psa 58:6; Psa 74:4; Sa1 17:37; Job 4:10; Jer 4:7; Jer 49:19; Joe 1:6; Isa 29:1-2.

3. Compare Isa 46:11; Jer 4:13; Jer 48:40; Jer 49:22; Lam 4:19; Hab 1:8.

4. Barnes, ibid, Daniel 7:4.

5. Barnes, ibid, Daniel 7:4.

6. Barnes, ibid, Daniel 7:5.

7. Compare Jer 5:6; Hos 13:7; Isa 11:6,; Jer 5:6; Hab 1:8; Hos 13:7.

8. Barnes, ibid, Daniel 7:28.

9. Isaac Newton, "Observations upon the Prophecies of Daniel, and the Apocalypse of St. John", Chapter 6.
    Available online at https://www.newtonproject.ox.ac.uk/view/texts/normalized/THEM00200

10. Barnes, ibid, Daniel 7:28.

11. See Barnes, ibid, Daniel 7:28.

12. Fred Miller, "Revelation: A Panorama of the Gospel Age", 36.
     Available online at http://moellerhaus.com/rev666.htm

13. Malachi Martin, "The Decline And Fall Of The Roman Church", 94.
     Available online at https://archive.org/details/TheDeclineAndFallOfTheRomMalachiMartin/page/n93/mode/2up

14. Quoted in Thomas Newton, "Dissertations on the Prophecies", 394. His footnote reads: "Dominus Deus noster papa. Alter Deus in terra. Rex regum, dominus dominorum. Idem est dominium Dei et papæ. Credere Dominum Deum nostrum papam non potuisse statuere, prout statuit, hæreticum censeretur. Papæ potestas est major omni potestate creata, extenditque se ad cœlestia, terrestria, et infernalia. Papa facit quicquid libet, etiam illicita, et est plus quam Deus. [Translated in the text.] See these and the like instances quoted in Bishop Jewel's Apology and Defence, in Downham's Treatise de Antichristo, and Poole's English Annotations. See likewise Barrow's Treatise of the Pope's Supremacy in the Introduction." Available online at https://play.google.com/store/books/details?id=mMe88JMxx9cC
     Some bloggers will try to deny that Popes accepted these titles, but the evidence is overwhelming. See documents on Michael Scheifler's Bible Light site: https://www.biblelightinfo.com/Extravagantes.htm

15. Barnes, ibid, Daniel 7:28.

16. Martin, ibid, 94.

17. This number may seem sensational, and it would be if the scope was limited to specific events and regions (like the Spanish Inquisition). Historical theologian Nathan Busenitz remarks, "If the term is used in a broad sense—to represent all Roman Catholic activity against non-Catholics—then the numbers rise dramatically. If the historian includes forms of torture and killing that did not involve a formal trial, along with religious wars and other forms of Catholic violence enacted against Protestants and other non-Catholics (in areas outside of Spain and Portugal), then one can easily speak in terms of millions of people who were killed."
Available online at https://thecripplegate.com/how-many-people-died-in-the-inquisition/

For a detailed view of these numbers, see David A. Plaisted's "Estimates of the Number Killed by the Papacy in the Middle Ages and Later".
Available online at https://static1.1.sqspcdn.com/static/f/827989/1511 6787/1321289366180/50+million+protestants+killed.pdf

18. Barnes, ibid, Daniel 7:28.

19. Barnes, ibid, Daniel 7:28.

20. Barnes, ibid, Daniel 7:28.

21. Barnes, ibid, Daniel 7:28.

22. Timothy Flanders, "The Third Pornocracy: What We Are Living Through".
Available online at https://onepeterfive.com/third-pornocracy/

23. Martin, ibid, 11.

24. Pope Pius IV qtd. in Robert Fleming, "The Rise and Fall of Papacy", 49.
    Available online at
    https://books.google.com/books?id=4CUEAAAAQAAJ
    Twelve 'articles of faith' including this one were added to the Apostles
    Creed by Rome and are found at the end of the decrees of the Council of
    Trent.

25. Tim Challies, "The People's Pope, The Man of the Year".
    Available online at https://www.challies.com/articles/the-peoples-pope
    -the-man-of-the-year/

26. Barnes, ibid, Daniel 7:28.

Chapter Six

The Man of Sin and That Which Restrains

2 Thessalonians 2

Many secular scholars today believe Jesus and Paul are failed prophets, and their eschatology was one of 'imminence' and urgency that failed to be realized. The Day of the Lord and the Kingdom of God were preached, but they did not come as promised, according to these scholars.

The Thessalonian church was dismayed for much the same reason- they also thought Paul was saying that the coming of Christ was imminent, so much so that he had already returned and they had somehow missed it. But Paul was quick to address this misunderstanding (or devious twisting of his words from others):

> Now, brothers, concerning the coming of our Lord Jesus Christ and our gathering together to him, we ask you 2 not to be quickly shaken in your mind, and not be troubled, either by spirit, or by word, or by letter as if from us, saying that the day

of Christ has already come. 3 Let no one deceive you in any way. For it will not be, unless the rebellion comes first, and the man of sin is revealed, the son of destruction, 4 he who opposes and exalts himself against all that is called God or that is worshiped, so that he sits as God in the temple of God, setting himself up as God. 5 Don't you remember that, when I was still with you, I told you these things? 6 Now you know what is restraining him, to the end that he may be revealed in his own season. (2 Thessalonians 2:1-6, WEB)

The coming of Christ was not imminent in the way they understood it to be- there were significant events that had to happen first. Namely, there would be an apostasy, or falling away from true faith in Christ, and the 'man of sin' would be unrestrained by whatever was holding him back, setting himself up as God in the temple of God.

These major events could be intimated long before they happened by a good understanding of Daniel chapter 7. If this man of sin is the same character as the little horn of Daniel 7, then there would have to be tremendous upheaval in the Roman Empire before he could appear. If you followed along in the last chapter of this book, you can see how that played out in history.

But we have the benefit of hindsight. Paul understood enough from the prophecy in Daniel to be able to share a significant future event before it happened: *something* was holding back the coming of the man of sin, and had to be taken out of the way first. *Something* that he couldn't mention by name or they would all get in trouble (if it was the Holy Spirit who restrained the man of sin, he could just say so). *Something* that he was able to tell them in person, but only hint at in a letter ("Don't you remember that, when I was still with you, I told you these things?"). *Something* that wouldn't be wise to write down explicitly with all of the eyes of the Empire on them: *The Roman Empire would be gone before the man of sin could be revealed.*

Here was a marker that was impossible to miss. Rome was thought to be eternal- how could such a mighty empire fall? But it had been foretold centuries before, recorded in Scripture in Daniel's dream of the four beasts. It was plain to see that the fourth beast, the Roman Empire, would be split apart into ten kingdoms, and that the little horn who opposes God and persecutes the saints would grow in power and take over three of them, marking the beginning of his campaign of apostasy.

Apostasy and the New Temple

The apostasy of the man of sin was another marker to watch out for. This Antichrist would be a "power rising out of the church, for that is the meaning of apostasy. It refers to an enemy, not from without but one who rises up from within."[1] He would not just rise up from within the church, but also attempt to take it over, exalting himself "against all that is called God or that is worshiped, so that he sits as God in the temple of God, setting himself up as God" (2 Thessalonians 2:4). This verse brings up another important topic- which temple is Paul talking about here? While the Temple in Jerusalem would still be around for a few more years when he wrote this letter, it has now been destroyed for over 1,950 years.

In the New Testament, the temple- the house of God, where he is worshiped- is no longer a building in Jerusalem, even if it were still standing. After Jesus had cleansed the old Temple in Jerusalem, the Jews there asked him:

> "What sign do you show us, seeing that you do these things?"
> Jesus answered them, "Destroy this temple, and in three days I
> will raise it up." The Jews therefore said, "It took forty-six years
> to build this temple! Will you raise it up in three days?" But he
> spoke of the temple of his body. When therefore he was raised
> from the dead, his disciples remembered that he said this, and
> they believed the Scripture, and the word which Jesus had said.
> (John 2:18-22, WEB)

Jesus is the Most Holy (Daniel 9:24), the chief cornerstone of God's new temple, which we who follow him are a part of:

> For through him we both have our access in one Spirit to the Father. So then you are no longer strangers and foreigners, but you are fellow citizens with the saints and of the household of God, being built on the foundation of the apostles and prophets, Christ Jesus himself being the chief cornerstone; in whom the whole building, fitted together, grows into a holy temple in the Lord; in whom you also are built together for a habitation of God in the Spirit. (Ephesians 2:18-22, WEB)

Paul repeats this truth more than once, and explains that it was foretold long ago:

> What agreement is there between the temple of God and idols? *For we are the temple of the living God.* As God has said:
>
> "I will live with them
> and walk among them,
> and I will be their God,
> and they will be my people." (2 Corinthians 6:16, emphasis mine)

And again:

> Don't you know that you yourselves are God's temple and that God's Spirit dwells in your midst? 17 If anyone destroys God's temple, God will destroy that person; for God's temple is sacred, and you together are that temple. (1 Corinthians 3:16-17)

The time has come that Jesus spoke of, when worship would no longer be in a specific building or place, because together we are the temple in which God is worshiped:

> Jesus said to her, "Woman, believe me, the hour comes, when neither in this mountain, nor in Jerusalem, will you worship the Father. You worship that which you don't know. We worship that which we know; for salvation is from the Jews. But the hour comes, and now is, when the true worshippers will worship the Father in spirit and truth, for the Father seeks such to be his worshippers. God is spirit, and those who worship him must worship in spirit and truth. (John 4:21-24, WEB)

Therefore, the temple in which the man of sin attempts to set himself up as the ultimate authority is the *church*, the entire body of believers, the new temple. How fittingly this prophecy describes what the Papacy has done, and still declares itself to be! Antichrist does not set himself up in a future rebuilt third temple building and proclaim to be God- but after Rome fell, the Papacy rose within the ensuing power vacuum and declared itself to be the head of the entire church. Not long after that, it acquired civil authority over three out of ten kingdoms that were left in the ruins of the Empire. It then proclaimed itself to be 'God on earth, head of all kingdoms, both civil and spiritual.' All of this was foretold by Scripture, and is verified by historical facts.

The Lost Interpretation

This understanding of the passage in 2 Thessalonians 2 used to be common knowledge among Christians who have the benefit of historical hindsight. But as the traditional interpretation has diminished and been nearly forgotten in the last century, these passages have become a greater enigma than ever. Somehow, even the early church could make greater sense of them than we can today, and they did so centuries before the events came to pass! We know this because some of their writings are preserved, and many showed remarkable foresight into the events that would herald the rise of the man of sin. Fred Miller gathered most of the following quotes in his commentary,[2] and I have added a few other relevant quotes. All of these works can be read in their context online for free.

Irenaeus (130 - 202 AD)

In his book *Against Heresies*, Irenaeus wrote about how "John and Daniel have predicted the dissolution and desolation of the Roman Empire, which shall precede the end of the world."[3] He understood "what shall happen in the last times, and concerning the ten kings who shall then arise, among whom the empire which now rules [the earth] shall be partitioned."[4] When Irenaeus wrote this, the Roman Empire was at the strongest and most peaceful time in its history. How could he have known that 'Eternal Rome' would fall and be replaced by ten kingdoms? Only by understanding the prophecies in Daniel and Revelation.

Irenaeus also had insight into the nature of the little horn's kingdom. Out of those ten kingdoms Rome would be broken up into, Antichrist would arise, and he "shall slay three, and subject the remainder to his power, and that he shall be himself the eighth among them."[5] As shown in the previous chapter of this book, history affirms the papal kingdom did just that. Irenaeus also knew that Antichrist, or the man of sin, would be an apostate. Referencing the passage of Scripture about the man of sin, Irenaeus wrote that "the apostle therefore clearly points out his apostasy, and that he is lifted up above all that is called God, or that is worshipped... and that he will endeavour in a tyrannical manner to set himself forth as God."[6] How well Irenaeus understood the prophecies, as the papacy indeed rose from within the church, and claimed such titles as 'God on earth' throughout its history.

Irenaeus went even further. He speculated that the mark of the beast- the number 666- was probably code for the name 'Roman,' or in the Greek, *Lateinos*:

It is not through a want of names containing the number of that name that I say this, but on account of the fear of God, and zeal for the truth: for the name Evanthas (ΕΥΑΝΘΑΣ) contains the required number, but I make no allegation regarding it. Then also Lateinos (ΛΑΤΕΙΝΟΣ) has the number six hundred and sixty-six; and it is a very probable [solution], this being the name of the last kingdom [of the four seen by Daniel]. For the Latins are they who at present bear rule: I will not, however, make any boast over this [coincidence].[7]

He calls 'Roman' a probable solution to the gematria of 666 (we will look into this more in the next chapter of this book). This solution would continue to be put forth by early Christian writers as likely, because "Roman is the name of both the empire, the beast, and a citizen, a single person, who is also a Roman."[8] Remarkably, Irenaeus had such insight into the identity of the Antichrist hundreds of years before he appeared.

Tertullian (155 - 220 AD)

Tertullian wrote about the coming man of sin when he commented on the passage in 2 Thessalonians:

> *'For that day shall not come, unless indeed there first come a falling away,'* he means indeed of this present empire... *'only he who now hinders must hinder, until he be taken out of the way.'* What obstacle is there but the Roman state, the falling away of which, by being scattered into ten kingdoms, shall introduce Antichrist upon (its own ruins)?[9]

Understanding the connection between 2 Thessalonians 2 and Daniel 7, Tertullian explicitly mentions the Roman Empire as being that which prevents the coming of the man of sin, knowing that it will be split into ten kingdoms.

Hippolytus (170 - 235 AD)

Hippolytus of Rome has been called one of the most important second-third century Christian theologians, and his commentary on Daniel is the oldest Christian biblical commentary to survive in its entirety. He understood the identity of the four beasts through interpreting the book of Daniel:

> The golden head of the image and the lioness denoted the Babylonians; the shoulders and arms of silver, and the bear, represented the Persians and Medes; the belly and thighs of brass, and the leopard, meant the Greeks, who held the sovereignty from Alexander's time; the legs of iron, *and the beast dreadful and terrible, expressed the Romans, who hold the sovereignty at present;* the toes of the feet which were part clay and part iron, *and the ten horns, were emblems of the kingdoms that are yet to rise; the other little horn that grows up among them meant the Antichrist in their midst;* the stone that smites the earth and brings judgment upon the world was Christ.[10]

He also put this understanding together with his interpretation of 2 Thessalonians 2: "And so who is 'He who restrains until now,' except the fourth beast, which, when it is set aside and is taken from the midst, the deceiver shall come?"[11] He knew the Roman Empire had to be taken out of the way, when ten kingdoms would appear in its ruins- only then would the man of sin start to appear. "These things, then, shall be in the future, beloved; and when the three horns are cut off, he will begin to show himself as God."[12]

Like Irenaeus before him, Hippolytus attempts to explain the mark of the beast. In fact, he "takes for granted that all the church understood that Lateinos is the name of the beast":[13]

> The wound of the first beast was healed and he (the second beast) was to make the image speak, that is to say to become powerful; and it is manifest to all, that those who at present still hold power are Latins. If then we take the name as the name of a single man it becomes Latinus. Wherefore we ought neither to give it out as if this were certainly his name, nor again ignore the fact that he may not be otherwise designated.[14]

This shows that Hippolytus was looking for an Antichrist that would point to the wounded first beast- the ruins of the Roman Empire- and cause it to be revived under the same identity, keeping the name 'Latinus.' This foresight is stunning, as centuries later the Papacy did arise and 'give breath' (Revelation 13:15) to the beast under the name of the Holy Roman Empire. The wounded Roman Empire received new life!

Scholia (ca. 250 - 300 AD)

Following in the same vein, an unnamed person wrote notes called 'scholia' in the margins of Hippolytus' writings. This person also understood the identity of the four beasts, and explicitly concluded that no other united world empires would arise after the Roman Empire:

> "And behold a fourth beast." Now, that there has arisen no other kingdom after that of the Greeks except that which stands sovereign at present, is manifest to all. This one has iron teeth, because it subdues and reduces all by its strength, just as iron does. And the rest it did tread with its feet, for there is no other

kingdom remaining after this one, but from it will spring ten horns.

"And it had ten horns." For as the prophet said already of the leopard, that the beast had four heads, and that was fulfilled, and Alexander's kingdom was divided into four principalities, so also now we ought to look for the ten horns which are to spring from it, when the time of the beast shall be fulfilled, and the little horn, which is Antichrist, shall appear suddenly in their midst...[15]

The author of the scholia understood that just as the kingdom of the Greeks was divided into four principalities, the same type of symbol of ten horns on the fourth beast revealed that the Roman Empire would be split into ten principalities. Only then would Antichrist appear among them.

As time went on, it became clear that these prophecies would not be fulfilled quickly. Even still, because of God's past faithfulness in fulfilling prophecies, he knew they would surely come to pass:

So that we ought not to anticipate the counsel of God, but exercise patience and prayer, that we fall not on such times. We should not, however, refuse to believe that these things will come to pass. For if the things which the prophets predicted in former times have not been realized, then we need not look for these things. But if those former things did happen in their proper seasons, as was foretold, these things also shall certainly be fulfilled.[16]

St. John Chrysostom (347 - 407 AD)

Chrysostom wrote about 2 Thessalonians 2, and why Paul was not able to speak plainly about 'that which withholds':

> One may naturally enquire, what is that which withholds, and after that would know, why Paul expresses it so obscurely. What then is it that withholds, that is, hinders him from being revealed? Some indeed say, the grace of the Spirit, but others the Roman empire, to whom I most of all accede. Wherefore? Because if he meant to say the Spirit, he would not have spoken obscurely, but plainly, that even now the grace of the Spirit, that is the gifts, withhold him... But because he said this of the Roman empire, he naturally glanced at it, and speaks covertly and darkly. For he did not wish to bring upon himself superfluous enmities, and useless dangers. For if he had said that after a little while the Roman empire would be dissolved, they would immediately have even overwhelmed him, as a pestilent person, and all the faithful, as living and warring to this end. And he did not say that it will be quickly, although he is always saying it — but what? "that he may be revealed in his own season..."[17]

He points to the clearness of the prophecies in Daniel as the reason they can be sure that the Roman Empire will end before the man of sin is revealed:

> But [Paul] did not also wish to point [Antichrist] out plainly: and this not from cowardice, but instructing us not to bring upon ourselves unnecessary enmities, when there is nothing to call for it. So indeed he also says here. "Only there is one that restrains now, until he be taken out of the way," that is, when

the Roman empire is taken out of the way, then he shall come. And naturally. For as long as the fear of this empire lasts, no one will willingly exalt himself, but when that is dissolved, he will attack the anarchy, and endeavor to seize upon the government both of man and of God... And these things Daniel delivered to us with great clearness.[18]

Careful study of the Scriptures made it clear to Chrysostom that Antichrist would claim both civil and ecclesiastical power in the anarchy that followed the removal of the Roman Empire. This is precisely what would happen, as history confirms!

Jerome (ca. 342 - 420 AD)

Jerome confirms the same interpretations as all of the previous, and even at such an early date calls it the 'traditional interpretation':

We should therefore concur with the traditional interpretation of all the commentators of the Christian Church, that at the end of the world, when the Roman Empire is to be destroyed, there shall be ten kings who will partition the Roman world amongst themselves. Then an insignificant eleventh king will arise, who will overcome three of the ten kings... after they have been slain, the seven other kings also will bow their necks to the victor.[19]

About 50 years after Jerome's death, the Roman Empire would fall, and ten kingdoms would quickly be formed in its place.

Regarding 2 Thessalonians 2, Jerome explains how the man of sin exalts himself in God's new temple- the church- and why Paul could not speak openly of the Roman Empire's downfall:

The man of sin... "sits in the temple of God" -- either in the temple of Jerusalem, as some think, or in the church, as we think more correctly -- he might sit and show himself, as if he were Christ and the son of God. If, he says, the Roman Empire is not devastated and if the antichrist does not come first, Christ will not come, who is going to come to destroy the antichrist. You remember, he says, that these things which now I write in a letter, I said in person when I was with you, and I said to you that Christ will not come unless the antichrist had preceded him. "And now you know what detains him, so that he might be revealed in his time," that is, you fully know what the reason is that the antichrist does not come in the present time. He does not mean to speak openly of the Roman Empire's destruction, which its rulers think is eternal.... For if openly and brazenly he had said: "The antichrist will not come until the Roman Empire is destroyed," a reasonable cause for persecution against the church, which was rising at that time, seemed to spring up.[20]

Pope Gregory the Great (ca 540 - 604)

There are many other early church examples of the foresight afforded to those who understood the traditional interpretation of Daniel, Revelation, and 2 Thessalonians. "Justyn Martyr, Origen, Cyril of Jerusalem, Lactantius, Ambrose, Austin, and others, left writings with similar views."[21] As a final example, we should understand what an early Pope himself thought about apostasy and the coming Antichrist.

By the time of Pope Gregory I, the Western Roman Empire had fallen and been partitioned into ten kingdoms. The Roman bishops were beginning to be recognized as leaders in the power vacuum that ensued- "in 443, Leo the First declared that the bishops of Rome were direct successors of Peter and, therefore, heirs to unique powers over heaven and hell."[22] In 533, Emperor Justinian I published an edict that acknowledged the Pope as 'Head of all the Churches.' Despite this, Gregory shunned these lofty titles and styled himself 'Servant of the Servants of God.'

Gregory was concerned when Bishop John 'the Faster' of Constantinople accepted the title 'Ecumenical Patriarch' from Emperor Maurice. Gregory understood the title to mean 'Universal Patriarch' and warned Maurice just how dangerous this was:

> "Is it not the case that, when Antichrist comes and calls himself God, it will be very frivolous, and yet exceedingly pernicious? If we regard the quantity of the language used, there are but a few syllables; but if the weight of the wrong, there is universal disaster. Now I confidently say that whosoever calls himself, or desires to be called, Universal Priest, is in his elation the precursor of Antichrist, because he proudly puts himself above all others."[23]

It was expected that the man of sin would try to exalt himself from within the church, and Gregory saw it happening in his day.

Emperor Maurice ignored Pope Gregory's warning, and John continued to claim the title. Even further, just a few short years after Gregory's death, Emperor Phocas appointed Boniface III as the new Pope, declaring him the 'Head of all Churches' and 'Universal Bishop.' This cemented Papal supremacy over the entire church, and eventually, they claimed authority over all earthly kings and kingdoms. It happened just as the Scriptures foretold.

Traditional Vs. Modern Interpretation

As with most of the prophecies we've looked at, the modern popular interpretation pushes the events of 2 Thessalonians 2 into the future: the apostasy is "the departure from the Christian faith of professing (not genuine) Christians soon after the Rapture;"[24] the removal of the restrainer is the Holy Spirit 'taken out of the way' during the three and a half year tribulation after the Rapture; the man of sin is the Antichrist who will proclaim himself to be God in a rebuilt third Temple. If the little horn of Daniel 7 is still future, then it only follows that this passage would also be unfulfilled.

This view begs the question- if the Holy Spirit is the one who restrains, why didn't Paul just say so? There was no reason to be so cryptic if that were the case.

Where else in the Scriptures is such an event mentioned? Clearly the earliest expositions of this passage have been linked with the prophecy of the four beasts in Daniel 7. Even futurists admit that the Roman Empire is what came before the ten kingdoms- only then does Antichrist appear. Yes, if the Roman Empire is what had to be taken out of the way, there would be a great need to use careful hints in the way that Paul did. The earliest Christian writers saw this, and it was the sign they were looking for.

Their incredible insight into the prophecies was spot on- the Roman Empire fell and was split into ten kingdoms. The man of sin was an apostate- he came from within the church- claiming authority over all churches. He slowly grew in power, eventually gaining kingship over three of the ten kingdoms. He even kept the name 'Roman'. The brutal facts of history show how he opposed God and the saints from there. Even apart from Revelation, all of this could be guessed at from careful study of Daniel 7 and 2 Thessalonians.

The book of Revelation does give us more details on these events, however, and it is there that we will go next.

---

1. Fred Miller, "Revelation: A Panorama of the Gospel Age", 48.

2. Miller, ibid, 46.

3. Irenaeus, "Against Heresies", Book 5, Chapter 26, Epilogue.
   Available online at https://www.newadvent.org/fathers/0103526.htm

4. Irenaeus, ibid, 5:26:1.

5. Irenaeus, ibid, 5:26:1.

6. Irenaeus, ibid, 5:25:1.

7. Irenaeus, ibid, 5:30:3.

8. Miller, ibid, 43.

9. Tertullian, "On the Resurrection of the Flesh", chap. XXIV.
   Available online at https://www.newadvent.org/fathers/0316.htm

10. Hippolytus, "On Christ and Antichrist", 28.
    Available online at https://www.newadvent.org/fathers/0516.htm

11. Hippolytus, "Commentary on Daniel", 4:21:3.
    Available online at https://docplayer.net/83945705-Hippolytus-of-rom
    e-commentary-on-daniel-t-c-schmidt-1-st-edition.html

12. Hippolytus, "On Christ and Antichrist", 53.

13. Miller, ibid, 50.

14. Hippolytus, "On Christ and Antichrist", 50.

15. Scholia on Daniel (Philip Schaff, Trans.), "Ante-Nicene Fathers - Volume
    5", 7:7.
    Available online at https://www.ccel.org/ccel/schaff/anf05.iii.iv.i.x.iii.ht
    ml

16. Scholia, ibid, 7:7.

17. St. John Chrysostom, "Homily 4 on Second Thessalonians", 2 Thessalo-
    nians 2:6-9.
    Available online at https://www.newadvent.org/fathers/23054.htm

18. Chrysostom, ibid, 2 Thessalonians 2:6-9.

19. St. Jerome (Gleason Archer, Trans.), "Commentary on Daniel", Daniel 7:8.
Available online at https://www.tertullian.org/fathers/jerome_daniel_0 2_text.htm

20. Jerome, "A Letter to Algasia."
Available online (including an English translation with the Latin below it) at https://epistolae.ctl.columbia.edu/letter/1291.html

21. Miller, ibid, 55.

22. Dan Graves, "Article #19 - Precursor of Antichrist."
Available online at https://christianhistoryinstitute.org/incontext/articl e/gregory-the-great

23. Gregory the Great (James Barmby, Trans.), "Nicene and Post-Nicene Fathers, Second Series, Vol. 12", Book VII, Letter 33.
Available online at https://www.newadvent.org/fathers/360207033.htm

24. Thomas Constable, "Constable's Expository Notes", 2 Thessalonians 2:3-4.
Available online at https://www.studylight.org/commentaries/eng/dcc/ 2-thessalonians-2.html

Chapter Seven

A Closer Look at the Beast and its Mark

Revelation 13 and 17

Quite a bit can be learned about the beast and Antichrist[1] before ever leaving the pages of the Old Testament. In the vision of the statue in Daniel 2 (covered in the first chapter of this book), we learn that there would be four world Empires before the Kingdom of God was inaugurated, starting with Babylon, then Persia, Greece, and ending with the Roman Empire. In the vision of the four beasts in Daniel 7 (covered in chapter five of this book), we learn more about the fate of the Roman Empire, and are introduced to the 'little horn' who will persecute the saints until the Son of Man comes again.

Through a close study of Daniel 7, the early church could see that Christ would not return until the Roman Empire was gone (see chapter six of this book). With incredible foresight, they realized that one day it would be split into ten kingdoms. They knew that an apostate would then grow powerful, eventually claiming three of the ten kingdoms. This enemy from within the church would blaspheme God by claiming all authority, while making war against the true church. Only after the time allotted to this little horn would the Son of Man come again and consummate the Kingdom of God, taking hold of all authority in heaven and on earth.

History has proven just how accurate their conjectures were. The Roman Empire-once thought to be 'eternal'- did fall and was split into ten kingdoms. The Papacy began to grow in its authority over both church and state in the ensuing power vacuum. Eventually, they were recognized as head of all churches, and given power over three of the ten kingdoms. They gladly accepted and used blasphemous titles such as "Our Lord God the Pope; another God upon earth; king of kings and lord of lords," claiming in their own words that "everything created in the human universe is subject to the Roman Pontiff."[2] The number of those killed after refusing to acknowledge such claims is in the millions.[3]

As we jump to the New Testament in Revelation, the same beast and Antichrist are reintroduced, but with more details confirming their identity, their method of exercising authority, and their final destruction. This closer look is found in Revelation 13 and 17.

The Beast Out of the Sea

Revelation 13 starts with a nearly identical description of the fourth beast in Daniel 7, signifying the different stages of the Roman Empire in its relation to Antichrist:

> Then I stood on the sand of the sea. I saw a beast coming up out of the sea, having ten horns and seven heads. On his horns were ten crowns, and on his heads, blasphemous names. 2 The beast which I saw was like a leopard, and his feet were like those of a bear, and his mouth like the mouth of a lion. The dragon gave him his power, his throne, and great authority. 3 One of his heads looked like it had been wounded fatally. His fatal wound was healed, and the whole earth marveled at the beast. 4 They worshiped the dragon, because he gave his authority to the beast, and they worshiped the beast, saying, "Who is like the beast? Who is able to make war with him?"

5 A mouth speaking great things and blasphemy was given to him. Authority to make war for forty-two months was given to him. 6 He opened his mouth for blasphemy against God, to blaspheme his name, and his dwelling, those who dwell in heaven. 7 It was given to him to make war with the saints, and to overcome them. Authority over every tribe, people, language, and nation was given to him. 8 All who dwell on the earth will worship him, everyone whose name has not been written from the foundation of the world in the book of life of the Lamb who has been killed. (Revelation 13:1-8, WEB)

Here is the same fourth beast of Daniel 7, having characteristics of each of the three beastly empires that came before it: generally resembling a leopard like Greece; feet like those of a bear matching Persia; the mouth of a lion like Babylon. It also came from the sea, representing the nations in commotion, as in the other passage. It has ten horns, just as before, symbolizing the eventual splitting of the united Roman Empire into ten kingdoms. It is given authority to make war for the same amount of time, as 42 months is another way of saying the 'times, time, and half a time' of Daniel 7. This beast is the terrifying might of the Roman Empire, just as powerful and blasphemous as before.

Seven Heads, Seven Governments

The extra details we are given in Revelation 13 and 17 reveal the changes the Roman Empire would undergo in its relationship with the Antichrist. In both passages, it is written that the beast has seven heads. In Revelation 17, an angel explains what these seven heads symbolize:

9 Here is the mind that has wisdom. The seven heads are seven mountains on which the woman sits. 10 They are seven kings. Five have fallen, the one is, the other has not yet come. When he comes, he must continue a little while. 11 The beast that was,

and is not, is himself also an eighth, and is of the seven; and he goes to destruction. (Revelation 17:9-11, WEB)

So the angel says that these seven heads represent two different things:

Seven Mountains- Or more accurately, 'seven hills' as translated in the NIV. This is an allusion to Rome, which was built on seven hills. "Rome was built, as is well known, on seven hills... and was called the seven-hilled city (Septicollis), from having been originally built on seven hills."[4] The seven heads of the beast represent the seat of its power, the city of Rome.

Seven Kings- Additionally, the angel said the seven heads of the beast represent seven kings. The word translated as 'kings' also means governments, or forms of government. The common traditional interpretation is that Rome had seven different forms of government in its history:

1. Kings

2. Republic

3. Council of 10

4. Military Triumites

5. Dictators

6. Imperial

7. Exarchate

When John wrote Revelation, the first five of those governments had passed, and they were then under the imperial form- emperors ruled the Roman Empire. It was just as the angel told John, "Five have fallen, the one is, the other has not yet come" (Revelation 17:10b, WEB). This was common knowledge in John's day, and contemporary classical historians even marked the dates of these six forms of Roman government they had witnessed.[5]

The seventh form of government would appear after the sixth was 'wounded'- the Roman emperors could not withstand the barbarian invasions that eventually caused the fall of the Empire in 476. Rome would then be ruled from the outside (the meaning of *exarchate*) by the Byzantine emperors, called the Exarchate of Ravenna. This was the seventh head, the final official form of government of the beast who *was* (Revelation 17:8, 11). It was to rule for "only a little while" (Revelation 17:10), less than 200 years. And so the beast who *was* is the Roman Empire, ruled by outsiders, fighting to stay alive, breathing its dying breath. It was about to become the beast who *is not*, lying as if in death, waiting for the eighth 'king' to give it new life.

The Beast out of the Earth

The first beast in Revelation 13 is nearly identical to the description given in Daniel 7, but there is one missing detail: the little horn is not mentioned. Instead, we are shown a different image of that same power: another beast, the beast out of the earth.

> I saw another beast coming up out of the earth. He had two horns like a lamb, and he spoke like a dragon. 12 He exercises all the authority of the first beast in his presence. He makes the earth and those who dwell in it to worship the first beast, whose fatal wound was healed. 13 He performs great signs, even making fire come down out of the sky to the earth in the sight of people. 14 He deceives my own people who dwell on the earth because of the signs he was granted to do in front of the beast, saying to those who dwell on the earth that they should make an image to the beast who had the sword wound and lived. 15 It was given to him to give breath to it, to the image of the beast, that the image of the beast should both speak, and cause as many as wouldn't worship the image of the beast to be killed. (Revelation 13:11-15, WEB)

Here is the same 'little horn,' the same 'man of sin,' now symbolized in the form of a beast who comes out of the earth. By the time this new beast rises, the Roman Empire is all but dead, already divided into ten kingdoms, and ruled from outside its own territory. So what does this new beast do? He makes an image of the first beast- the fallen Roman Empire- and gives it breath. He resurrects the Roman Empire in its imperial form of government, healing the fatally wounded head. He makes a spitting image of the Roman Empire and exercises all of the same authority. He unites the power of the ten kingdoms again, adding only one word to the same name: The *Holy* Roman Empire.

The facts of history confirm this new perspective of the beast and the little horn in Revelation 13. The creation of the Holy Roman Empire is stated so simply, and yet as if it were written with these very prophecies in mind:

> On 25 December 800, Pope Leo III crowned the Frankish king Charlemagne as emperor, *reviving the title in Western Europe,* more than three centuries after the fall of the earlier ancient Western Roman Empire in 476.[6]

The slogan of the day was *renovatio Romanorum imperii* ("renewal of the empire of the Romans"), which Charlemagne used in his imperial seal.

A monk that wrote about the newly crowned Emperor Charlemagne just 44 years after this event obviously has the statue of Daniel 2 in mind, but didn't realize it was closer to the beast in Revelation 13! He likens it to the creation of a new *image* of the Roman Empire:

> He who ordains the fate of kingdoms and the march of the centuries, the all-powerful Disposer of events, having destroyed one extraordinary image, that of the Romans, which had, it was true, feet of iron, or even feet of clay, then raised up, among the Franks, *the golden head of a second image,* equally remarkable, in the person of the illustrious Charlemagne.[7]

This was the ultimate integration of Church and State, the beginning of an *imperium Christianum*- a Christian Empire. The beastly Roman Empire was alive again, or at least an image of it was. The papacy healed the wounded sixth head of the beast by bestowing the title of Emperor and giving the beast new breath. The Holy Roman Empire would go on to become the most powerful force in Europe and rule for 1000 years, and the little horn would be the power behind the throne, killing all who would not bow down before them.

The Mark of the Beast

The last part of Revelation 13 is about the mark of the beast:

> He causes all, the small and the great, the rich and the poor, and the free and the slave, to be given marks on their right hands, or on their foreheads; 17 and that no one would be able to buy or to sell, unless he has that mark, which is the name of the beast or the number of his name. 18 Here is wisdom. He who has understanding, let him calculate the number of the beast, for it is the number of a man. His number is six hundred sixty-six. (Revelation 13:16-18, WEB)

Earlier in Revelation, the servants of God had been sealed: "I saw another angel ascend from the sunrise, having the seal of the living God. He cried with a loud voice to the four angels to whom it was given to harm the earth and the sea, saying, 'Don't harm the earth, the sea, or the trees, until we have sealed the bondservants of our God on their foreheads!'" (Revelation 7:2-3, WEB). This seal of God is said to be the name of the Lamb and the Father in Revelation 14: "I saw, and behold, the Lamb standing on Mount Zion, and with him a number, one hundred forty-four thousand, having his name, and the name of his Father, written on their foreheads" (14:1, WEB). So the mark of the beast is a mockery of this seal, as it is the name of the beast written on their right hand or forehead.

In symbolic prophecy like this, these marks are a figure of ownership. "This 'mark' on their foreheads or on their right hand is simply Satan's way of mimicking the seal of God on God's people. If you have the name of Jesus and God the Father written on your forehead, it simply means that they own you, that you belong to them, that you are loyal to the Lord God Almighty. But if you have 'the name of the beast' (Rev. 13:17) written on your forehead, it signifies that he owns you, that you belong to him, that you are loyal to the Antichrist."[8] It would not need to be a visible mark, because the actions of our obedience and loyalty will clearly show who we belong to.

This symbolic mark of ownership is given in the form of a code: "the number of his name" (Revelation 13:17). This type of code is called *gematria*, where each letter of the Greek alphabet is given a number value. As it turns out, early Christians were able to guess the name of the beast based on their interpretation of this chapter as well as Daniel 7. Both Irenaeus and Hippolytus mention *Lateinos* (ΛΑΤΕΙΝΟΣ)- Greek for 'Roman'- as being the probable solution, because it was the name of the beast in their own day.[9] They wrote this centuries before the Roman Empire was revived or the Roman bishops were declared to have universal authority over the church.

As mentioned in the previous chapter of this book on 2 Thessalonians 2, it is given in a cryptic form like this rather than being written out explicitly, so that the persecution of the early church was not made even worse than it already was:

> The Roman Empire waged ten official persecutions against the church for almost 300 years. These were legally sanctioned by the senate and carried out under the Roman legal system. The Christians were tortured, whipped, burned, torn apart, beheaded, thrown to lions, and crucified by official Roman authority according to law, for three centuries. Pastors were killed, Bibles confiscated and burned, church buildings destroyed, and the flocks scattered.

How much worse might the Roman persecutors have been if

they found their nation named by name as a beast in the Holy writings of those they persecuted? The conditions were bad enough without adding more fuel to the fire. So God couched the name in a mystery. He called the fourth beast 666, so no one could know it except the mind that has wisdom.[10]

The number 666 has many other solutions in gematria, but none of them match the simplicity and fullness of context that 'Roman' does. It is simply "the name of the beast" (Revelation 13:17). In every major interpretation, the beast in Daniel 7 and Revelation 13 is identified as the Roman Empire, at least at one stage or another. It also meets all of the criteria of the passage: "Roman is the name of both the empire, the beast, and a citizen, a single person, who is also a Roman."[11] Everything the papacy did was 'romanized' through using the Latin language:

> They *latinize* in every thing. Mass, prayers, hymns, litanies, canons, decretals, and bulls are conceived in Latin. The papal councils speak in Latin. Women themselves pray in Latin. Nor is the Scripture read in any other language under popery, than Latin. Wherefore the council of Trent commanded the vulgar Latin to be the only authentic version. Nor do their doctors doubt to prefer it to the Hebrew and Greek text itself, which was written by the prophets and apostles. In short all things are Latin: the pope having communicated his language to the people under this dominion, as the mark and character of his empire.[12]

Gematria is also a code used in the Hebrew language, and the name for Roman beast or Roman kingdom (*Romiith)* also has the exact number 666. Concerning this remarkable fact, Thomas Newton writes, "It is really surprising that there should be such a fatal coincidence in both names in both languages...

no other word in any language whatever, can be found to express both the same *number*, and the same *thing*."[13] This must be more than mere coincidence.

The Beast and the Whore

In Revelation chapter 17, the beast makes another appearance in much the same form, but the Antichrist is now shown as a prostitute that rides the beast:

> One of the seven angels who had the seven bowls came and spoke with me, saying, "Come here. I will show you the judgment of the great prostitute who sits on many waters, 2 with whom the kings of the earth committed sexual immorality. Those who dwell in the earth were made drunken with the wine of her sexual immorality."
>
> 3 He carried me away in the Spirit into a wilderness. I saw a woman sitting on a scarlet-colored beast, full of blasphemous names, having seven heads and ten horns. 4 The woman was dressed in purple and scarlet, and decked with gold and precious stones and pearls, having in her hand a golden cup full of abominations and the impurities of the sexual immorality of the earth. 5 And on her forehead a name was written,
>
> "MYSTERY, BABYLON THE GREAT, THE MOTHER OF THE PROSTITUTES AND OF THE ABOMINATIONS OF THE EARTH."
>
> 6 I saw the woman drunken with the blood of the saints, and with the blood of the martyrs of Jesus. When I saw her, I wondered with great amazement. (Revelation 17:1-6, WEB)

Specifically, here the prostitute is a representation of the seat of Antichrist's power, the city of Rome. The last verse of this chapter reads, "The woman whom you saw is the great city, which reigns over the kings of the earth" (Revelation 17:18, WEB). The papacy has always ruled from Rome, and still holds some civil authority there in Vatican City, their independent city-state in the middle of Rome.

How can we be sure that Rome is meant here, instead of Babylon or some other city? There are several reasons:

- When Revelation was written, Babylon was no longer a city; it was desolate. But it was the symbol of a power that set itself against God, and was judged because of it.

- The interpretation given by the angel in this chapter points to Rome. "Here is the mind that has wisdom. The seven heads are seven mountains on which the woman sits" (Revelation 17:9, WEB). In other versions, the word 'mountains' here is translated as 'hills.' Rome is known as the city of seven hills.

- The description of "the great city, which reigns over the kings of the earth" fits Rome's historical status.

- The context of Revelation and Daniel 7 points to Rome. These chapters have always been interpreted as the Roman Empire, and a power that comes from within it. The papacy fulfills the descriptions of that power, and has always operated from Rome.

- The Apostle Peter confirms that the early church called Rome 'Babylon.' At the end of his first epistle, he gives these closing remarks: "She who is in Babylon, chosen together with you, greets you" (1 Peter 5:13a, WEB). For him, Babylon is code for Rome. Keener writes regarding this verse:

Jewish people by this period viewed Rome as the fourth of the four kingdoms in Daniel 7 that would oppress Israel, a successor to Babylon. Some elements of contemporary Judaism had readily transferred prophecies of Babylon's demise in the Old Testament to the new empire of Rome (a transferral readily highlighted after A.D. 70). "Babylon" had thus become a fairly common cryptogram for Rome (although "Edom" was more popular with later rabbis).[14]

This chapter must have been a big clue for the early Christian church that the Antichrist would be an apostate- an enemy that rises up from within the church- because the Scriptures have often represented the unfaithful among God's people as a prostitute. Israel is likened to one multiple times in Hosea and Jeremiah. The city of Jerusalem is also called a harlot in Ezekiel and Isaiah. Barnes writes about the use of such imagery in this chapter:

> It is not uncommon in the Scriptures to represent a city under the image of a woman - a pure and holy city under the image of a virgin or chaste female; a corrupt, idolatrous, and wicked city under the image of an abandoned or lewd woman... and the design here is to represent it as resembling an abandoned female - fit representative of an apostate, corrupt, unfaithful church.[15]

Antichrist would not literally be a female prostitute, or just any great city in the world. Instead, they would be corrupt, unfaithful leaders from within the church.

This is precisely what happened when the papacy sought spiritual and political power at all costs, altogether abandoning the servant leadership Jesus called the church to. Remember, it was a pope who warned against seeking such authority: "Now I confidently say that whosoever calls himself, or desires to be called, Universal Priest, is in his elation the precursor of antichrist, because he proudly puts himself above all others."[16] Gregory's successors ignored this warning, cozying up to kings and emperors to secure power in Rome, and the Bishop of Rome was called exactly that just a few years after it was penned.

Not too long after claiming spiritual authority over all churches, the papacy secured political power. This was prophesied in Daniel 7, Revelation 13, and here in Revelation 17- the leaders of the church of Rome would gain real political power over kingdoms, likened to committing adultery with the kings of the earth in this chapter. As shown in chapter 5 of this book, many Popes were also literally sexually depraved throughout their history in periods called the pornacracies. Because of their unfaithfulness to God, Rome would be considered "THE MOTHER OF PROSTITUTES AND OF THE ABOMINATIONS OF THE EARTH" (Revelation 17:5). She was "drunken with the blood of the saints, and with the blood of the martyrs of Jesus" (Revelation 17:6) because many Christians would refuse to bow before this wicked power, and were killed for standing against them.

The Fate of the Prostitute

While Daniel 7 introduces us to the papal Antichrist, and Revelation 13 expands on its rule, this chapter reveals its ultimate fate. Explaining what John saw, the angel continues:

> The ten horns that you saw are ten kings who have received no kingdom as yet, but they receive authority as kings with the beast for one hour. 13 These have one mind, and they give their power and authority to the beast. 14 These will war against the Lamb, and the Lamb will overcome them, for he is Lord of lords, and King of kings, and those who are with him are called chosen and faithful."

> 15 He said to me, "The waters which you saw, where the prostitute sits, are peoples, multitudes, nations, and languages. 16

The ten horns which you saw, and the beast, these will hate the prostitute, will make her desolate, will strip her naked, will eat her flesh, and will burn her utterly with fire. 17 For God has put in their hearts to do what he has in mind, to be of one mind, and to give their kingdom to the beast, until the words of God should be accomplished. 18 The woman whom you saw is the great city, which reigns over the kings of the earth." (Revelation 17:12-18, WEB)

The papacy in Rome today is a shadow of what it once was, but it still hangs on to real political power as a city-state, the smallest sovereign country in the world. This is because it has already faced many of the judgments prepared for it as written in Revelation 16, covered in more detail later in this book. The same ten kingdoms that gave the papacy its political power will also destroy it. "These have one mind, and they give their power and authority to the beast" (Revelation 17:13, WEB), and yet "these will hate the prostitute, will make her desolate, will strip her naked, will eat her flesh, and will burn her utterly with fire" (Revelation 17:16b, WEB). Commenting on this verse, Albert Barnes writes:

This statement will be accomplished if these same powers, represented by the ten horns, that were formerly in alliance with the papacy, shall become its enemy, and contribute to its final overthrow. That is, it will be accomplished if the nations of Europe, embraced within the limits of those ten kingdoms, shall become hostile to the papacy, and shall combine for its overthrow.[17]

He had seen much of it happen already in his day:

> Is anything more probable than this? France has already struck
> more than one heavy blow on that power; England has been
> detached from it; many of the states of Italy are weary of it, and
> are ready to rise up against it; and nothing is more probable than
> that Spain, Portugal, France, Lombardy, and the papal States
> themselves, will yet throw off the yoke forever, and put an end
> to a power that has so long ruled over people. It was with the
> utmost difficulty, in 1848, that the papal power was sustained,
> and this was done only by foreign swords; the papacy could not
> probably be protected in another such outbreak.[18]

How right he was. In the year of Barnes' death (1870), the Italian army captured Rome and ended the Papal States, which had existed since 756. However, the papacy would not let go of its claim to temporal power, and was granted control of only Vatican City nearly 60 years later, in 1929.

So the destruction of the great prostitute is not entirely fulfilled, as would be expected by the symbols of being made desolate, stripped naked, flesh eaten, and the rest burned utterly with fire. Popes still rule from Rome. Perhaps this end will come soon, as the papacy gained control over the three kingdoms by 800 under Charlemagne. The little horn and the beast are given a time limit of 1260 years, bringing us to 2060 if that is the correct date.

In any case, it is not too difficult to imagine how this will happen. The Roman Catholic Church is embroiled in sexual and even *genocidal* scandals that only seem to get worse year after year as more is revealed. The kingdoms of the world grow more and more secular, and also in their hatred of all religions, but especially the prostitute. What shocking deed will be uncovered next that will cause them to finally snap? Eventually they will band together in their fury and strip the Roman Catholic Church of all wealth, lands, and titles- or simply make them pay taxes- and in some way, the papacy will lose temporal power for good.

Traditional Vs. Modern Interpretation

In the modern popular futurist interpretation of Revelation 13 and 17, the Roman Empire is identified as only the beginning of the beast out of the sea, or the beast that the prostitute rides. The rest of the vision has been paused for over a millennium until the ten 'kings' are revealed, whom a personal Antichrist will overpower through charm and deceit. This Antichrist will go on to create a New World Order or alliance among nations, and shortly after claim to be God in a yet-to-be-built third Temple in Jerusalem. The Antichrist is bound to be someone with political or religious power, and fingers are pointed at every president, king, Imam, or single Pope the world over.

There is much anxiety and paranoia over the identity of the mark of the beast. Technology is usually considered to be the culprit. The most common speculation is a payment method embedded in our skin. A newer favorite is vaccines, sometimes said to include 'RNA-modifying transhumanism nanotechnology.' Fear-mongering is rampant as we try our hardest to avoid 'accidentally' taking the mark of the beast and damning our souls.

Very few of us learn enough church history to understand how the fulfillment of these visions is not 'paused,' but that there are recognizable events that correspond with how these symbols are used in the Bible. We understand the Roman Empire as the beast's beginning well enough, but do we realize it split into ten kingdoms when it fell, or that an apostate power from within the church claimed authority over three of them? How many of us are aware of the papacy's hand in creating an image of the wounded beast, revived in the Holy Roman Empire? What about the persecution and death of *millions* of 'heretics' who would not bow to that power? These are not hidden or obscure events, but it's easy enough to get through our education by only giving them a cursory glance and then quickly forgetting about them.

Instead, we believe the currently popular interpretation we're taught by the people we trust, without even realizing there was ever anything else. There is little incentive to understand the history of the church when all of these prophecies are yet to come. What often results is either an unnatural obsession over the 'end times' filled with speculation, or on the opposite end, a deep aversion to that tendency and to the unknown.

As you continue to read this book, my hope is that you will understand that there has been a very different yet cohesive understanding of these prophecies in the church throughout history. The papacy was not simply a villain that Protestants called Antichrist in order to defame them- rather, they genuinely saw the prophecies in Daniel and Revelation fulfilled in them, and for good reason. The Scriptures pointed to their rise to power, and they have predicted their imminent downfall. Sooner or later, God's people will look back in wonder at how he has sovereignly revealed these things to us before they happened.

---

1. 'Antichrist' has become a catch-all term for what the Scriptures call the 'little horn' in the Old Testament, and 'the man of sin/lawlessness' and the 'beast out of the earth' in the New Testament.

2. Malachi Martin, "The Decline And Fall Of The Roman Church", 94. Available online at https://archive.org/details/TheDeclineAndFallOfTh eRomMalachiMartin/page/n93/mode/2up

3. This number may seem sensational, and it would be if the scope was limited to specific events and regions (like the Spanish Inquisition). Historical theologian Nathan Busenitz remarks, "If the term is used in a broad sense—to represent all Roman Catholic activity against non-Catholics—then the numbers rise dramatically. If the historian in- cludes forms of torture and killing that did not involve a formal trial, along with religious wars and other forms of Catholic violence enacted against Protestants and other non-Catholics (in areas outside of Spain and Portugal), then one can easily speak in terms of millions of people who were killed."
Available online at https://thecripplegate.com/how-many-peo-

ple-died-in-the-inquisition/

For a detailed view of these numbers, see David A. Plaisted's "Estimates of the Number Killed by the Papacy in the Middle Ages and Later". Available online at https://static1.1.sqspcdn.com/static/f/827989/1511 6787/1321289366180/50+million+protestants+killed.pdf

4. Albert Barnes, "Notes, Critical, Illustrative, and Practical", Revelation 12:3.
   Available online at https://www.sacred-texts.com/bib/cmt/barnes/rev0 12.htm

5. The historians Livy and Tacitus are quoted in Fred Miller, "Revelation: A Panorama of the Gospel Age", 154.
   Available online at http://moellerhaus.com/scar-wom.htm

6. Wikipedia, "Holy Roman Empire".
   Available online at https://en.wikipedia.org/wiki/Holy_Roman_Empire

7. Einhard and Notker the Stammerer (Lewis Thorpe, Trans.), "Two Lives of Charlemagne", 93.
   Another translation is available online at https://sourcebooks.fordham. edu/basis/stgall-charlemagne.asp

8. Sam Storms, "Perplexing Passages: What Is the Mark of the Beast in Revelation 13?".
   Available online at https://www.thegospelcoalition.org/article/perplexi ng-passages-what-is-the-mark-of-the-beast/

9. See more on this in the previous chapter of this book.

10. Miller, ibid, 44-45.

11. Miller, ibid, 43.

12. Henry Moore quoted in Thomas Newton, "Dissertations on the Prophe-

cies", 539. The footnote there reads: "Moore's Mystery of Iniquity, Part ii. B. i. chap. xv. sect. i. et Petri Molinæi Vates p. 500, & c. Missa, preces, hymni, litaniæ, canones, decreta, bullæ, Latine conceptæ sunt. Concilia papalia Latine loquuntur. Ipsæ Mulierculæ precantur Latine. Nec alio sermone scriptura legitur sub papismo quam Latino. Quapropter Concilium Tridentinum jussit solam versionem vulgatam Latinam esse authenticam. Nec dubitant doctores eam præferre ipsi textui Hebraico et Græco ab ipsis apostolis et prophetis exarato. Denique sunt omnia Latina; nempe Papa populis a se subactis dedit suam linguam, ut sui imperii notam et characterem. [Translated in the text.]"

13. Thomas Newton, also quoting a 'Mr. Pyle', ibid, 540. The full quote is "It is really surprising that there should be such a fatal coincidence in both names in both languages. Mr. Pyle asserts, and I believe he may assert very truly, that no other word, in any language whatever, can be found to express both the same number and the same thing." The footnote reads "See Pyle's Paraphrase, p. 104."

14. Craig Keener, "The IVP Bible Background Commentary: New Testament", 697.

15. Barnes, ibid, Revelation 17:1.

16. Gregory the Great (James Barmby, Trans.), "Nicene and Post-Nicene Fathers, Second Series, Vol. 12", Book VII, Letter 33.
Available online at https://www.newadvent.org/fathers/360207033.htm

17. Barnes, ibid, Revelation 17:16.

18. Barnes, ibid, Revelation 17:16.

Chapter Eight

Eastern Antichrist

Revelation 9

Due to the popularity of the modern interpretation of Revelation, all eyes are on Israel. Many of the major signs of the end times are thought to occur there: a future Antichrist is expected to come after another Temple is built in Jerusalem. He sets his sights on the Holy Land to conquer it and proclaim himself as God. Jews are among those who are 'left behind' after the rapture to suffer under Antichrist, while a remnant of them marked by God resist and turn to Jesus.

Because Israel is the focal point, the surrounding Muslim population is also in view. Will Antichrist come from one of these nations that hate Israel? Haven't they always declared Jews to be their enemies, and don't they want to wipe Israel off of the map? Among the many guesses of who Antichrist might be, perhaps it will be an Islamic king or religious leader. It seems only logical, and so Christians pay close attention to news of the Middle East.

It turns out that the rise of Islam as an antichristian power *is* foretold in Revelation, and with surprising detail. Not only its rise, but also its ultimate downfall alongside the beast.

So far, most of our attention has been on the Western part of the Roman Empire (the fourth beast), the changes it went through in its history, and especially its appropriation by the little horn (a.k.a. the man of sin, the beast out of the earth, the whore of Babylon). But Revelation introduces another power that rises out of the East simultaneously, bringing about the downfall of that portion of the old Roman Empire known as the Byzantine Empire. It terrorizes that part of the world for centuries, and casts a darkness over the whole region that remains to this day.

The Fifth Trumpet

The book of Revelation is God's view of the church age. In the traditional historicist interpretation of prophecy, Revelation is a divine view of history from the time when it was written (96 A.D) to the current day. The first seven seals tell the story of the pagan Roman Empire and its eventual conversion to Christianity. The next four trumpets foretold the judgment of the Western Roman Empire, and its eventual downfall in 476. A sweeping summary of these and other events in Revelation is given in chapter 11 of this book, but it is worth studying these remarkable fulfillments in detail (free resources are listed in Appendix A).

The fifth, sixth, and seventh trumpets are distinctly devastating, called 'woes' by the angels (Revelation 8:13, 9:12). They complete the judgments started against the Roman Empire, as two-thirds of it still remained.[1] In Revelation 9, the sounding of the fifth trumpet releases strange beings that reveal a new setting in the East:

> The fifth angel sounded, and I saw a star from the sky which had fallen to the earth. The key to the pit of the abyss was given to him. 2 He opened the pit of the abyss, and smoke went up out of the pit, like the smoke from a burning furnace. The sun and the air were darkened because of the smoke from the pit. 3 Then out of the smoke came locusts on the earth, and power was given to them, as the scorpions of the earth have power. 4 They were told that they should not hurt the grass of the earth, neither any green thing, neither any tree, but only those people who don't

have God's seal on their foreheads. 5 They were given power, not to kill them, but to torment them for five months. Their torment was like the torment of a scorpion when it strikes a person. 6 In those days people will seek death, and will in no way find it. They will desire to die, and death will flee from them.

7 The shapes of the locusts were like horses prepared for war. On their heads were something like golden crowns, and their faces were like people's faces. 8 They had hair like women's hair, and their teeth were like those of lions. 9 They had breastplates, like breastplates of iron. The sound of their wings was like the sound of chariots, or of many horses rushing to war. 10 They have tails like those of scorpions, and stings. In their tails they have power to harm men for five months. 11 They have over them as king the angel of the abyss. His name in Hebrew is "Abaddon", but in Greek, he has the name "Apollyon".

12 The first woe is past. Behold, there are still two woes coming after this. (Revelation 9:1-12, WEB)

Commentators of the traditional interpretation of Revelation are unanimous in their understanding of the fifth trumpet: the setting, timing, and descriptions given in this prophecy point to the Muslim conquests starting with Muhammad, the Arab religious, social, and political leader, and founder of Islam.

The Setting

In the Bible, the source of locusts is from the East. In Exodus, the Lord commands Moses:

"Stretch out your hand over the land of Egypt for the locusts, that they may come up on the land of Egypt, and eat every herb of the land, even all that the hail has left." Moses stretched out his rod over the land of Egypt, and Yahweh brought an east wind on the land all that day, and all night; and when it was morning, the east wind brought the locusts. (Exodus 10:12b-13, WEB).

When used as a symbol in apocalyptic prophecy, a plague of locusts naturally draws our minds to their common source, and the place where they chiefly occur- in this case, Arabia. The Bible often uses symbols like this that are relevant to the location of the subject: "When Judah is to be symbolized, the olive, the vine, and the fig-tree are selected; when Egypt is referred to, the reed is chosen; when Babylon, the willow. And so, in the animal kingdom, the lion is the symbol of Judah; the wild ass, of the Arabs; the crocodile, of Egypt, etc."[2]

The Timing

The timing is right because this point of Revelation comes after the downfall of the Western Roman Empire in 476. Interestingly, the Papacy and Islam grew in power and influence at very similar times: the Pope was declared 'Universal Bishop' by Emperor Phocas in 606, while Muhammad received his visions that led to the writing of the Quran in 610. The Papacy gained control over kingdoms starting in 756, while the Muslim conquests reached their apex at about 750. According to Revelation 16, both are destroyed at about the same time (see chapter 11 of this book for more on that future event).

The plague of locusts is allowed to torment people for five months, which is the natural life cycle of the locust "from the springtime hatching of the egg to the death of the locust in the fall."[3] This is the same amount of time as 150 days. When the day-year principle is followed, that would mean 150 years. From the time when Muhammad first began to preach in 612, to the end of Muslim conquests with the founding of the capital of Baghdad in 762, is exactly 150 years.

The Fallen Star

This plague of locusts comes from a cloud of smoke rising out of the abyss, opened by "a star from the sky which had fallen to the earth" (Revelation 9:1, WEB). "A star is a common metaphor for kings in the ancient Near East."[4] Barnes writes that "A star is a natural emblem of a prince, of a ruler, of one distinguished by rank or by talent,"[5] and it is used that way in the Bible in Numbers 24:17 and Isaiah 14:12. A leader is given the key to the abyss, unleashing smoke and darkness over the land, and a plague of locusts. Muhammad is best suited to these descriptions. According to Barnes:

> He was like a star that fell from heaven (Revelation 9:1), a bright and illustrious prince, as if heaven-endowed, but fallen. Would anything better characterize the genius, the power, and the splendid but perverted talent of Muhammed? Muhammed was, moreover, by birth, of the princely house of the Koreish, governors of Mecca, and to no one could the term be more appropriate than to one of that family... there was to be one monarch - one ruling spirit to which all these hosts were subject. And never was anything more appropriate than this title as applied to the leader of the Arabic hosts. All those hosts were subject to one mind - to the command of the single leader that originated the scheme.[6]

The Locusts

The description of the locusts released by the fifth trumpet are fitting symbols for the armies led by Muhammad and those after him who conquered Arabia and beyond. An interesting tradition of Muhammad states that "there is an inscription on the locust's chest that says: 'The greatest army of God.'"[7] A similar tradition speaks of locusts dropping into the hands of Muhammad, "bearing on their wings this inscription; 'We are the army of the great God.'"[8]

Their numbers - Locusts are known for swarming in great numbers and covering the land. This is used to symbolize great armies in the Bible. Below are two out of many examples:

> 'They will cut down her forest,' says Yahweh, 'though it can't be searched; because they are more than the locusts, and are innumerable.' (Jeremiah 46:23, WEB)

> The sword will cut you off. It will devour you like the grasshopper. Multiply like grasshoppers. Multiply like the locust. (Nahum 3:15b, WEB)

According to Barnes, "Nothing would better represent the numbers of the Saracenic hordes that came out of Arabia, and that spread over the East - over Egypt, Libya, Mauritania, Spain, and that threatened to spread over Europe - than such an army of locusts."[9]

Their mounts - Locusts are an appropriate symbol for horses, and a plague of locusts for armies that are known for their cavalry. The verses directly mention horses: "The shapes of the locusts were like horses prepared for war" (Revelation 9:7a, WEB). Throughout history, locusts have been compared to horses due to similar head shapes, and the Italian word for grasshopper is *cavaletta*, or 'little horse.' A later verse says, "The sound of their wings was like the thundering of many horses and chariots rushing into battle" (Revelation 9:9b). The armies of Muhammad were famous for their cavalry, and the sound of their horses' charging would have been terrifying.

Their faces - The verse says, "their faces were like people's faces" (Revelation 9:7b, WEB), but it could also be translated specifically like *men* (as it is in the KJV) instead of *people* generically. The Arabic armies had a special regard for their facial hair, and to this day the beard and mustache are regulated by the Quran. They had faces that were distinctly 'manly' rather than being shaved.

Their hair - The verse says, "They had hair like women's hair" (Revelation 9:8a, WEB). They have faces like men, perhaps denoting masculine facial hair, but their hair is like women's hair, long and effeminate. Many contemporary historians before, during, and after this period describe this style of a beard and mustache combined with the long, uncut hair the Arabs wore.

Their 'golden crowns' - The verse says, "On their heads were something like golden crowns" (Revelation 9:7, WEB). John states that they were not literally gold crowns, but 'something like' them- the general shape encircled their heads, and the color resembled gold. Barnes writes:

> The writer saw such head-ornaments as he was accustomed to see. They were not exactly crowns or diadems, but they had a resemblance to them, and he therefore uses this language: "and on their heads were as it were crowns." Suppose that these were turbans, and that they were not in common use in the time of John, and that they had, therefore, no name, would not this be the exact language which he would use in describing them? The same remarks may be made respecting the other expression... they were not pure gold, but they had a resemblance to it. Would not a yellow turban correspond with all that is said in this description?[10]

A saying often attributed to Muhammad goes, "The turbans are the crowns of the Arabs."[11] Muhammad is said to have encouraged the wearing of turbans: "The turban distinguishes the Muslims from the Mushriks (polytheists)."[12] There is no unanimous consensus on what color they wore, but yellow is among the likely traditions. In the Arabian peninsula, the most famous type of colored turban is yellow.[13]

Their armor - The verse says, "They had breastplates, like breastplates of iron" (Revelation 9:9a, WEB). The Arabic armies were noted for wearing steel and iron breastplates (a.k.a. cuirasses). The pre-Islamic *Poem of Antar* makes at least four references to a warrior's cuirass or breastplate.[14] The Quran says, "God hath given you coats of mail to defend you in your wars."[15]

Their limits - Verse four says, "They were told that they should not hurt the grass of the earth, neither any green thing, neither any tree..." (Revelation 9:4a, WEB). Unlike the normal behavior of a plague of locusts, or even of literal armies, they were commanded not to harm the land. This is precisely what was commanded of the Arabic armies:

> Remember that you are always in the presence of God, on the verge of death, in the assurance of judgment, and the hope of paradise. Avoid injustice and oppression; consult with your brethren, and study to preserve the love and confidence of your troops. When you fight the battles of the Lord, acquit yourselves like men, without turning your backs; but let not the victory be stained with the blood of women or children. Destroy no palm-trees, nor burn any fields of grain. Cut down no fruit-trees, nor do any mischief to cattle, only such as you kill to eat. When you make any covenant or article, stand to it, and be as good as your word. As you go on, you will find some religious persons who live retired in monasteries, and propose to themselves to serve God in that way; let them alone, and neither kill them, nor destroy their monasteries," etc.[16]

Their mission - They were not to hurt the land, "...but only those people who don't have God's seal on their foreheads" (Revelation 9:4b). The armies under Muhammad were commanded to harm those who they considered to be idolators- first among their own people, and then against all infidels. "They were given power, not to kill them, but to torment them for five months" (Revelation 9:5, WEB): those who would not convert to Islam were allowed to live if they paid tribute. As quoted above, they were commanded not to destroy monasteries, or women and children- they were not allowed to destroy the church- but they would definitely harm it for the 150 years given to them. This is exactly what they did in their history of conquest.

The Sixth Trumpet

With the sounding of the fifth trumpet, the first woe spread a cloud of darkness over the East. Muhammad 'the Prophet' preached the Quran, becoming a powerful king and warlord. Islam was established as an oppressive new religious and political force that spread from Arabia and even penetrated Europe. They successfully conquered another third of the remaining Roman (Byzantine) Empire.[17] But the plague of locusts eventually subsided, and they settled in the Eastern territories they had won in swift conquest. "The first woe is past. Behold, there are still two woes coming after this" (Revelation 9:12, WEB).

With the sounding of the sixth trumpet, Eastern Antichrist would be unleashed once more in the form of "one of the mightiest and longest-lasting dynasties in world history"[18]: the Ottoman (or Turkish) Empire.

> 13 The sixth angel sounded. I heard a voice from the horns of the golden altar which is before God, 14 saying to the sixth angel who had the trumpet, "Free the four angels who are bound at the great river Euphrates!"

> 15 The four angels were freed who had been prepared for that hour and day and month and year, so that they might kill one third of mankind. 16 The number of the armies of the horsemen was two hundred million. I heard the number of them.

> 17 Thus I saw the horses in the vision, and those who sat on them, having breastplates of fiery red, hyacinth blue, and sulfur yellow; and the horses' heads resembled lions' heads. Out of their mouths proceed fire, smoke, and sulfur. 18 By these three plagues were one third of mankind killed: by the fire, the smoke,

and the sulfur, which proceeded out of their mouths. 19 For the power of the horses is in their mouths and in their tails. For their tails are like serpents, and have heads, and with them they harm. 20 The rest of mankind, who were not killed with these plagues, didn't repent of the works of their hands, that they wouldn't worship demons, and the idols of gold, and of silver, and of brass, and of stone, and of wood; which can't see, hear, or walk. 21 They didn't repent of their murders, their sorceries, their sexual immorality, or their thefts. (Revelation 9:13-21, WEB)

Once again, the setting, timing, and descriptions in this passage pinpoint the identity of this massive army and its leaders. This army would finish what the locusts started, completing the divine judgment over the last remaining third of the Byzantine Empire.

The Setting

This woe also starts in the East, where the four angels are bound at the river Euphrates. "The River Euphrates is called great because in ancient times it served as the primary boundary between the great threatening powers to the east and the more western world, including the Roman Empire."[19] The Arabic armies under Muhammad and afterward did not get very far past 'the great river'- they were defeated in their attempts to conquer Constantinople and subjugate Europe. After tormenting those regions for 150 years, they would settle in the more Eastern territories they had won with the founding of Baghdad, which is near the Euphrates.

This new power had been 'prepared', however, to be unleashed for this very purpose. They would cross over the great river Euphrates into the remainder of the Byzantine Empire "so that they might kill one third of mankind" (Revelation 9:15b)- that is, they would cause the downfall of the last third of the Eastern Roman world, culminating in the downfall of its capital, Constantinople.

The Timing

The times and successive events given in this prophecy coincide remarkably with history. The rise of the Turkmen is also the reunification of the Muslim world, revived to conquer once again. It is the next major Islamic power to rise in the East, making it a natural fit for the fulfillment of the sixth trumpet. Barnes writes:

> If the previous trumpet referred to the Saracens, or to the rise of the Muhammedan power among the Arabs, then the Turkish dominion, being the next in succession, would be what would most naturally be symbolized. The Turkish power rose on the decline of the Arabic, and was the next important power in affecting the destinies of the world.[20]

The beginning of this rise is traced to a man named Tughril Beg: "After the death of the Prophet Muhammad, Islam took a firm hold on the region. Succession struggles between local Caliphs (kings) came to an end in 1055 when Tughril Beg, a warrior from the Turkish steppes, established a Seljuk dynasty."[21] Tughril gained the title of 'temporal lieutenant of the prophet [Muhammad]' after conquering Baghdad in 1055, uniting the Turks and other Muslims under an Islamic banner. Soon after this preparation, they crossed the Euphrates River to wage war against the Byzantine Empire in 1057.

The time given to this conquering force is an "hour and day and month and year" (Revelation 9:15), when added together would be about 396 days. When the 'day-year' principle is applied, this would be about 396 years. This united Islamic army would have 396 years to bring about the downfall of the Byzantine Empire.

Amazingly, this is precisely what happened. From the time Tughril Beg led the renewed Muslim army under the banner of Muhammad across the Euphrates in 1057, the resulting Turkish Empire would go on win battle after battle in Europe for centuries. In 1453, they would go on to conquer the capital of the Byzantine Empire, Constantinople, the date that marks its end in history. The time between these two events is 396 years![22]

So another incredible time prophecy is fulfilled exactly as laid out in Scripture. From the 2300 'evenings and mornings' of Daniel 8, fulfilled exactly to the day; to the 'seventy weeks' in Daniel 9, where we see clearly how a day equals a year in prophecy; to the prophecy of Jesus in Matthew 24, when the Temple was destroyed within a generation; the 150 years given to the locusts to conquer in this chapter; and once again, the 396 years foretold when the remaining third of the Roman Empire would be destroyed by the revived Eastern Antichrist.

There are still more to marvel at as well. All of these are labeled 'unfulfilled' and pushed into the future with the modern popular interpretation, but history reveals that God gave us these time prophecies for a good reason. The majority of the church today only finds confusion and uncertainty in these prophecies- we can no longer afford to ignore the fact that God is truly faithful to his promises. Understanding them fills us with faith and assurance, knowing that the 'times, time, and half a time' will also be fulfilled.

The Armies of the Horsemen

The description of the powers released by the sixth trumpet also confirms the identity of this revived Eastern Antichrist:

Four Angels - The trumpet blow is said to release four angels, symbolic of four different powers. Barnes comments that this would be the most natural sense of the text: "It has been made a question why the number four is specified, and whether the forces were in any sense made up of four divisions, nations, or people.... it must be admitted that the most obvious interpretation would be to refer it to some combination of forces, or to some union of powers."[23]

Tughril Beg is noted above as the 'temporal lieutenant of the prophet', but he is the warlord of a union of four different kingdoms: "the original power that had established itself in Persia, under Malek Shah, and the three subordinate powers that sprung out of that of Kerman, Syria, and Roum."[24] It is appropriate that four angels symbolize this union of four kingdoms that crosses the Euphrates.

Prepared, yet bound - The verses in this passage show that the angels had been prepared to conquer the remaining third of the Roman Empire, but were somehow bound at the Euphrates. God told the sixth angel who had the trumpet, "'Free the four angels who are bound at the great river Euphrates!' The four angels were freed who had been prepared for that hour and day and month and year..." (Revelation 9:14b-15a, WEB). Miller explains the fulfillment of these symbols:

> The Turks had most of the dominions east of the Euphrates under their control by the eleventh century and seemingly were restrained there. The Euphrates was no barrier to them but they did not cross it for further conquests, until the mid eleventh century.[25]

Barnes also writes:

> These Turkish hordes had been long restrained in the East. They had subdued Persia. They had then achieved the conquest of India. They had conquered Bagdad, and the entire East was under their control. Yet for a long time they had now been inactive, and it would seem as if they had been bound or restrained by some mighty power from moving in their conquests to the West.[26]

The biblical image of the revived Eastern Antichrist being prepared, yet bound until released by God, matches what happened in history.

Armies of horsemen - The Turkish armies were known for being composed primarily of cavalry. According to Collins:

The description of the sixth trumpet forces as "mounted troops" (NIV) is most apt for the Turkish invaders, as they are well-known for use of horses in warfare. With the contemporary armies of Western Europe, the majority of the fighting men were foot soldiers, with a minority of knights as cavalry, whereas the Turkish armies consisted of cavalry and were therefore very swift and powerful.[27]

When historians describe the Turkish armies, they note the massive amount of horsemen in them. Gibbon said that even as early as 1050, "The myriads of the Turkish horse overspread a frontier of six hundred miles, from Taurus to Arzeroum."[28]

Two hundred million - This number is translated literally as "twice ten thousand times ten thousand,"[29] or "two myriads of myriads."[30] It would be the largest force ever fielded in history if the number is taken literally, but Collins writes that "this symbolic language probably should be understood to mean 'too many to count.'"[31] According to Haynes:

> This is the only time this number, "twice-ten-thousand" is used in the New Testament. "Twice-ten-thousand" is unique, and oddly specific. Like it's a clue. And it is. The Hebrew equivalent only occurs in Psalm 68:17, where the Hebrew reads, *"The chariots of God are twice-ten-thousand and multiplied thousands"* [my trans.]. In Hebrew it's not a precise number, just a vast number. That's how we should read the quotation here also.[32]

The Turkish Empire's armies of horsemen were indeed vast throughout its history. But even if the number just means an innumerable host, there is another connection to the Turkish hosts: they would number their forces by 'myriads', or tens of thousands. That is why the historian Gibbon used 'myriads' to describe their numbers in the quote above. Barnes remarks, "One thing is clear, that to no other invading hosts could the language used here be so well applied, and if it were supposed that John was writing after the event, this would be the language which he would be likely to employ - for this is nearly the identical language employed by the historian Gibbon."[33]

Breastplates of red, blue, and yellow - The verse says, "Thus I saw the horses in the vision, and those who sat on them, having breastplates of fiery red, hyacinth blue, and sulfur yellow" (Revelation 9:17a, WEB). The English scholar Charles Daubuz writes that "this has a literal accomplishment, for the Ottomans, from the first time of their appearance, have affected to wear such warlike apparel of scarlet, blue, and yellow."[34] When looking for confirmation of this in other sources, I saw paintings of Ottoman battles from many different eras, and their uniform was nearly always a striking mix of red, blue, and yellow.

Fire, smoke, and sulfur - The verse says that "the horses' heads resembled lions' heads. Out of their mouths proceed fire, smoke, and sulfur" (Revelation 9:17b, WEB). This is symbolic of the Turks' introduction of the use of gunpowder in warfare. "It was their use of enormous cannon that they succeeded in 1573 in breaking down the great walls of Constantinople and taking both the city and the empire."[35] Among the many cannons they used in the assault, they had made the largest cannon in history up to that point: twenty-seven feet long, a barrel lined with eight inches of solid bronze and a diameter of thirty inches, capable of firing stones weighing over half a ton.[36] A Turkish historian's description of their use brings to mind the fire, smoke, and sulfur mentioned in Scripture:

> The Moslems placed their *cannon* in an effective position. The gates and ramparts of Constantinople were pierced in a thousand places. The flame which issued from the mouths of those instruments of warfare, of brazen bodies and fiery jaws, cast grief and dismay among the miscreants. The smoke which spread itself in the air rendered the brightness of day sombre as

night; and the face of the world soon became as dark as the black fortune of the unhappy infidels.[37]

Mouths and tails - The verse says, "For the power of the horses is in their mouths and in their tails. For their tails are like serpents, and have heads, and with them they harm" (Revelation 9:19, WEB). It was previously shown how the power out their mouths was the fire, smoke, and sulfur of their cannons. As for the tails, the Turkish forces used the strange standard of horsetails to signify ranks. The 'heads,' or commanders, of their armies would ride into battle with these standards. Barnes writes:

> This remarkable standard or ensign is found only among the Turks, and, if there was an intended reference to them, the symbol here would be the proper one to be adopted. The meaning of the passage where it is said that "their power is in their tails" would seem to be, that their tails were the symbol or emblem of their authority - as in fact the horse's tail is in the appointment of a pasha. The image before the mind of John would seem to have been, that he saw the horses belching out fire and smoke, and, what was equally strange, he saw that their power of spreading desolation was connected with the tails of horses. Anyone looking on a body of cavalry with such banners or ensigns would be struck with this unusual and remarkable appearance, and would speak of their banners as concentrating and directing their power.[38]

They Did Not Repent

With the fall of Constantinople, the entire Roman world was destroyed, both East and West. Despite these woes, those who lived did not repent of their evil deeds. The verses say:

> 20 The rest of mankind, who were not killed with these plagues, didn't repent of the works of their hands, that they wouldn't worship demons, and the idols of gold, and of silver, and of brass, and of stone, and of wood; which can't see, hear, or walk. 21 They didn't repent of their murders, their sorceries, their sexual immorality, or their thefts. (Revelation 9:20-21 WEB)

All of these sins could be found in both old pagan Rome before its destruction, but also in the revived Papal Rome.

Worship of demons and idols - "Homage rendered to the spirits of departed people, and substituted in the place of the worship of the true God, would meet all that is properly implied here,"[39] i.e., praying to saints and their images. Collins writes,

> During the entire period of the fifth and sixth trumpet, the sixth through the fifteenth centuries, the worship of saints was widely practiced in both the Eastern and Western churches, as having its beginnings in the fourth century. Philip Schaff comments that the worship of saints "was a Christian substitute for heathen idolatry and hero worship, and well suited to the tastes and antecedents of the barbarian races, but was equally popular among the cultivated Greeks."[40]

Murders - The Papacy would persecute and kill anyone who dissented from their commands. A prime example of this is the 12th-century Christian movement of the Waldensians. They were severely persecuted for rejecting some of the teachings of the Roman Catholic Church:

> The confession of sins was guided by their leaders but did not require a priest; they rejected the use of indulgences. Baptism was to be by full immersion in water and was not administered to infants. Eventually, the elements of the Eucharist (bread and wine) were understood as symbols only, and the Waldenses denied the doctrine of transubstantiation. They also rejected the notion of purgatory and of prayers offered for the dead. Their views were based on a simplified biblicism, moral rigour, and criticism of abuses in the contemporary church. They accepted the Bible as the sole, total authority of all doctrine. Additionally, a formal church building was not viewed as necessary to worship God, and thus many Waldenses held services in their homes, stables, or other locations.[41]

The Papacy called a crusade against them for holding these beliefs, and entire towns and villages of Waldensians were slaughtered. It is estimated that a million people were killed.[42] There are many more cases like this one:

> It is supposed that fifty million of persons have perished in these persecutions of the Waldenses, Albigenses, Bohemian Brethren, Wycliffites, and Protestants; that some fifteen million of Indians perished in Cuba, Mexico, and South America, in the wars of the Spaniards, professedly to propagate the Catholic faith; that three million and a half of Moors and Jews perished, by Catholic persecution and arms, in Spain; and that thus, probably no

less than sixty-eight million and five hundred thousand human beings have been put to death by this one persecuting power.[43]

Sorceries - This is fulfilled in Catholicism with supposed miracles: "Puppets, relics, images of the saints, and other paraphernalia were commonly alleged to perform miracles in exchange for payment."[44] Barnes points out that "false and pretended miracles; arts adapted to deceive through the imagination; the supposed virtue and efficacy of relics; and frauds calculated to impose on mankind, have characterized those portions of the world where the Roman religion has prevailed, and been one of the principal means of its advancement."[45]

Sexual immorality - The list of sexual immorality among the clergy in the Roman Catholic Church during this period is long; the periods of the most evil Popes called the Pornacracies have been mentioned in an earlier chapter of this book. The history of Octavianus, elected Pope John XII in 955, is enough to illustrate the magnitude of the depravity here:

> In his first years as pope, the people of Rome accused John XII of incest, murder, and rape. John used the papal treasury as his personal spending account to finance his many vices. He indulged in the city's prostitutes, housing many of them in the Lateran Palace for his own pleasure. When he wasn't in his brothel, John seduced Roman widows and kidnapped female pilgrims on their way to St. Peter's Basilica. As stories of his inclinations spread throughout Europe, the number of women traveling on pilgrimage significantly decreased.

> The pope was a man ruled by his passions. Lavishing wealth and power on one of his mistresses, he made her governor of Rome. No woman was safe from John's lust. When he seduced his father's long-time mistress, she became pregnant, and she bled to death during childbirth. After almost a decade of his sexual antics, Pope John XII died in the bed of his latest mistress.

Although the Church records state that he died of a stroke, other sources claim that the woman's husband broke into the room and caught the lovers together. The cuckolded husband beat John to death in a jealous rage.[46]

Thefts - Fulfilled in the money extorted from Catholics in different ways- charging them to handle relics of saints; elevating patron saints and charging for their favor; the sale of indulgences; mandatory pilgrimages; pressuring laymen to gift their estate to the church in their will; charging for masses to be held for dead relatives said to be in purgatory.[47]

Traditional Vs. Modern Interpretation

It was noted at the beginning of this chapter that many Christians today *sense* that Muslim nations or leaders play a role in the end times, even if they can't quite pin down which Scriptures foretell it. Yet Revelation 9 clearly speaks to the darkness of understanding that originates in the East, and still covers the nations gripped by Islam.

The mistake we often make, however, is to pit ourselves against Muslims as enemies. This is evident in our distrust of immigrants and refugees from these nations, such as President Trump's executive order in 2017 banning people from six Muslim-majority countries from entering the USA. We act out of fear, demanding that our nation's leaders take proactive measures against Muslim nations in our Global War On Terror.

One thing that should become clear from the historical interpretation of these passages is that *our battle is not against flesh and blood*- it is not against Muslims, it is not against Catholics, it is not against Atheists. Antichrist is not just one single person. Our battle is "against the principalities, against the powers, against the world's rulers of the darkness of this age, and against the spiritual forces of wickedness in the heavenly places" (Ephesians 6:12b, WEB). These Antichristian powers are *spiritual*, and our primary weapon against them is prayer. According to Haynes,

We should never be afraid of Islam, or think about it the same way again. Like the Babylonians against Judah, God raised up invaders who deny Jesus Christ to punish so-called believers who were disloyal to Jesus Christ. It's the same irony Habakkuk complained about when God sent Babylon to punish Judah: God used a more wicked nation to punish the wicked nation (Hab 1:13)... Before you look down on apostate Christians, or on Muslims, look at your own prayer life: Judging from our love for Jesus, how Christian are we?[48]

Our hearts should be filled with compassion and mourning for the suffering these nations have endured under the first and second woe. Miller writes,

Islamic nations have been so held in the bondage of this false doctrine for over 1300 years. One cannot preach the gospel in those lands. If one could preach the gospel, there is still the confusion of Islam in the minds of its adherents that darkens the understanding. One would pray that this will soon change; that in those lands, freedom from religious coercion could soon be a fact of life and political freedom might follow.[49]

But our hope is real- the Kingdom of God prevails, and all nations, East and West, will one day bow to Christ. The beast and the false prophet will be destroyed, and the dragon bound. Therefore, "Love your enemies, and pray for those who persecute you!"

---

1. Called the Byzantine Empire, the Eastern Roman Empire, or Byzantium. It was "the continuation of the Roman Empire primarily in its eastern provinces during Late Antiquity and the Middle Ages, when its capital city

was Constantinople. It survived the fragmentation and fall of the Western Roman Empire in the 5th century AD and continued to exist for an additional thousand years until the fall of Constantinople to the Ottoman Empire in 1453." From Wikipedia, "Byzantine Empire". Available online at https://en.wikipedia.org/wiki/Byzantine_Empire

2. Albert Barnes, "Notes, Critical, Illustrative, and Practical", Revelation 9:3. Available online at https://www.sacred-texts.com/bib/cmt/barnes/rev0 09.htm

3. Oral Collins, "The Final Prophecy of Jesus", 204.

4. John Walton, Victor Matthews, Mark Chavalas, "The IVP Bible Background Commentary: Old Testament", 162.

5. Barnes, ibid, Revelation 8:10.

6. Barnes, ibid, Revelation 9:11.

7. M. J. Kister, "The Locust's Wing: Some Notes on Locust in the Hadith", 351.
Available online at http://www.kister.huji.ac.il/sites/default/files/Locus t_0.pdf

8. Charles Forster, "Mahometanism Unveiled Vol. 1", 217.
Available online at https://archive.org/details/in.ernet.dli.2015.31686/p age/n267/mode/2up

9. Barnes, ibid, Revelation 9:11.

10. Barnes, ibid, Revelation 9:7.

11. Kister, "'The Crowns of this Community'... Some Notes on the Turban in the Muslim Tradition", 217.
Available online at http://www.kister.huji.ac.il/sites/default/files/crown s.pdf

12. Shaykh Fadl al-Rahman al-A'zami, "The Status of the Turban in Light of the Sunnah."
Available online at https://www.ilmgate.org/the-status-of-the-turban-in-light-of-the-sunnah/

13. Wikipedia, "Turban."
Available online at https://en.wikipedia.org/wiki/Turban

14. Barnes, ibid, Revelation 9:11.

15. Barnes, ibid, Revelation 9:11.

16. Edward Gibbon, "Decline and Fall of the Roman Empire, Vol. 5", Chapter LI: Conquests By The Arabs. Part II.
Available online at https://www.sacred-texts.com/cla/gibbon/05/daf05016.htm

17. The Western Roman Empire had fallen in 476. Two thirds of it remained in the form of the Eastern/'Byzantine Empire, and the initial Muslim conquests took another. A third was left.

18. History.com, "Ottoman Empire."
Available online at https://www.history.com/topics/middle-east/ottoman-empire

19. Collins, ibid, 208.

20. Barnes, ibid, Revelation 9:20.

21. Felicity Arbuthnot, Nikki van der Gaag, "A History of Iraq".
Available online at https://newint.org/features/1999/09/05/history

22. Collins writes, "'This very hour and day and month and year' may be understood on the year-day principle as a composite period of 396 years, 118 days. Togrul Beg, the Seljuk Turk launched his campaign to conquer the Greek Empire from Baghdad on January 18, A.D. 1057... Constantinople

fell on May 29, 1453- 396 years and 130 days... just 12 days more than the forecast period of 396 years and 118 days... On the year-day time scale, the fall of Constantinople exceeded this period by less than one-half hour! Although one might well be satisfied with this as an adequate and remarkable fulfillment of the symbolic formula, Elliott takes this a step further and notes that if one subtracts 12 days of the siege, one arrives at the 40th day, about which Gibbon states, "After a siege of forty days the fate of Constantinople could no longer be averted" (1.527). Thus, we can be satisfied that from God's point of view, the time formula may well have been fulfilled to the very day!" Ibid, 216-217

23. Barnes, ibid, Revelation 9:14.

24. Barnes, ibid, Revelation 9:20.

25. Fred Miller, "Revelation: a Panorama of the Gospel Age", 86. Available online at http://moellerhaus.com/turkish.htm

26. Barnes, ibid, Revelation 9:20.

27. Collins, ibid, 214.

28. Edward Gibbon, ibid, Chapter LI: Conquests By The Arabs. Part II. Available online at https://sacred-texts.com/cla/gibbon/05/daf05043.ht m

29. Collins, ibid, 210.

30. Barnes, ibid, Revelation 9:16.

31. Collins, ibid, 210.

32. Joe Haynes, "Revelation 9:13-21 The Sixth Trumpet (NOTES)", 1. Available online at http://bcchurch.ca/SermonNotes/Revelation9-13-2 1-The%20Sixth%20Trumpet.pdf

33. Barnes, ibid, Revelation 9:20.

34. Charles Daubuz, "A perpetual commentary on the Revelation of St. John", 444.
Available online at https://babel.hathitrust.org/cgi/pt?id=mdp.390150 14811064&view=1up&seq=5

35. Collins, ibid, 215.

36. Roger Crowley, "The Guns of Constantinople."
Available online at https://www.historynet.com/the-guns-of-constantin ople/?r

37. From Edward Bishop Elliott, "Horae Apocalypticae Vol 1", 512. The footnote reads "Cited appropriately by Dr. Keith (in Apoc. Vol. ii. p. 46) from the Tadg al Tivarikh (or Diadem of Histories) of Saadeddin, 'the preceptor and historiographer of Murad 3 , and prince of Ottoman historians,' as translated in David's Grammar of the Turkish language." Available online at https://play.google.com/store/books/details?id=4yJ NAQAAMAAJ&rdid=book-4yJNAQAAMAAJ&rdot=1

38. Barnes, ibid, Revelation 9:20.

39. Barnes, ibid, Revelation 9:20.

40. Collins, ibid, 218.

41. Britannica, "Waldenses".
Available online at https://www.britannica.com/topic/Waldenses

42. This number may seem sensational, and it would be if the scope was limited to specific events and regions (like the Spanish Inquisition). Historical theologian Nathan Busenitz remarks, "If the term is used in a broad sense—to represent all Roman Catholic activity against non-Catholics—then the numbers rise dramatically. If the historian includes forms of torture and killing that did not involve a formal trial,

along with religious wars and other forms of Catholic violence enacted against Protestants and other non-Catholics (in areas outside of Spain and Portugal), then one can easily speak in terms of millions of people who were killed."
Available online at https://thecripplegate.com/how-many-peo-ple-died-in-the-inquisition/

For a detailed view of these numbers, see David A. Plaisted's "Estimates of the Number Killed by the Papacy in the Middle Ages and Later". Available online at https://static1.1.sqspcdn.com/static/f/827989/1511 6787/1321289366180/50+million+protestants+killed.pdf

43. Barnes, ibid, Revelation 9:20.

44. Collins, ibid, 221.

45. Barnes, ibid, Revelation 9:20.

46. Jennifer Conerly, "17 Popes Who Didn't Practice What They Preached." Available online at https://historycollection.com/17-popes-who-didnt -practiced-what-they-preached/14/

47. Barnes, ibid, Revelation 9:20.

48. Haynes, ibid.

49. Miller, ibid, 82.

Chapter Nine

The Fate of the Church

Revelation 12

It can be discouraging to dwell on the state of the church today. In the United States, political partisanship has caused a deep divide in denominations and congregations. High-profile believers are leaving the faith and calling for *deconstruction*. More pastors are suffering burnout and retiring earlier than ever. Secularism and atheism have been steadily rising in the West for decades. Worldwide, critics claim that there are 40,000 Christian denominations, and even though that number is massively overinflated, the fracturing of the church can seem overwhelming.

And this is in countries where we are relatively prosperous and have religious freedom. In many nations, it is illegal to preach the gospel. There are more Christians persecuted now than have ever been in the world. As encouraging as it is that believers in these countries stand firm even in the face of death, it is hard to imagine the sheer amount of pain and suffering they go through daily.

The bride of Christ is in rough shape. One begins to wonder how God could let it get so bad. How much longer will we be an object of mockery, the target of the world's disdain?

It stings a little less when we realize that our current condition was foretold in Scripture. It's also comforting that he promised to protect and take care of us in the midst of it, to the very end. It's downright encouraging when we see that there truly is an end in sight, a time limit he set that we may very well be in the last stages of. The story of our low estate is found in Revelation 12, the great sign of the woman and the dragon. The first six verses summarize the story, and the rest of the chapter goes into a little more detail.

The Woman...

A great sign was seen in heaven: a woman clothed with the sun, and the moon under her feet, and on her head a crown of twelve stars. 2 She was with child. She cried out in pain, laboring to give birth. 3 Another sign was seen in heaven. Behold, a great red dragon, having seven heads and ten horns, and on his heads seven crowns. 4 His tail drew one third of the stars of the sky, and threw them to the earth. The dragon stood before the woman who was about to give birth, so that when she gave birth he might devour her child. 5 She gave birth to a son, a male child, who is to rule all the nations with a rod of iron. Her child was caught up to God, and to his throne. 6 The woman fled into the wilderness, where she has a place prepared by God, that there they may nourish her one thousand two hundred sixty days. (Revelation 12:1-6, WEB)

The first thing that might come to mind when reading this prophecy is the Nativity story, when the virgin Mary gave birth to Jesus Christ. There are a few reasons why this prophecy is not about that event in particular:

- John received this prophecy almost 100 years after the birth of Christ, and he was told to write things "which will happen hereafter" (Revelation 1:19b, WEB).

- Jesus was not "caught up to God" (Revelation 12:5b, WEB, the word is 'snatched up' in the NIV) as a helpless baby or child. "The verb, 'to snatch'..., here in the passive voice, conveys the idea of taking up by an outside force or even by aggressive action in which the subject is passive... The ascension of Jesus is described in the Gospels as a deliberate and voluntary act of our Lord, surely not suitably described by the passive mode."[1]

- There is no corresponding event of Mary fleeing into the wilderness for 1260 days after Jesus ascends into heaven.

Instead, the woman in this prophecy has been generally agreed on by interpreters to symbolize the church. This is a familiar symbol in the Bible, where a woman represents God's people. The 'daughter of Zion' is mentioned throughout the Old Testament representing Israel as the people of God (2 Kings 19:21; Isaiah 1:8; Jeremiah 4:31; Isaiah 62:11; Micah 4:13; Zechariah 9:9). In the New Testament, the church is called 'the bride of Christ' (Ephesians 5:24-27; 2 Corinthians 11:2; Revelation 19:7-9, 21:1-2).

In this beautiful picture, the woman is "clothed with the sun, and the moon under her feet, and on her head a crown of twelve stars" (Revelation 12:1b, WEB). Solomon speaks of his bride similarly: "Who is she who looks out as the morning, beautiful as the moon, clear as the sun, and awesome as an army with banners?" (Song of Solomon 6:10, WEB). Here the church is pictured as shining with the brightness of the gospel, the "comparatively feeble light"[2] of the Old Covenant underneath her feet, bejeweled with the twelve tribes of Israel- or rather the twelve apostles now- shining in her diadem.

This is the church, nearly ready to give birth to a generation of Christians who would see "increase and prosperity - as if a child were born that was to rule over all nations."[3] This is how the same symbol is used elsewhere in the Bible:

"Before she goes into labor, she gives birth; before the pains come upon her, she delivers a son. 8 Who has ever heard of such things? Who has ever seen things like this? Can a country be born in a day or a nation be brought forth in a moment? Yet no sooner is Zion in labor than she gives birth to her children. (Isaiah 66:7-8)

"Sing, barren woman, you who never bore a child; burst into song, shout for joy, you who were never in labor; because more are the children of the desolate woman than of her who has a husband," says the Lord. (Isaiah 54:1)

The children born during your bereavement will yet say in your hearing, 'This place is too small for us; give us more space to live in.' (Isaiah 49:20)

This destiny of the church was assured, for the child "'will rule all the nations with an iron scepter'"(Revelation 12:5a). For now, however, she was crying out in the pain of labor- the church was being severely persecuted.

...And the Dragon

The source of this persecution was the dragon. One who is familiar with Daniel 7 and other parts of Revelation will recognize this beast, as it is described in nearly the same way in those places. It is explained in more detail in this book in chapters five, six, and seven, but a summary is as follows:

The dragon is Satan - The identity of the dragon is explained later in the chapter: "The great dragon was hurled down—that ancient serpent called the devil, or Satan, who leads the whole world astray" (Revelation 12:9). The dragon is identified again in chapter 20: "He seized the dragon, the old serpent, which is the devil and Satan, who deceives the whole inhabited earth, and bound him for a thousand years" (Revelation 20:2, WEB). This dragon is the devil working through the nations of this world, deceiving them into doing his bidding of persecuting the people of God. "There can be no doubt, therefore, that the reference here is to Satan, considered as the enemy of God, and the enemy of the peace of man, and especially as giving origin and form to some mighty power that would threaten the existence of the church."[4]

The dragon is enormous - In the other passages of Scripture where a beast like this is mentioned, it symbolizes empires. It is insinuated in the Bible that the devil has some sway over kingdoms: the devil took Jesus "to an exceedingly high mountain, and showed him all the kingdoms of the world and their glory. He said to him, 'I will give you all of these things, if you will fall down and worship me'" (Matthew 4:8-9, WEB). Satan deceives those in power into doing his bidding, and he had long worked within the Roman Empire, persecuting the church in hopes of destroying her. The Roman Empire was enormous, the largest empire the world had ever seen.

The dragon is red - The beast in Revelation 17:3 is also red. Red was a favorite color in Rome, and the one that appears the most in modern depictions connected to their armies. Red could also symbolize the dragon's bloody persecutions of the church.

The dragon has seven heads - The beast in Revelation 17:3 also has seven heads. There it was explained by the angel that "The seven heads are seven hills on which the woman sits. They are also seven kings. Five have fallen, one is, the other has not yet come; but when he does come, he must remain for only a little while." (Revelation 17:9b-10). This is explained in more detail in chapter 7 of this book, and to summarize, the seven heads represent Rome as 'the city of seven hills'. They also symbolize that in John's time, the Roman Empire had seen five forms of government come and go; they were currently under the imperial form, and there would be one more to come later. The dragon is once again identified as Rome.

The dragon has ten horns - Just like the beast in Daniel 7 and Revelation 13 and 17, the dragon has ten horns. This is explained more in chapters five and six of this book. To summarize, this symbolizes the ten kingdoms that would arise after the Roman Empire fell.

The dragon has seven crowns - According to Barnes, "this would merely denote that kingly or royal authority was claimed."[5] However, Collins points out that there is likely something more to it than that- diadems were not in use until Emperor Diocletian introduced them as his imperial crown in the year 293. "Prior to that time the laurel wreath crown was ordinarily used."[6] This small detail synchronizes with all of the other descriptions perfectly, and pinpoints the time period the prophecy is speaking of.

One more interesting fact is that Rome used a dragon as its royal standard in the same period:

> The dragon was first used as an ensign near the close of the second century of the Christian era, and it was not until the third century that its use had become common; and the reference here, according to this fact, would be to that period of the Roman power when this had become a common standard, and when the applicability of this image would be readily understood. It is simply Rome that is referred to - Rome, the great agent of accomplishing the purposes of Satan toward the church.[7]

The dragon "stood in front of the woman who was about to give birth, so that it might devour her child the moment he was born" (Revelation 12:4b). Satan, using the power of the Roman Empire, was ready to take down the church once and for all, before it could prosper and increase in the world.

Snatched from the Jaws of Defeat

The dragon failed, however. The rest of chapter 12 gives us more details:

> 7 There was war in the sky. Michael and his angels made war on the dragon. The dragon and his angels made war. 8 They

didn't prevail. No place was found for them any more in heaven. 9 The great dragon was thrown down, the old serpent, he who is called the devil and Satan, the deceiver of the whole world. He was thrown down to the earth, and his angels were thrown down with him. 10 I heard a loud voice in heaven, saying, "Now the salvation, the power, and the Kingdom of our God, and the authority of his Christ has come; for the accuser of our brothers has been thrown down, who accuses them before our God day and night. 11 They overcame him because of the Lamb's blood, and because of the word of their testimony. They didn't love their life, even to death. 12 Therefore rejoice, heavens, and you who dwell in them. Woe to the earth and to the sea, because the devil has gone down to you, having great wrath, knowing that he has but a short time."

13 When the dragon saw that he was thrown down to the earth, he persecuted the woman who gave birth to the male child. 14 Two wings of the great eagle were given to the woman, that she might fly into the wilderness to her place, so that she might be nourished for a time, and times, and half a time, from the face of the serpent. 15 The serpent spewed water out of his mouth after the woman like a river, that he might cause her to be carried away by the stream. 16 The earth helped the woman, and the earth opened its mouth and swallowed up the river which the dragon spewed out of his mouth. 17 The dragon grew angry with the woman, and went away to make war with the rest of her offspring, who keep God's commandments and hold Jesus' testimony. (Revelation 12:7-17, WEB)

The dragon could not stop the sudden increase and prosperity of the church that the birth of the male child symbolized. The child was 'snatched up' to heaven, and the dragon and his angels were thrown down. In other words, the church was given power and protection, while Satan's use of power in government was taken away.

Even still, the dragon takes down a third of the stars as he goes: "His tail drew one third of the stars of the sky, and threw them to the earth" (Revelation 12:4a, WEB). The majority of Satan's persecuting power through kingdoms and rulers was taken away, and yet he was able to retain a third of them.

In his fury, the dragon still pursues the woman and her offspring- the church, those "who keep God's commands and hold fast their testimony about Jesus" (Revelation 12:17b). The woman flees into the wilderness to escape, and she is aided in getting there: "two wings of the great eagle were given to the woman, that she might fly into the wilderness to her place" (Revelation 12:14a, WEB). This is an act that represents "the obscure, and humble, and persecuted state of the church... this would well represent the fact, that the true church became for a time obscure and unknown - as if it had fled away from the habitations of people, and had retired to the solitude and loneliness of a desert."[8]

In the wilderness she is kept safe, nourished for "one thousand two hundred sixty days" (Revelation 12:6b, WEB), or "a time, and times, and half a time" (Revelation 12:14, WEB)- two different ways of saying the same amount of time. This is the same time period given in Daniel 7:25 that the little horn oppresses the church; also in Revelation 13:5 where the beast does the same. The group of these passages refer to the same events: the church is kept safe during the 1,260 years that the dragon (a.k.a. the beast, the man of sin, and the prostitute- Satan using Roman powers in all of their different forms) persecutes the people of God. See chapters five, six, and seven of this book for more details on these passages and this time period.

During these 1,260 years, Satan still attempts to destroy the church through various means: "The serpent spewed water out of his mouth after the woman like a river, that he might cause her to be carried away by the stream" (Revelation 12:15, WEB). Yet the earth helped the woman: "The earth opened its mouth and swallowed up the river which the dragon spewed out of his mouth" (Revelation 12:16b, WEB). Floods in the Bible typically symbolize armies that invade like a 'flood,' like a river overflowing into the surrounding lands: "Now

therefore, behold, the Lord brings upon them the mighty flood waters of the
River: the king of Assyria and all his glory. It will come up over all its channels,
and go over all its banks" (Isaiah 8:7, WEB); see also Jeremiah 47:2 and Jeremiah
46:7-8. Somehow the earth swallowed up the flooding river- the armies were
dispersed and absorbed, and were not allowed to hurt the church.

The Historical Fulfillment

The use of symbols in this prophecy is consistent with other parts of the Bible-
the woman is used in many parts of both the Old and New Testament to
symbolize God's people, the birth of a child as their increase, and the dragon
matches its other appearances in Daniel and Revelation. But does this passage
have a specific historical fulfillment?

It turns out that as 'simple' as this vision is, there is a very specific period of
church history that it points to! It also speaks to the current plight of the church,
and why we are in such a humble estate centuries later.

For a little over two-hundred years after Jesus founded the church, persecution of Christians was fierce at times, but largely localized- "persecution
came mainly at the instigation of local rulers, albeit with Rome's approval."[9]
Claudius (41–54), perhaps the first to persecute Christians, expelled them from
Rome. Nero (54–68) blamed Christians for starting a major fire in Rome and
burned many of them alive in retaliation; Peter and Paul are said to have been
martyred under his reign. Domitian (81–96), the emperor who banished John
to Patmos where he authored Revelation, insisted on being acclaimed as 'God
the Lord' and killed those who refused to do so. Trajan (98–117) specifically
targeted Christians as fully distinct from Jews, calling for them to be punished
if they would not worship Roman gods. Marcus Aurelius (161–180) followed
in Trajan's footsteps, and fueled greater persecutions that continued under
Hadrian and Antoninus Pius. Finally, Septimius Severus (193–211) forbade
further conversions to Judaism and Christianity, killing many believers in North
Africa and Egypt.

Later persecutions, however, became Empire-wide. The church's continued growth bothered Decius (249–251), who sought to reinstate the deification of Roman rulers. Everyone in the Empire was expected to perform pagan religious observances, receiving a 'Certificate of Sacrifice' for doing so. Many faithful believers were killed for refusing to compromise. After him, Valerian (253–260) blamed Christians for the plagues and barbarian invasions that racked the Empire, intensifying the policies of Decius. Finally, we come to the point where Revelation 12 begins- the 'Great Persecution' of Diocletian (284–305):

> It was the first time in almost 50 years that an emperor had taken the trouble. Yet, as never before, the motive of this Great Persecution was the total extinction of Christianity. *It was, it seems, the final struggle between the old and new orders, and therefore the fiercest.*

> The first of Diocletian's edicts prohibited all Christian worship and commanded that churches and Christian books be destroyed. Two further edicts, required in the eastern provinces, ordered clergy to be arrested unless they sacrificed to pagan deities. By 304 this edict was extended to all Christians and was particularly vicious in Africa, under Diocletian co-Augustus Maximian.[10]

This was the "final struggle between the old and new orders" as Galli puts it, the war in heaven between the dragon and his angels, and Michael and his angels.

These fierce persecutions continued until 311, when Galerius issued an edict canceling them. More famously, in 312, Constantine the Great won the battle at Milvian Bridge while purportedly bearing the sign of the *Chi* (X) *Rho* (P), representing the first two letters of the Greek word ΧΡΙΣΤΟΣ (Christos). He became the first Roman Emperor to endorse Christianity, and in 313 issued the Edict of Milan, which decreed full legal toleration of Christianity.

The Roman Empire's persecution of the church finally ended. Under Constantine,

> Gradually, Rome became Christianized. On his own instructions, the statue of the emperor erected in the Forum depicts Constantine bearing a cross – "the sign of suffering that brought salvation," according to the inscription provided by Constantine. In 321, Constantine decreed that Sundays should become public holidays. Christian symbols began to appear on Roman coins. Christianity was now more than just legitimate; it was on its way to becoming the established religion of the empire.[11]

This monumental historical event matches the setup to the vision in Revelation 12 perfectly: the woman clothed with the sun, a symbol of the church, is suffering the pain of labor- she is experiencing fierce persecution. She is about to give birth to a child, symbolizing the prosperity and increase of the church. The dragon, symbolizing Satan's power over a pagan Roman Empire, lies in wait, hoping to wipe out the church completely in his greatest campaign of persecution to date. The dragon loses the war in heaven, however, and the increase of the church is assured. Stripped of its authority over the Roman Empire, the dragon is thrown down to heaven (but not without taking down 'one third of the stars' with him- that is, retaining some earthly authority in the East, continuing persecution).[12]

Two seemingly small details also confirm this period of history- the use of the symbol of the dragon, and also the presence of diadems. As stated previously, the Roman battle standard of the dragon was not common until about this time in the third century. Also, the dragon wears seven crowns on its seven heads in this vision, and the Roman use of crowns starts precisely with Diocletian, the very emperor who initiates the 'Great Persecution' of the church! "The appearance of the diadems on the heads of the dragon is clear indication of the detailed accuracy of this temporal prophecy."[13]

Filled With Fury

The dragon, having been thrown down, is filled with fury. "Woe to the earth and to the sea, because the devil has gone down to you, having great wrath, knowing that he has but a short time" (Revelation 12:12b, WEB). He continues to persecute the church in every way he can. This is when the woman flees to the wilderness, being brought safely there and nourished for 1,260 years.

This next stage of persecution is clear: the very next chapter of Revelation concerns the continuation of the Roman Empire, wounded nearly to death, and resurrected in the form of the Holy Roman Empire (see chapter 7 of this book). Even though the survival of the church is guaranteed, more Christians will die under this persecution than ever before:

> What's most interesting is when the heroic age stopped and when the Church itself converted into being a form of Roman imperial culture, after the conversion of Constantine in 312... Christianity's effort to reclaim its own heroic history after it had already become an arm of government, itself, and was, of course, persecuting other Christians. *More Christians were persecuted by the Roman Government after the conversion of Constantine, than before.* The difference is that it's a Christian government who's persecuting the other Christians.[14]

Both good and bad things came from the rise of Constantine. While there was much-needed relief from persecution and important doctrinal debates were settled, the corruption of the church and the rise of Antichrist had also begun. It was understood by the early church that Daniel 7 foretold the fall of the Roman Empire. It would be split into ten kingdoms, and the little horn would claim direct authority over three of them- then his campaign against the church would last for 1,260 years (see chapters five and six of this book). The rise of the church into high stature in government foreshadowed this fate.

The church continues to survive in the wilderness to this very day. Remember, this exile is "emblematic of the long period of obscurity and persecution in the true church, and yet of the fact that it would be protected and nourished."[15] The true church has been through some extremely brutal times at the hands of the beast (Papal Rome), the false prophet (Islam), and the dragon (satanic secular power). This exile will not fully end until the 1,260 years are over, when the dragon is bound (Revelation 20:2), and the beast and false prophet are thrown into the lake of fire (Revelation 19:20). The beast has already received some of the judgments apportioned to it, and the true church has benefited from it- but we are not out of the wilderness yet (for more, see chapter 11 of this book),

Traditional Vs. Modern Interpretation

In the modern futurist interpretation, the woman symbolizes Israel, and the child she bears is Jesus Christ. "Satan failed to destroy Jesus at His birth, and because he also failed to destroy Him during His life and in His death, Jesus Christ ascended victoriously into heaven."[16] Satan then turns to persecute Israel- in the future, of course. The rest of the chapter is pushed into the mysterious and unknown future.

Earlier in this chapter, it was shown how this is unlikely for a few reasons: God told John to write down what would happen in the future, and the birth and ascension of Christ were decades in the past when John wrote it. The baby in this vision is passive while being actively 'snatched up', but Christ ascended to the Father as a man, in a deliberate and voluntary act rather than passively.[17] Additionally, the woman had other children (Revelation 12:17), making the symbol hardly appropriate if it references Jesus, demeaning the uniqueness of his birth.

The modern futurist interpretation results in confusion over how these symbols are used elsewhere in Scripture, and a staggering amount of conjecture. For example, take this explanation of the flood that comes out of the dragon's mouth (Revelation 12:15) from Dr. Constable:

Perhaps Satan will use literal water to try to drown this group of Israelites. If they take refuge in a place such as Petra this might seem to be a possibility. Another possibility is that he will pursue them with soldiers as a river (cf. Jeremiah 46:7-8; Jeremiah 47:2-3). A flood is also a biblical metaphor for overwhelming evil, persecution (Psalms 18:4; Psalms 124:2-4; Isaiah 43:2). Probably this is a picturesque way of describing Satan's attempt to destroy the Jews who will have congregated in Palestine following the Antichrist's covenant with them. He may seek to do it with deceptive false teaching, since the water comes out of his mouth. Both water and fire (cf. Revelation 9:17; Revelation 11:5) proceeding from the mouth picture punishment in Scripture.[18]

This attempt at an explanation reveals a strange hybrid of hyper-literal and symbolical interpretation that results in an inconsistent hermeneutic. Dispensationalists take pride in using a "consistently literal method of interpretation" but apply it inconsistently in the biblical apocalyptic genre. The truly 'literal, grammatical' approach in this case is to recognize that Revelation is full of biblical symbols foretelling chronological events. It *is* to be interpreted literally, meaning:

The text should be understood in its normal or ordinary sense. Accordingly, a literal understanding includes figures of speech and any other language phenomena that would normally be found in the particular kind of literature as they were known and recognized when they were written. As it is an apocalyptic writing, one should expect the Revelation to abound in figurative language, yet the book to be taken literally- that is, according to the norms by which at the time of writing that kind of language was understood. This is the method which must be pursued when seeking an authoritative message from any part of the Bible.[19]

The type of example commonly used today is to compare modern genres: we are going to interpret a cookbook differently than say a poem, or a romance novel differently than a legal document. We understand the rules of each genre, and interpret them appropriately. *Context matters.*

The modern hyper-literal interpretation has led to confusion over the timing of these prophecies. Futurists will accept the day-year principle- where a day equals a year in prophetic language- in Daniel 9, but ignore it elsewhere in Daniel and Revelation. Confusion abounds in these passages: as seen above, is the flood literal, or symbolic? Are the locust-scorpion-man-beasts literal demon monsters that will appear, incomprehensible modern machinery, or are they symbolic?

The traditional historicist interpretation takes Scripture *literally*, letting it speak for itself in its own grammatical-historical context. The angels often explain the symbols, and the symbols are applied consistently. Other passages of Scripture set the ground rules for their usage. Speculation is kept in check until the historical fulfillment appears, revealing the remarkable power and sovereignty of our God.

This includes understanding Israel's place in prophecy. As seen in the modern futurist interpretation of the woman in this passage, Jews and national Israel play a major part in their understanding of the end times. Historicists are accused of ignoring or downplaying God's future plans for Israel, but traditionally this was not the case. In the next chapter we will explore the exciting and hopeful future of the Jews in prophecy.

---

1. Oral Collins, "The Final Prophecy of Jesus", 280.

2. Albert Barnes, "Notes, Critical, Illustrative, and Practical", Revelation 12:1.
Available online at https://www.sacred-texts.com/bib/cmt/barnes/rev0 12.htm

3. Barnes, ibid, Revelation 12:5.

4. Barnes, ibid, Revelation 12:3.

5. Barnes, ibid, Revelation 12:3.

6. Collins, ibid, 287.

7. Barnes, ibid, Revelation 12:3.

8. Barnes, ibid, Revelation 12:6.

9. Mark Galli, "Persecution in the Early Church: A Gallery of the Persecuting Emperors."
Available online at https://christianhistoryinstitute.org/magazine/article /persecution-in-early-church-gallery

10. Galli, ibid, emphasis mine.

11. Alister McGrath, "Historical Theology", 36.

12. According to Barnes, "There were times under the emperors when, in a considerable part of the empire, after the establishment of Christianity, the church enjoyed protection, and the Christian religion was tolerated, while in other parts paganism still prevailed, and waged a bitter warfare with the church... 'In two-thirds of the empire, embracing its whole European and African territory, Christians enjoyed toleration; in the other, or Asiatic portion, they were still, after a brief and uncertain respite, exposed to persecution, in all its bitterness and cruelty as before' (Elliott)."
See Barnes, ibid, Revelation 12:4; Edward Bishop Elliott, "Horae Apocalypticae - Volume 3", 17.

Available online at https://play.google.com/store/books/details?id=ZL8
7AAAAcAAJ

13. Collins, ibid, 287.

14. Wayne Meeks, "The Martyrs", emphasis mine.
Available online at https://www.pbs.org/wgbh/pages/frontline/shows/r
eligion/why/martyrs.html

15. Barnes, ibid, Revelation 12:2.

16. Thomas Constable, "Constable's Expository Notes", Revelation 12:5.
Available online at https://www.studylight.org/commentaries/eng/dcc/r
evelation-12.html

17. Collins, ibid, 280.

18. Constable, ibid, Revelation 12:15.

19. Collins, ibid, 18.

Chapter Ten

Future Hope for Israel

Romans 11

I t would be an understatement to say that national Israel and Jews play a significant role in the popular modern interpretation of end times prophecy today. This is because many prophecies in the Bible concerning Israel are seen as unfulfilled, so they are pushed into the future (even when there is a clear historical fulfillment). One example of this is Daniel 9, where futurists insert an unmentioned 'pause' between the 69th and 70th week (see chapter three of this book for more details). So they explain that another Temple must be built in Jerusalem that a future Antichrist will invade, beginning a campaign of persecution against the Jews in Israel.

In this view, the Church plays little to no role in these prophecies. Believers would have already been raptured, and the Jews left behind. Israel and the church are said to be completely different entities. In fact, this is one of the two main principles of dispensational theology, which are "(1) maintaining a consistently literal method of interpretation, and (2) *maintaining a distinction between Israel and the church.*"[1] Israel is seen as *separate* from the church. Sometimes this view can go so far as to claim that Jews are on a separate path to salvation by following the Law or by works apart from Christ, known as 'dual covenant' theology.

On the other end of the spectrum, modern mainline protestant and reformed theologians are accused of believing in supersessionism (derogatively called 're-placement theology' by dispensationalists),[2] which teaches that the church has essentially *replaced* Israel. Those who hold to this view do not see any future prophecies that apply specifically to Jews anymore, but rather to the church at large (including both Jews and Gentiles).

Sadly, finding a balanced interpretation of Israel in Scripture between the two extremes of *separation* or *replacement* is difficult today. Yet it was not always this way, and the traditional interpretation of prophecy in Scripture saw a clear future hope for Jews. This prophecy is not found in the apocalyptic passages of the Bible like Daniel or Revelation, but in Paul's epistle to the Romans.

Israel, but not Israel

One of the main reasons Paul wrote his epistle to the Romans was to address the tensions that had arisen between the Jew and Gentile believers, "who probably meet in separate house churches and who appear to be at odds regarding Gentile adherence to the Jewish law."[3] Paul wanted them both to understand that in Christ, Jew and Gentile together form one people of God- the Church.

In Romans, Paul speaks of Israel in two different ways: *physical* Israel, made up of ethnic Jews, many of whom have not responded to the call of God; and *spiritual* Israel, those Jews who have responded to God's plan in Christ. They are the remnant of believers that God has kept for himself. Paul compares them:

> A person is not a Jew who is one only outwardly, nor is circum-
> cision merely outward and physical. No, a person is a Jew who
> is one inwardly; and circumcision is circumcision of the heart,
> by the Spirit, not by the written code. Such a person's praise is
> not from other people, but from God. (Romans 2:28-29).

> For not all who are descended from Israel are Israel. (Roman
> 9:6b)

Paul confirms that a Jew could be part of physical Israel- that is, ethnically Jewish, and even in good standing with the Jewish religious community- yet still not be a part of spiritual Israel, the community of Christ followers, which now includes Gentile believers.

Jews who are a part of spiritual Israel are not separate from or replaced by Gentiles, rather, Israel is expanded: "Jesus brought the blessings of Abraham 'first to the Jew' and then expanded the blessing 'also to the Gentile' (see Galatians 3:14 and Romans 1:16)... The concept of "Spiritual Israel" is a Biblical doctrine. It doesn't mean "replacement"...it means EXPANSION! God has joined Gentiles to the true faith of Israel --He has expanded the nation spiritually!"[4] Gentiles share in this blessing by submitting to the King of Israel, Jesus Christ. This concept is made clear in Ephesians:

> Therefore remember that once you, the Gentiles in the flesh, who are called "uncircumcision" by that which is called "circumcision" (in the flesh, made by hands), 12 that you were at that time separate from Christ, alienated from the commonwealth of Israel, and strangers from the covenants of the promise, having no hope and without God in the world. 13 But now in Christ Jesus you who once were far off are made near in the blood of Christ. 14 For he is our peace, who made both one, and broke down the middle wall of separation, 15 having abolished in his flesh the hostility, the law of commandments contained in ordinances, that he might create in himself one new man of the two, making peace, 16 and might reconcile them both in one body to God through the cross, having killed the hostility through it. 17 He came and preached peace to you who were far off and to those who were near. 18 For through

him we both have our access in one Spirit to the Father. (Ephesians 2:11-18, WEB)

When it comes to our standing before God, there is no inherent advantage to being a Jew, "For there is no distinction between Jew and Greek; for the same Lord is Lord of all, and is rich to all who call on him. For, 'Whoever will call on the name of the Lord will be saved'" (Romans 10:12-13, WEB). We are one through the Holy Spirit: "For in one Spirit we were all baptized into one body, whether Jews or Greeks, whether bond or free; and were all given to drink into one Spirit" (1 Corinthians 12:13, WEB). Jew and Gentile are heirs to the same promises:

> "For you are all children of God, through faith in Christ Jesus. 27 For as many of you as were baptized into Christ have put on Christ. 28There is neither Jew nor Greek, there is neither slave nor free man, there is neither male nor female; for you are all one in Christ Jesus. 29 If you are Christ's, then you are Abraham's offspring and heirs according to promise." (Galatians 3:26-29, WEB)

Yet Paul wrote that there *is* a benefit to being a Jew: "Then what advantage does the Jew have? Or what is the profit of circumcision? Much in every way! Because first of all, they were entrusted with the revelations of God" (Romans 3:1-2, WEB). Jews are those "whose is the adoption, the glory, the covenants, the giving of the law, the service, and the promises; of whom are the fathers, and from whom is Christ as concerning the flesh, who is over all, God, blessed forever" (Romans 9:4, WEB). Paul is a Christian, an apostle of the Church, but he retains his Jewish identity: "I also am an Israelite, a descendant of Abraham, of the tribe of Benjamin" (Romans 11:1b, WEB). We are one before God, yet we do not lose our ethnic or cultural identities. It will not be a monoculture that worships before God, rather "a great multitude, which no man could count, out of every nation and of all tribes, peoples, and languages, standing before the throne and before the Lamb" (Revelation 7:9, WEB)

Understanding Paul's definitions of Israel and the Church goes a long way in dispelling common notions we have of both, which for many Christians is typically as follows:

> The Church= Gentiles, separate from Israel and Jews.
> Israel= Jews, separate from Gentiles.

Instead, it should be:

> The Church= *Spiritual* Israel, or New Covenant believing Jews expanded with Gentile believers.
> *Physical* Israel= Ethnic Jews, many of whom are currently unbelievers.

The Olive Tree

In Romans 9-11, Paul expresses how desperately he hopes for the salvation of physical Israel, going so far as to say that he "could wish that I myself were accursed from Christ for my brothers' sake, my relatives according to the flesh" (Romans 9:3, WEB). And in chapter 10: "Brothers, my heart's desire and my prayer to God is for Israel, that they may be saved" (Romans 10:1, WEB). Yet he saw so many of them reject Christ and the gospel.

In Romans 11, Paul explains this situation, referencing both physical and spiritual Israel. He calls his mostly unbelieving ethnic family of Jews 'Israel,' while spiritual Israel is compared to an olive tree, with both natural and wild branches- Jews and Gentiles, respectively- all nourished by the root of the olive tree, which is Christ. Speaking to Gentiles (verse 13), Paul says:

If the root is holy, so are the branches. 17 But if some of the branches were broken off, and you, being a wild olive, were grafted in among them and became partaker with them of the root and of the richness of the olive tree, 18 don't boast over the branches. But if you boast, it is not you who support the root, but the root supports you. 19 You will say then, "Branches were broken off, that I might be grafted in." 20 True; by their unbelief they were broken off, and you stand by your faith. Don't be conceited, but fear; 21 for if God didn't spare the natural branches, neither will he spare you. 22 See then the goodness and severity of God. Toward those who fell, severity; but toward you, goodness, if you continue in his goodness; otherwise you also will be cut off. 23 They also, if they don't continue in their unbelief, will be grafted in, for God is able to graft them in again. 24 For if you were cut out of that which is by nature a wild olive tree, and were grafted contrary to nature into a good olive tree, how much more will these, which are the natural branches, be grafted into their own olive tree? (Romans 11:16b-24, WEB)

Some of the natural branches- physical Israel- have been broken off, and "by their fall salvation has come to the Gentiles" (Romans 11:11, WEB). There were still Jewish believers in Christ: "Even so then at this present time also there is a remnant according to the election of grace" (Romans 11:5, WEB), and at first the Church was exclusively Jewish. But now Gentiles were coming into the church in droves, and more and more Jewish leaders and synagogues were rejecting the gospel. The olive tree was being filled with 'wild branches.'

Paul insists that the fallen natural branches can still be grafted on, "for God is able to graft them in again" (Romans 11:23b). If they turn from their unbelief and put their faith in Christ, they will join the remnant and be a part of spiritual Israel once more. And amazingly, this is precisely what Paul says is going to happen.

All Israel Will Be Saved

25 For I don't desire you to be ignorant, brothers, of this mystery, so that you won't be wise in your own conceits, that a partial hardening has happened to Israel, until the fullness of the Gentiles has come in, 26 and so all Israel will be saved. Even as it is written,

"There will come out of Zion the Deliverer,
and he will turn away ungodliness from Jacob.
27 This is my covenant with them,
when I will take away their sins." (Romans 11:25-27, WEB)

At some point in the future, after "the fullness of the Gentiles has come in" (Romans 11:25b, WEB), there will be a massive revival among Jews. At that time they will turn from their unbelief, putting their faith in Christ. The natural branches will once again be grafted onto the olive tree.

Albert Barnes, a 19th-century Reformed theologian, wrote the following about this passage:

And so - That is, in this manner; or when the great abundance of the Gentiles shall be converted, then all Israel shall be saved.

All Israel - All the Jews. It was a maxim among the Jews that "every Israelite should have part in the future age." (Grotius.) The apostle applies that maxim to his own purpose; and declares the sense in which it would be true. He does not mean to say that every Jew of every age would be saved; for he had proved that a large portion of them would be, in his time, rejected and lost. But the time would come when, as a people, they would be recovered; when the nation would turn to God; and when it could be said of them that, as a nation, they were restored to the divine favor. It is not clear that he means that even then every individual of them would be saved, but the body of them; the great mass of the nation would be. Nor is it said when this would be. This is one of the things which "the Father hath put in his own power;" Acts 1:7. He has given us the assurance that it shall be done to encourage us in our efforts to save them; and he has concealed the time when it shall be, lest we should relax our efforts, or feel that no exertions were needed to accomplish what must take place at a fixed time.

Shall be saved - Shall be recovered from their rejection; be restored to the divine favor; become followers of the Messiah, and thus be saved as all other Christians are.

Many more quotes from both classic and modern theologians could be given saying much the same, from every denominational background.[5] However, as mentioned previously, many modern believers interpret this differently now: "Not everyone agrees that 'all Israel' refers to the nation as a whole alive in some future generation. Some take 'all Israel' to refer to the true spiritual Israel including Jews and Gentiles. Others take it to refer to the remnant of believing ethnic Israel that is being saved all along through faith in Christ."[6] John Piper continues with five reasons why the passage clearly points to "a great and stupendous national conversion of Israel some day":

Five Reasons Why I Believe Romans 11:26 Refers to the Nation of Israel as a Whole

So let me draw out several reasons again why I believe verse 26 ("And in this way all Israel will be saved") means that someday the nation as a whole (not necessarily every individual; see 1 Kings 12:1; 2 Chronicles 12:1) will be converted to Christ and join the Christian church and be saved...

1. I think the term "Israel" in verse 25 and 26 most naturally refer to the same thing.

Verse 25: "Lest you be wise in your own conceits, I want you to understand this mystery, brothers: a partial hardening has come upon Israel. . . ." That must refer to the nation as a whole from generation to generation. He continues, ". . . until the fullness of the Gentiles has come in. 26 And in this way all Israel will be saved." I don't think the meaning of Israel changes between verse 25 and 26. The hardened Israel (the nation as a whole) will be the saved Israel (the nation as a whole).

2. The reference in verse 26 to banishing ungodliness from Jacob fits with the national view of "all Israel."

Verse 26: "And in this way all Israel will be saved, as it is written, 'The Deliverer will come from Zion, he will banish ungodliness from Jacob.'" This seems most naturally to be a picture of Christ's return at the second coming, and banishing ungodliness from Jacob refers most naturally to the removal of the hardening referred to in verse 25. "Jacob" is not a natural or typical reference to the elect remnant of Israel. The hardening lasts until the full number of the Gentiles comes in (the climax of world missions), and then Christ comes and lifts the veil and removes the hardening — he banishes ungodliness from Jacob, from "all Israel."

3. The parallel between the two halves of verse 28 point to all Israel as the nation as a whole.

Verse 28: "As regards the gospel, they are enemies of God for your sake." Now that half of the verse surely refers to the nation as a whole — they are enemies of God. So the second half of the verse surely refers to the nation as a whole as well: "But as regards election, they are beloved for the sake of their forefathers." The point of this verse is to show that even though Israel now is a covenant-breaking, unbelieving nation, that is going to change. The nation that are enemies now, will be converted later because of election and love.

4. The parallels in verse 12 point in the same direction.
Verse 12: "Now if their [the Jewish nation's] trespass means riches for the world [salvation for the Gentiles], and if their [the Jewish nation's] failure means riches for the Gentiles, how much more will their full inclusion!" Here "their full inclusion" most naturally refers to the same nation as "their trespass" and "their failure." So "their full inclusion" refers to the salvation of "all Israel" and is national.

5. The same thing is true about the parallels in verse 15.
"For if their [Jewish nation's] rejection means the reconciliation of the world, what will their [Jewish nation's] acceptance mean but life from the dead?" The nation now rejected will be accepted. So the "acceptance" of the Jewish nation most naturally refers to the salvation of "all Israel" — the salvation of the nation as a whole some day.[7]

The context of the astounding statement that "all Israel will be saved" is clear, and it points to the mass conversion of Jews at some point in the future.

But When?

Paul does not say when this event will occur, only that it will be after "the fullness of the Gentiles has come in" (Romans 11:25b). In Luke, there is a mention of the 'times of the Gentiles':

> 20 "But when you see Jerusalem surrounded by armies, then know that its desolation is at hand. 21 Then let those who are in Judea flee to the mountains. Let those who are in the middle of her depart. Let those who are in the country not enter therein. 22 For these are days of vengeance, that all things which are written may be fulfilled. 23 Woe to those who are pregnant and to those who nurse infants in those days! For there will be great distress in the land, and wrath to this people. 24 They will fall by the edge of the sword, and will be led captive into all the nations. *Jerusalem will be trampled down by the Gentiles, until the times of the Gentiles are fulfilled.* (Luke 21:20-24, WEB, emphasis mine)

This is the parallel passage to Matthew 24 (covered in chapter 4 of this book), talking about the razing of Jerusalem and the destruction of the Temple in 70 A.D. Jerusalem has been overrun by 'Gentiles' ever since, and even though Jews control much of the city, the supposed site of the Temple is home to the Islamic shrine, the Dome of the Rock. But according to Jesus' words, this state of affairs will come to an end. Barnes states:

> The meaning of the passage clearly is,

> 1. That Jerusalem would be completely destroyed.

2. That this would be done by Gentiles - that is, by the Roman armies.

3. That this desolation would continue as long as God should judge it proper in a fit manner to express his abhorrence of the crimes of the nation - that is, until the times allotted to "them" by God for this desolation should be accomplished, without specifying how long that would be, or what would occur to the city after that.

> It "may" be rebuilt, and inhabited by converted Jews. Such a thing is "possible," and the Jews naturally seek that as their home; but whether this be so or not, the time when the "Gentiles," as such, shall have dominion over the city is limited. Like all other cities on the earth, it will yet be brought under the influence of the gospel, and will be inhabited by the true friends of God. Pagan, infidel, anti-Christian dominion shall cease there, and it will be again a place where God will be worshipped in sincerity - a place "even then" of special interest from the recollection of the events which have occurred there. "How long" it is to be before this occurs is known only to Him "who hath put the times and seasons in his own power," Acts 1:7.[8]

Again, the details of when this will occur are not given, only that it is sure to happen.

Another time given to the Gentiles is in Revelation 11:

> A reed like a rod was given to me. Someone said, "Rise, and measure God's temple, and the altar, and those who worship in it. 2 Leave out the court which is outside of the temple, and don't measure it, for it has been given to the nations. They will tread the holy city under foot for forty-two months. 3 I will give power to my two witnesses, and they will prophesy

one thousand two hundred sixty days, clothed in sackcloth."
(Revelation 11:1-3, WEB)

With Revelation being of the apocalyptic genre and symbolic throughout, the temple here is interpreted in the same way it is used in the rest of the New Testament- as a symbol for the Church. The outer court is given to 'the nations,' which is interpreted as 'the Gentiles' in other versions like the KJV and NIV. The time period given here is the same used throughout the Old and New Testament, and it is recognized as the same time that the little horn, the beast, and the dragon have power over the saints- the Roman Antichrist in all of its forms, namely the Papacy, Rome, and the Holy Roman Empire (see chapters 5, 6, 7, and 9 of this book for more on this time).

Perhaps these 'times of the Gentiles' are tied to the period of the desolation of Jerusalem and the 'partial hardening' of Israel. This is what Fleming believed:

> ...Being satisfied that the Jews were to be converted, and that this great event could not be wholly left out in the Revelation, I did at last conclude that this must not be, whatever particular conversions of some part of them might happen, until the final destruction of the Popish party; whose idolatry, villainies, lies and legends, and bloody temper, is the chief thing that prejudices them against Christianity. So that I did at length conclude, that the resurrection or revival of the ancient Jewish church is understood by the resurrection of the martyrs, [Revelation 20:4], who, being thus added to the true reformed Christian church, and making up one body together with those gentile believers, in the fulness or ripened state of the gentile church, shall be to them as life from the dead. See Rom. 11:15-25.[9]

Even still, "'how long' it is to be before this occurs is known only to Him 'who hath put the times and seasons in his own power.'"[10]

Traditional Vs. Modern Interpretation

In the modern popular interpretation, the future of Israel is a mixed bag. Blessings are seen for *national* Israel, Jews that are a part of the modern nation of Israel, and especially Jerusalem. The fact that they are at least mostly back in their homeland is seen as a major fulfillment of prophecy. Many Christians keep Jerusalem under the microscope, because they are expectantly waiting for the Temple to be rebuilt, thus kicking off the Apocalypse.

But very little attention and effort is given regarding their actual salvation, which can only come through their recognition of the Messiah, Jesus Christ. Only a tiny future remnant of Jews are believed to be saved- 144,000 to be exact- and the 'Gentile' Church expects to be long gone by then, already having been raptured at that point. The rest of the unsaved Jews are thought to face the same grim fate as all unbelievers during the tribulation and Armageddon.

This is not the miracle that is promised for Israel in Romans 11. As much of a blessing as the land promises are, how could they ever compare to salvation through their Messiah? And what worth is a physical Temple now, when the blood of a million animal sacrifices would do nothing to cover their sins? The Church is the new Temple- the place where the Spirit of God lives- and Christ is the chief cornerstone. When Jews around the world turn to Christ, they will become living stones in this new Temple! In the New Jerusalem that comes down from heaven, there is no temple building: "I saw no temple in it, for the Lord God, the Almighty, and the Lamb, are its temple" (Revelation 21:22, WEB).

The true miracle is the re-grafting of the natural branches back onto the olive tree, a mass revival of millions of Jews worldwide, not just a tiny remnant. "God is able to graft them in again" (Romans 11:23b), to open their eyes to see Him "whom they have pierced; and they shall mourn for him as one mourns for his only son, and will grieve bitterly for him as one grieves for his firstborn" (Zechariah 12:10b, WEB). This prophecy fills our hearts with hope for Israel, instead of putting a nation in the Middle East on morbid display as some sort of 'doomsday clock'. The new sign of the end times is a mass conversion of Jews to Christ, and our mission is to be a witness to them of the Savior of Israel, rather than contributing to their temple-rebuilding fund.

In God's plan, Jews are neither *separate* nor *replaced* by the Church. Spiritual/ remnant Israel is expanded, now including Gentiles into the same plan of salvation set into motion since the Fall. Now we pray and labor (like Paul did) for their full inclusion once more, knowing that God has promised to graft them in again.

---

1. Paul Enns, "The Moody Handbook of Theology", 740, emphasis mine.

2. This is an unfair accusation, and the view I propose is largely from Reformed teaching on Israel. See R. Scott Clark, "Covenant Theology Is Not Replacement Theology" for more on this. Available online at https://heidelblog.net/2013/08/covenant-theology-is-not-replacement-theology/
It's true, however, that the interpretation I propose for Romans 11 is not universal among Reformed/mainline protestants, and it used to be more common than it is today.
For the three main views on Israel in Romans 11, please see Matt Waymeyer, "The Dual Status of Israel in Romans 11:28", available online at https://tms.edu/wp-content/uploads/2021/09/tmsj16c.pdf

3. Gordon Fee, "How to Read the Bible Book by Book", 319.

4. Fred Klett, "Not Replacement... Expansion".
Available online at https://chaim.org/xpansion

5. Charles Hodge, John Murray, Geerhardus Vos, A. B. Simpson, John Gill, Jonathan Edwards, Charles H. Spurgeon, William Perkins, Samuel Rutherford, John Piper, F. F. Bruce, William Sanday, Arthur C. Headlam, C. E. B. Cranfield, Robert H. Mounce, Douglas J. Moo, Leon Morris, James D. G. Dunn, Thomas R. Schreiner, Robert L. Saucy, S. Lewis Johnson, Jr., Harold W. Hoehner, Everett F. Harrison, to name a few.

6. John Piper, "All Israel Will Be Saved."
Available online at https://www.desiringgod.org/messages/all-israel-will-be-saved

7. Piper, ibid.

8. Barnes, ibid, Luke 21.24.

9. Robert Fleming, "Apocalyptical Key", 95-96.
Available online at https://play.google.com/store/books/details?id=zWEJAQAAMAAJ

10. Barnes, ibid, Luke 21.24.

Chapter Eleven

Where Are We Now?

Revelation 16

"…This book [of Revelation] represents to us, as in a small but exact map, the steadiness and exactness of Providence, and Christ's government of the world."[1]

If the prophecies in Revelation truly are like a map- a divine history of the world that spans centuries- then we should be able to see where we are currently in God's timeline. Just as the prophecies in Daniel revealed events that would span the '400 years of silence' and beyond from when they were given to Daniel, Revelation has revealed the future from when John received the vision to the current day.

It was shown in chapters 1-3 and 5 of this book that the prophecies in Daniel revealed to God's people the worldly empires they would see rise and fall; the rebuilding of Jerusalem and the Temple; the future desecration of that Temple by a specific Greek king; even the revealing of the Messiah who would be 'cut off.' These predicted events were so precise that the Jews were able to recognize events that were unfolding around them and beyond. The first-century

Jewish historian Josephus gives one example: when Alexander the Great visited Jerusalem.

According to Josephus, Alexander had written a letter to the Jewish high priest asking for soldiers and provisions to support his siege of Tyre. The high priest answered that he could not give Alexander what he asked for, as he would not betray the oath they had given the Persian king Darius while he was still living. Alexander did not appreciate this response, and threatened to take down Jerusalem after he was done with Tyre.

After taking Tyre and Gaza, Alexander started making his way to Jerusalem. Jaddus, the high priest, was terrified at the news, and had everyone in the city pray and seek God's help with him as he made sacrifices. God answered him in a dream, "that he should take courage, and adorn the city, and open the gates; that the rest should appear in white garments, but that he and the priests should meet the king in the habits proper to their order, without the dread of any ill consequences, which the providence of God would prevent."[2] Jaddus rejoiced at this word from God, and did exactly as he was told to do.

When Alexander arrived near the city, Jaddus, the priests, and a procession of citizens went out to meet him. Everyone with Alexander was shocked by what happened next: "Alexander, when he saw the multitude at a distance, in white garments, while the priests stood clothed with fine linen, and the high-priest in purple and scarlet clothing, with his mitre on his head, having the golden plate whereon the name of God was engraved, he approached by himself, and adored that name, and first saluted the high-priest."[3] Instead of coming with wrath and vengeance, fresh from conquests, Alexander the Great arrived in peace and reverence! When asked why he did this, he told them that he wasn't adoring the high priest, but rather "that God who has honored him with his highpriesthood."[4] He explained further that God had given him a dream that had this very high priest in it, confirming him in his further conquest of the Persians.

The priests knew precisely where Alexander's conquest was confirmed in the Scriptures: "And when the Book of Daniel was showed him wherein Daniel declared that one of the Greeks should destroy the empire of the Persians, he supposed that himself was the person intended."[5] God had revealed his future plans for Alexander and the Greeks over 200 years earlier (see chapter 2 of this book), and the Jews were able to recognize it.

The nature of apocalyptic prophecy in Scripture has remained the same from Daniel to Revelation. Just as God showed Daniel what major events would occur (relevant to his people and plans) in the centuries before the advent of Christ, he also showed John what would happen (still relevant to his people and plans) in the centuries before the return of Christ. We should be able to point to the place we are at in God's timeline of the world, with perhaps a glimpse of what is to occur, just as the Jews were able to show Alexander what plans God had for him.

This type of understanding is vastly different from the rampant speculation that is inherent to the current trend of shoving every fulfillment of prophecy into the future. It is only possible in the traditional interpretation when we understand what events have already been fulfilled. We cannot expect to understand where we are or where we're headed *if we don't even know where we've been*.

Where We've Been

Just like the example given above for Alexander the Great's appearance in Daniel, traditional interpreters from the past were able to recognize where they were in the grand timeline God had ordained for the Church. We have shown in chapter six of this book that early Christian writers from the second century- less than a century after Revelation was written in about 96- recognized what was to occur before the appearance of the Antichrist. They knew that the Roman Empire had to first fall and be split into ten kingdoms before the little horn from Daniel 7 would come and take power over three of them. They also knew that the Antichrist would be an apostate power- coming from within the Church- and that they would call themselves God in the new temple, the Church. They even guessed what the mark of the beast signified- *Lateinos*, the 'Roman' power in a new form. They predicted all of this from their knowledge of Daniel, 2 Thessalonians, and Revelation, centuries before the events came to pass.

When the Papacy began to seize both spiritual and political power, Christians recognized the prophetic implications. Pope Gregory (540 - 604) called out the bishops who would claim the title of 'Universal Patriarch'- the ultimate head of the Church- as a precursor of the Antichrist. Just a few years after his death, the Roman bishop did just that, accepting the title of the 'Head of all Churches' and 'Universal Bishop' from Emperor Phocas in 607.

In 991, Arnulf (bishop of Orléans) decried the immoral Papacy of his day as Antichrist:

> Looking at the actual state of the papacy, what do we behold? ...Are there, indeed, any bold enough to maintain that the priests of the Lord over all the world are to take their law from monsters of guilt like these — men branded with ignominy, illiterate men, and ignorant alike of things human and divine? ...What would you say of such a one, when you behold him sitting upon the throne glittering in purple and gold? *Must he not be the 'Antichrist, sitting in the temple of God, and showing himself as God'?*[6]

Continuing from Arnulf's day to the height of the Reformation, many Christians recognized their place in the prophetic timeline as those believers under the persecuting powers of the Roman pontiff. Millions of them were killed for exposing and defying the commands of the Papacy, including the Waldenses, Albigenses, Bohemian Brethren, Wycliffites, and Protestants.[7]

During the Reformation and beyond, historicists began to gain consensus on the specific fulfillments of the symbols in Revelation as they looked back into history. What follows is the most common interpretation, which can be studied in detail, verse-by-verse, for free online (see Appendix A for further study resources):

- **The Seven Seals** - *Revelation 4-8:2*. The state of the Church up to the defeat of Paganism in the Roman Empire with Constantine (95 A.D.- 323 A.D.).

- **The Seven Trumpets** - *Revelation 8:2-13*. The judgment and fall of the Western Roman Empire under barbarian invasions with the first four trumpets; the judgment and fall of the Eastern Roman Empire under Islam (Arabs and Turks) with the fifth and sixth trumpets (397 - 1453. See chapter 8 of this book for more on these events).

- **The Little Scroll and the Two Witnesses** - *Revelation 10-11*. This period is commonly understood to be the events surrounding the Protestant Reformation.

- **The Woman and the Dragon** - *Revelation 12*. This vision is understood to be the persecution of the Church by different Roman powers from the 3rd century onward.

- **The Beast out of the Sea** - *Revelation 13*. The civil powers of the Roman Empire in its different forms.

- **The Beast out of the Earth** - *Revelation 13*. The Papal power of Rome, especially related to the revived Holy Roman Empire.

- **The Seven Vials** - *Revelation 16*. The first four vials represent the events surrounding the French Revolution and the Revolutionary Wars that significantly diminished the Papal power in Europe and saw the end of the Holy Roman Empire.

Remarkable Predictions

As they became increasingly convinced of these prophetic fulfillments in their study of the history of the Church, some Christians made remarkable predictions of the Papacy's downfall as foretold in Scripture. In 1701, Robert Fleming mapped out the dates of fulfillment for each of the seals, trumpets, and vials, recognizing that he was living in the time before the fourth vial:

> The fourth poured out his bowl on the sun, and it was given to him to scorch men with fire. 9 People were scorched with great heat, and people blasphemed the name of God who has the power over these plagues. They didn't repent and give him glory. (Revelation 16:8-9, WEB)

Fleming was fairly confident in what had been fulfilled by his day, but he was careful to make any guesses about what lay ahead:

> And now, seeing I have marked out the time we are in at present, it is time also to put a stop to our Apocalyptical thoughts; seeing no man can pretend, upon any just grounds, to calculate *future* times. However, seeing I have come so far, I shall attempt to present you further with some conjectural thoughts on this head; for I am far from the presumption of some men, to give them any higher character.[8]

In reference to the fourth vial, Fleming wrote how the symbols might be fulfilled:

> Now seeing the bombarding of towns and cities was chiefly made use of in these latter wars, we may see how properly the scorching or burning men from above- as if the sun had sent down fire and heat from his own body- is made use of to characterize the time of this vial. But the chief thing to be taken notice of here, is, that the sun, and other luminaries of heaven, are the emblem of princes and kingdoms, as we took notice before. Therefore the pouring out of this vial on the sun

> must denote the humiliation of some eminent Potentates of the
> Romish interest, whose influence and countenance cherish and
> support the Papal cause... Now it is not unusual with God to
> make his enemies crush and weaken one another. And thus I
> suppose this vial is to be understood, when it is said, that upon
> the pouring of it out upon the sun, "power was given to him," i.
> e. the sun, (as most understand the words from the connection)
> "to scorch men with fire." And this is plain in what of the vial is
> fulfilled, and will be, perhaps, more so afterwards.[9]

He guessed that a ruler ('the sun') from a nation that was previously friendly to the Papacy would fight against it, weakening it severely. He went on to guess the time in which this would happen, adding the 1260 years that Scripture said the Antichrist would have power, to the year 552 "when Justinian, upon his conquest of Italy, left it in a great measure to the Pope's management, being willing to eclipse his own authority, to advance that of this haughty prelate."[10] He narrows it down to the year 1811 according to our calendar, or 1794 under the 'prophetic' calendar (360 days per year instead of 365).[11]

Amazingly, this is precisely what happened in history. France was a major ally of the Papacy, known as the 'the eldest daughter of the Church.' The year 1794 was the middle of the French Revolution (King Louis XVI was beheaded in January 1793) and the Revolutionary Wars that sent waves throughout Europe, led by the military and political leader Napoleon Bonaparte. Just as Fleming guessed, this 'sun' harassed the Pope throughout his career, invading Rome, taking the Pope prisoner, confiscating church lands, and eventually causing the end of the Holy Roman Empire, all within 1796-1809.

Fleming continued his guesses of what Revelation 16 foretold with the fifth vial:

> The fifth poured out his bowl on the throne of the beast, and
> his kingdom was darkened. They gnawed their tongues because
> of the pain, 11 and they blasphemed the God of heaven because

of their pains and their sores. They still didn't repent of their works. (Revelation 16:10-11, WEB).

Once again, he forges ahead carefully:

And now, my friends, I may be well excused, if I venture no further, in giving you any more conjectural thoughts upon this present period of time. But seeing I pretend to give my speculations, of what is future, no higher character than guesses, I shall still venture to add something to what I have already said.[12]

Fleming explains the symbol, and the time it might occur:

The fifth vial, verses 10, 11, which is to be poured out on the seat of the beast, or the dominions that more immediately belong to and depend upon the Roman See; that, I say, this judgment will probably begin about the year 1794, and expire about A. D. 1848; so that the duration of it, upon this supposition, will be the space of fifty-four years. For I do suppose, that, seeing the Pope received the title of Supreme Bishop no sooner than A. D. 606, he cannot be supposed to have any vial poured upon his seat immediately, so as to ruin his authority so signally as this judgment must be supposed to do, until the year 1848, which is the date of the twelve hundred and sixty years in prophetical account, when they are reckoned from A. D. 606. But yet we are not to imagine that this vial will totally destroy the Papacy, though it will exceedingly weaken it, for we find this still in being and alive, when the next vial is poured out.[13]

He identifies the fifth vial as a judgment on the Papacy's control over Rome, 'the throne of the beast.' He dates it as happening in 1848, which is 1260 years (using the older 360-day calendar, 1866 in the modern one) from when the Papacy claimed the title of Universal Bishop, head of the entire Church, in 606.

Once again, Fleming's guess is spot on! In the year 1848, there was a revolution in the Italian States. An Italian army of 60,000 soldiers went to Rome and defeated the Pope's army of 10,000 soldiers. "When the old Porta Pia was bombarded, opening a huge hole for the invaders, the Pope asked the white flag to be shown. It was his last act as King of the Papal States."[14] The very seat of the Pope's power was assaulted. "Garibaldi removed the first portion of the States from the Papacy in 1848, and then a piece at a time, the rest of the territory was lost to Papal dominion culminating in the complete loss of the States under Victor Emmanuel in 1870."[15] All of the Pope's civil power was taken from him by 1870, and in 1929 only the current 100-acre Vatican was returned to him:

> In an agreement made with Mussolini in 1929, Vatican city was recognized as a sovereign state and the Pope recognized the kingdom of Italy. The Pope formally accepted one billion, seven hundred fifty million lire for the territory which was taken from him in 1870. He had begun his return to political and temporal authority. They had not repented![16]

Already having such an amazing track record, Fleming continues with the sixth vial: "The sixth angel poured out his bowl on the great river Euphrates, and its water was dried up to prepare the way for the kings from the East" (Revelation 16:12). He writes the meaning and timing of it:

> The sixth vial, verse 12, etc., will be poured out upon the Mahometan anti-Christ, as the former on the Papacy. And seeing the sixth trumpet brought the Turks from beyond Euphrates, from their crossing which river they date their rise; this sixth vial dries up their waves, and exhausts their power, as the means and way to prepare and dispose the Eastern Kings and kingdoms to

> renounce their heathenish and Mahometan errors, in order to
> their receiving and embracing Christianity... Supposing, then,
> that the Turkish Monarchy should be totally destroyed between
> 1818 and 1900, we may justly assign seventy or eighty years
> longer to the end of the sixth vial.[17]

Fleming predicts that the Turkish (Ottoman) Empire- the Eastern Antichrist- will 'dry up' by 1900. Just as their rise was symbolized by being released at the great river Euphrates, their downfall is tied to that same river being dried up.

Once again, Fleming's predictions were strikingly close to what happened in history. The period of the Ottoman Empire's decline is noticeable by the middle of the 19th century- the once mighty and feared power becomes known as 'the sick man of Europe.' The Christian population of the Empire began to pull ahead of the Muslim majority. Between 1908-1922, the Empire was completely dissolved.

What astounding predictions Robert Fleming made over 200 years before they came to pass! And not just the events, but the timing of them as well! Because he understood the nature of apocalyptic prophecy in the Bible, he knew where we were on God's timeline of divine history. He saw what had been fulfilled- where we have been- and so he was able to guess where we were headed with alarming accuracy.

Where We Are

So where are we currently according to Revelation? If Fleming could tell where he was in 1700 with such clarity, shouldn't we be able to do the same today? After the sixth vial, Revelation continues:

> I saw coming out of the mouth of the dragon, and out of the
> mouth of the beast, and out of the mouth of the false prophet,
> three unclean spirits, something like frogs; 14 for they are spirits

of demons, performing signs; which go out to the kings of the whole inhabited earth, to gather them together for the war of that great day of God, the Almighty.

15 "Behold, I come like a thief. Blessed is he who watches, and keeps his clothes, so that he doesn't walk naked, and they see his shame." 16 He gathered them together into the place which is called in Hebrew, "Megiddo".

17 The seventh poured out his bowl into the air. A loud voice came out of the temple of heaven, from the throne, saying, "It is done!" 18 There were lightnings, sounds, and thunders; and there was a great earthquake, such as has not happened since there were men on the earth, so great an earthquake, and so mighty. 19 The great city was divided into three parts, and the cities of the nations fell. Babylon the great was remembered in the sight of God, to give to her the cup of the wine of the fierceness of his wrath. 20 Every island fled away, and the mountains were not found. 21 Great hailstones, about the weight of a talent, came down out of the sky on people. People blasphemed God because of the plague of the hail, for this plague is exceedingly severe. (Revelation 16:13-21, WEB).

We are living in the times before or during the seventh vial, the events of 'Armageddon' [Revelation 16:16, as it is translated in the KJV and NIV]. As Fleming foresaw, the sixth vial had passed when the Ottoman Empire dried up in the early 1900s. Now the powers of spiritual darkness under the symbol of the dragon (pagan/secular), the beast (Roman/Papal), and the false prophet (Islamic) are preparing for the final conflict, "for the war of that great day of God, the Almighty" (Revelation 16:14b, WEB). This war does not necessarily literally take place at the Mountain of Megiddo, rather, it has become a symbol for decisive battles "which would determine the question of the prevalence of true religion on the earth."[18]

What signs should we expect in the fulfillment of Armageddon and the pouring out of the seventh vial?

A Great Earthquake - Earthquakes in Revelation and the rest of the Bible typically symbolize "remarkable political convulsions and revolutions,"[19] just as the violent shaking of the earth changes the landscape. So we should expect revolutions and the changing of nations and governments to a degree that has never been witnessed before in history.

The Great City Divided - This is Babylon, symbolizing the city that has been in view throughout Revelation, the seat of the beast's power: Rome. We should expect Rome (or perhaps more specifically, Vatican City) to be utterly ruined by this threefold judgment- "either a different judgment in regard to some threefold manifestation of that power, or a succession of judgments, as if one part were smitten at a time."[20]

Great Hailstones - Barnes writes, "Perhaps this is an allusion to one of the plagues of Egypt, Exodus 9:22-26... the Attic talent was equal to about 55 lbs. or 56 lbs. Troy weight; the Jewish talent to about 113 lbs. Troy. Whichever weight is adopted, it is easy to conceive what must be the horror of such a storm, and what destruction it must cause."[21] In Barnes' day, there were no bombs with the destructive power that they are capable of now, and it is too easily imaginable that such weapons are what is symbolized by the hailstones. Either way, it will be a plague of mass destruction, centered primarily on the territory of the Papal power.

The Whore Destroyed - Revelation 17 is a closer look at the beast (see chapter 7 of this book), and it gives more details on the destruction of the whore (Roman Papal power) that rides the beast:

> The ten horns which you saw, and the beast, these will hate the
> prostitute, will make her desolate, will strip her naked, will eat
> her flesh, and will burn her utterly with fire. 17 For God has put
> in their hearts to do what he has in mind, to be of one mind,

and to give their kingdom to the beast, until the words of God should be accomplished. 18 The woman whom you saw is the great city, which reigns over the kings of the earth." (Revelation 17:16-18, WEB)

The nations that once served the papacy will be its ultimate downfall. With the description given here, it is easy to imagine how this might happen: it sounds as if they will turn on the papacy, take away the Roman Catholic Church's lands and wealth (make them pay taxes?), and ultimately destroy its presence within their nations. The Roman Catholic Church has already become obnoxious to many Western countries, with centuries-long periods of sexual abuse and genocide being uncovered year after year, all while secularism and atheism become more prevalent. One day these kingdoms will no longer tolerate the Papacy, and bring about its end, burning her 'utterly with fire.'

The Beast and False Prophet Destroyed - It is likely that the battle of Armageddon is referenced in Revelation 19. There it is said that the beast (Rome/Papacy) and the false prophet (Islam) are captured and thrown into the lake of fire:

I saw the beast, and the kings of the earth, and their armies, gathered together to make war against him who sat on the horse, and against his army. 20 The beast was taken, and with him the false prophet who worked the signs in his sight, with which he deceived those who had received the mark of the beast and those who worshiped his image. These two were thrown alive into the lake of fire that burns with sulfur. 21 The rest were killed with the sword of him who sat on the horse, the sword which came out of his mouth. So all the birds were filled with their flesh. (Revelation 19:19-21, WEB)

And so a major sign of the fulfillment of Armageddon and the seventh vial will be the complete destruction of the Papacy and Islam. To be clear, we are not talking about the deaths of 'Catholics' or 'Muslims,' but rather the end of their religious systems and the dark spiritual powers that influence millions worldwide. We would do well to remember that "our struggle is not against flesh and blood, but against the rulers, against the authorities, against the powers of this dark world and against the spiritual forces of evil in the heavenly realms" (Ephesians 6:12). Ultimately we hope for revivals among those populations, and mass conversions to Jesus Christ!

The Dragon Bound - At the end of the battle in Revelation 19, and before the Millennium in Revelation 20, the dragon is bound:

> I saw an angel coming down out of heaven, having the key of the abyss and a great chain in his hand. 2 He seized the dragon, the old serpent, which is the devil and Satan, who deceives the whole inhabited earth, and bound him for a thousand years, 3 and cast him into the abyss, and shut it, and sealed it over him, that he should deceive the nations no more, until the thousand years were finished. After this, he must be freed for a short time. (Revelation 20:1-3, WEB)

Pagan/secular influence in the world will be held in check during the Millennium (in whatever form it takes- see the next chapter of this book). The signs we are to look out for are clear: cataclysmic events are in store for humanity. Some of them are terrifying, such as massive revolutions, destructive storms, and a complete change in governments and nations. Others are much longed for, such as the final destruction of dark spiritual powers that deceive millions, and all pagan/secular influence held in check.

When?

The best traditional interpreters were very careful about dates. We saw above that Fleming did not put much weight behind his guesses, even though he showed amazing foresight. Isaac Newton (1643 - 1727), of mathematician and physicist fame, was also a historicist. He wrote the following about setting dates, and those who would speculate:

> The folly of Interpreters has been, to foretell times and things by this Prophecy, as if God designed to make them Prophets. By this rashness they have not only exposed themselves, but brought the Prophecy also into contempt. The design of God was much otherwise. He gave this and the Prophecies of the Old Testament, not to gratify men's curiosities by enabling them to foreknow things, but that after they were fulfilled they might be interpreted by the event, and his own Providence, not the Interpreters, be then manifested thereby to the world. For the event of things predicted many ages before, will then be a convincing argument that the world is governed by providence.[22]

Despite this caution, he did give a guess alongside another warning:

> So then the time times & half a time are 42 months or 1260 days or three years & an half, recconing [sic] twelve months to a year & 30 days to a month as was done in the Calendar of the primitive year. And the days of short lived Beasts being put for the years of lived [sic] kingdoms, the period of 1260 days, if dated from the complete conquest of the three kings A.C. 800, will end A.C. 2060. It may end later, but I see no reason for its ending sooner. This I mention not to assert when the time

of the end shall be, but to put a stop to the rash conjectures of fancifull men who are frequently predicting the time of the end, & by doing so bring the sacred prophesies into discredit as often as their predictions fail. Christ comes as a thief in the night, & it is not for us to know the times & seasons which God hath put into his own breast.[23]

Newton did not expect to see the end of the Antichrist in his own day, and set a date over 300 years into the future as the earliest it could be. He added 1260 years to when the Papacy fully gained control over three of the ten kingdoms that the Roman Empire had split into, which happened by 800. This brought the time of the end of Rome and the apostate church to 2060.

Some guessed earlier- Fleming had guessed the date from 758, when the Papacy first gained civil power. So he thought the end of the Papacy would be "in or about the year 2000" (Fleming 94). Barnes also felt that it would be around that time. But both of them were careful to label these dates as nothing more than guesses; besides, they lived centuries before those dates. Also, none of them dared to guess the time of the second coming of Christ, of which Jesus himself said, "No one knows of that day and hour, not even the angels of heaven, but my Father only" (Matthew 24:36, WEB).

We should show the same caution. Perhaps Newton is correct, and the Papacy will be destroyed around 2060. But no matter what, 'Christ comes as a thief in the night, & it is not for us to know the times & seasons which God hath put into his own breast.'

Traditional Vs. Modern Interpretation

For the futurist, these prophecies are useless as a map to show us where we are in God's timeline. By the time the events in Revelation begin, they expect the Church to be gone, having been raptured while everyone else is *Left Behind*. At its best, Revelation becomes a spoiler of the end times, confirming that indeed 'God wins.' At its worst, it becomes fuel for fear, speculation, and conspiracies.

Signs of imminent fulfillment are frantically sought after in the news headlines (what's happening in Israel?), astronomical signs (blood moons), and even extra-biblical prophecies are given undue attention (Nostradamus, the Mayan calendar, the prophecy of the Popes).

With the traditional interpretation, we can wait in hopeful patience, knowing that God's plan has been unfolding all of these 2000 years, and he has even given us a glimpse into what he's been doing. This way of understanding prophetic Scriptures could be compared to our parents going on a long trip, not able to say precisely when they would be coming back. But before they left, they gave us an itinerary with a general idea of what they were heading out to accomplish. We would be able to see when stages of their journey had begun or were completed. Sometimes there were even times listed, of how long it would take to complete certain items on the itinerary. What assurance would fill our hearts during the long wait, knowing that they are slowly but surely completing the things they set out to do! We do not know when they'll be home, but they are certain to return as they said they would.

Compare this to the modern futurist interpretation. Our parents leave for the same long journey- years long- and they cannot say when they'll be back. They give us very little indication of when they'll return, only a few ideas about what should happen the very last week of the trip. How anxiously we would look for the signs of this last week, latching on to any and every possibility that it would be the one to indicate their return that we desperately long for!

God has never treated his people like that- a thorough study of Daniel combined with even a cursory understanding of history confirms that God has always given us an idea of what he's doing in the world. Before Jesus ascended into heaven, he told the Church what to expect within one generation- and they listened and obeyed! After he ascended, he came to John to share even more: Christ is worthy to open the seals that reveal the future, and he graciously gave us his final prophecy. We are to wait patiently for Christ's return no matter what, but with growing faith and assurance as we watch events unfold throughout all of these 2000 years.

---

1. Robert Fleming, "Apocalyptical Key", 90.
   Available online at https://play.google.com/store/books/details?id=zW
   EJAQAAMAAJ

2. Flavius Josephus, "Antiquities of the Jews", 11:8:4.
   Available online at https://penelope.uchicago.edu/josephus/ant-11.html

3. Josephus, ibid, 11:8:5.

4. Josephus, ibid, 11:8:5.

5. Josephus, ibid, 11:8:5.

6. Quoted in Philip Schaff, "History of the Christian Church Volume 4",
   290.
   Available online at https://ia800200.us.archive.org/27/items/chris-
   tianchurchh04schauoft/christianchurchh04schauoft.pdf

7. This number may seem sensational, and it would be if the scope was
   limited to specific events and regions (like the Spanish Inquisition).
   Historical theologian Nathan Busenitz remarks, "If the term is used
   in a broad sense—to represent all Roman Catholic activity against
   non-Catholics—then the numbers rise dramatically. If the historian includes forms of torture and killing that did not involve a formal trial,
   along with religious wars and other forms of Catholic violence enacted
   against Protestants and other non-Catholics (in areas outside of Spain and
   Portugal), then one can easily speak in terms of millions of people who
   were killed."
   Available online at https://thecripplegate.com/how-many-peo-
   ple-died-in-the-inquisition/

   For a detailed view of these numbers, see David A. Plaisted's "Estimates of

the Number Killed by the Papacy in the Middle Ages and Later".
Available online at https://static1.1.sqspcdn.com/static/f/827989/1511
6787/1321289366180/50+million+protestants+killed.pdf

8. Fleming, ibid, 70.

9. Fleming, ibid, 68.

10. Fleming, ibid, 72.

11. The calendar that was used when the prophecy was given was 360 days a year. An example of this in the Bible is how the 'times, time, and half a time' (3.5 years) of Daniel and Revelation is related to the 1260 days in Revelation (1260 divided by 3.5 is 360). So Fleming, using the 'prophetic' calendar, comes to his calculation by multiplying 1260 x 360, divided by 365.

12. Fleming, ibid, 72.

13. Fleming, ibid, 80.

14. Wikipedia, "Pope Pius IX."
Available online at https://en.wikipedia.org/wiki/Pope_Pius_IX

15. Fred Miller, "The Incredible Predictions of Robert Fleming."
Available online at http://moellerhaus.com/fleming.htm

16. Miller, "A Panorama Of the Gospel Age", 138.
Available online at http://moellerhaus.com/7bowls.htm

17. Fleming, ibid, 80, 82.

18. Albert Barnes, "Notes, Critical, Illustrative, and Practical", Revelation 16:16.
Available online at https://www.sacred-texts.com/bib/cmt/barnes/rev0 16.htm

19. Barnes, ibid, Revelation 6:12.

20. Barnes, ibid, Revelation 16:19.

21. Barnes, ibid, Revelation 16:21.

22. Isaac Newton, "Observations Upon the Prophecies of Daniel and the
Apocalypse of St. John", 251.
Available online at https://play.google.com/store/books/details?id=rdp
CAQAAMAAJ

23. Newton, "Fragments on the rise of the papacy, with further draft fragments on Revelation", Yahuda MS 7.3g, folio 13 verso.
Available online at https://www.newtonproject.ox.ac.uk/catalogue/reco
rd/THEM00050

Chapter Twelve

The Millennium

Revelation 20

There is a great deal of confusion today when describing modern inter-pretations of Revelation. Most discussions, if they are had at all, revolve around the Millennium- is one premil, postmil, or amil? That is, does Jesus return before the Millennium, or after? Or is the Millennium just a description of the entire church age?

This is like trying to describe the building you live in by only giving details about the roof- "I have a flat roof, and it's white. There's a small parapet in the front"; or "it has a sloped roof with brown asphalt shingles. There's a chimney in the middle." One can make guesses about the architecture of a building based on the roof, but it would be much more helpful to hear about the framework of the building itself- "I live in a classic Chicago 3-story graystone apartment from 1920"; or "my home is a single-story modern ranch style with a two car garage."

The Millennium is only explicitly mentioned in one chapter of the whole Bible: Revelation 20. Additionally, this chapter is a relatively cursory glance at future events compared to the rest of the book:

> There is none of the detail which we have found in the previous
> portions of the book - for such detail was not necessary to the
> accomplishment of the design of the book. The grand purpose

was to show that Christianity would finally triumph, and hence the detailed description is carried on until that occurs, and beyond that we have only the most general statements.[1]

What we have done in these modern times is load our entire framework of interpreting Revelation using the most general description of a somewhat obscure future event. If you explain to someone that you are 'premil,' you've told them that you believe Jesus will return before the Millennium to rule on Earth in person for 1000 years. You've described the 'roof' of the house- what about the framework? We would understand your view of Revelation chapter 20- what about chapters 1-19?

Four Frameworks

Maybe you don't know what you believe about chapters 1-19 because you've only ever heard Revelation discussed in terms of the Millennium. This would be completely understandable, as most Christians today are unaware that there have been four historical frameworks for interpreting Revelation: historicist, preterist, futurist, and idealist. These are summarized by Steve Gregg as follows:

> The **historicist** approach, which is the classical Protestant interpretation of the book, sees the book of Revelation as a prewritten record of the course of history from the time of John to the end of the world. Fulfillment is thus considered to be in progress at present and has been unfolding for nearly two thousand years.

> The **preterist** approach views the fulfillment of Revelation's prophecies as having occurred already, in what is now the ancient past, not long after the author's own time. Thus the fulfillment was future from the point of view of the inspired author, but it is past from our vantage point in history. Some

[partial-preterists] believe that the final chapters of Revelation look forward to the second coming of Christ. Others think that everything in the book reached its culmination in the past.

The **futurist** approach asserts that the majority of the prophecies of Revelation have never yet been fulfilled and await future fulfillment. Futurist interpreters usually apply everything after chapter 4 to a relatively brief period before the return of Christ.

What is generally called the **idealist** approach to Revelation does not attempt to find individual fulfillments of the visions but takes Revelation to be a great drama depicting transcendent spiritual realities, such as the perennial conflict between Christ and Satan, between the saints and the antichristian world powers, the heavenly vindication of the martyrs and the final victory of Christ and his saints. Fulfillment is seen either as entirely spiritual or as recurrent, finding representative expression in various historical events throughout the age, rather than in onetime, specific fulfillments. The prophecy is thus rendered applicable to Christians in any age.[2]

The following chart is a simple visual representation of these views:

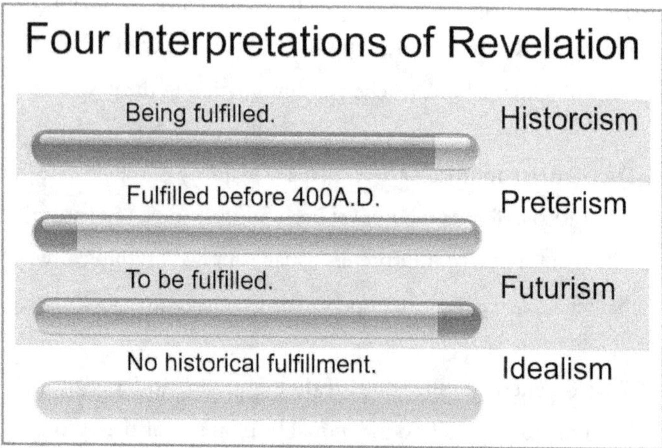

Historicism is the oldest developed framework out of these four views[3]. It is the 'traditional interpretation' given in this book. Developed preterism and futurism were both products of the Counter-Reformation, traced back to Jesuit theologians in a thinly-veiled attempt to keep the Papacy from being identified as the Antichrist.[4] Idealism started to take shape afterward in the late 1800s.[5] Around that same time, futurism gained traction among Christians, and the once ubiquitous historicist view began to diminish. With ideas like the modern interpretation of the rapture being introduced, futurism began to morph into the view most Christians seem to have today, which is called the 'popular modern interpretation' in this book.

Three Views of the Millennium

Once you identify the frameworks of interpreting Revelation, understanding the three views of the millennium becomes much easier. Put simply, Jesus either returns before the Millennium (pre-mil), or after (post-mil); or the Millennium is symbolic of the entire Church age (a-mil). Another chart with a simple overview:

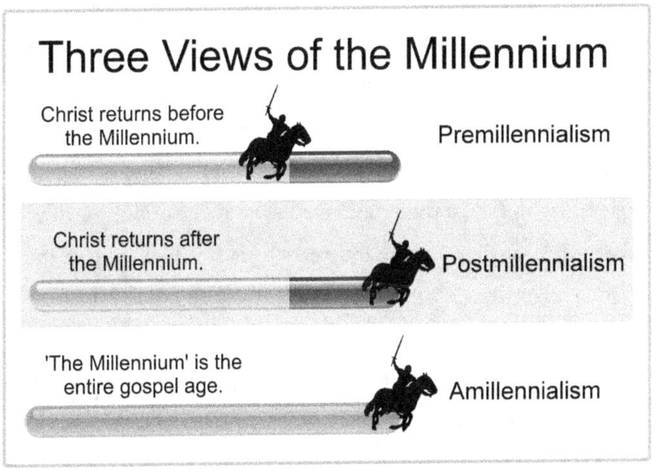

As stated previously, the Millennium is only mentioned in Revelation chapter 20, and in very general descriptions. Each of the three (basic) views has biblical support and reasoning behind them, and this book does not endorse one over the other- it would be better for Christians to understand the framework of what the Church has believed before delving into the confusion of loaded modern definitions of the Millennium. Historicism, the traditional framework of Revelation given in this book, is compatible with all three Millennial views.[6]

Revelation 20

I saw an angel coming down out of heaven, having the key of the abyss and a great chain in his hand. 2 He seized the dragon, the old serpent, which is the devil and Satan, who deceives the whole inhabited earth, and bound him for a thousand years, 3 and cast him into the abyss, and shut it, and sealed it over him, that he should deceive the nations no more, until the thousand years were finished. After this, he must be freed for a short time.

4 I saw thrones, and they sat on them, and judgment was given to them. I saw the souls of those who had been beheaded for the testimony of Jesus, and for the word of God, and such as didn't worship the beast nor his image, and didn't receive the mark on their forehead and on their hand. They lived and reigned with Christ for a thousand years. 5 The rest of the dead didn't live until the thousand years were finished. This is the first resurrection. 6 Blessed and holy is he who has part in the first resurrection. Over these, the second death has no power, but they will be priests of God and of Christ, and will reign with him one thousand years.

7 And after the thousand years, Satan will be released from his prison, 8 and he will come out to deceive the nations which are in the four corners of the earth, Gog and Magog, to gather them together to the war; the number of whom is as the sand of the sea. 9 They went up over the width of the earth, and surrounded the camp of the saints, and the beloved city. Fire came down out of heaven from God and devoured them. 10 The devil who deceived them was thrown into the lake of fire and sulfur, where the beast and the false prophet are also. They will be tormented day and night forever and ever.

11 I saw a great white throne, and him who sat on it, from whose face the earth and the heaven fled away. There was found no place for them. 12 I saw the dead, the great and the small, standing before the throne, and they opened books. Another book was opened, which is the book of life. The dead were judged out of the things which were written in the books, according to their works. 13 The sea gave up the dead who were in it. Death and Hades gave up the dead who were in them. They were judged, each one according to his works. 14 Death and Hades were

thrown into the lake of fire. This is the second death, the lake
of fire. 15 If anyone was not found written in the book of life,
he was cast into the lake of fire. (Revelation 20, WEB)

This chapter is the capstone of the book, the happy end (or as some view
it, a synopsis) of the gospel age. The beast and the false prophet are gone, and
the dragon is bound. The saints reign with Christ for 1000 years. Despite one
last rebellion, fire comes down to devour them, and the final judgment of all
people begins. What follows are brief definitions of the three major views of this
chapter, along with their modern loaded definitions:

Premillennialism - Basically, Christ returns in person before the Millennium. According to this view, the saints are raised to life bodily in "the first
resurrection" (Revelation 20:5), and they reign together with Christ on Earth
(Israel in particular) for 1000 years. At the end of the Millennium, after the
unleashing of Satan and the final rebellion is put down, the rest of the dead are
raised and judged.

The strength of this view is that it takes the plainest meaning of the first
resurrection, and a literal in-person reign of Christ. It is said to be the type
of fulfillment that prophecies given to Israel in the Old Testament point to.
A possible weakness is that it is a very literal interpretation in a book full of
symbols. It raises some questions- why is it said that only martyrs from the time
of the beast are raised, and not all saints? Also, the rest of Scripture points to
a single resurrection of all people simultaneously, not one for the saints and
another for everyone else.

Modern Premil - Today's definition of premillennialism is tied to the
framework of 'futurism'- the interpretation that the book of Revelation still
awaits fulfillment in a very short period of time yet to come. It is heavily associated with *Left Behind* theology, a 'secret' rapture in which Christians are taken
away either before, during, or after (pre-trib, mid-trib, or post-trib respectively)
a future 'great tribulation.' A remnant of Jews is saved during this tribulation,
standing up against a future Antichrist in the form of a charismatic, deceptive,
and maniacal leader.

Because of its focus on a third Temple and the land promises of Israel, modern premil and futurism are thought to be the only views that have a future hope for Israel and the Jews. These views are associated with dispensationalism, which sees the Church as separate from Jews (see chapter 10 of this book for more on that subject). This was not the case in the history of the church- Christians of every kind of eschatological view saw a future hope for Jews, and a clear prophecy of their mass conversion to Christ in Romans 11. Premillennialism was also not tied to futurism, and there are (and have been) many historicists that hold to the classic version of this view.

Postmillennialism - Christ returns after the Millennium, which is either literally 1000 years, or possibly symbolic for a long period of time. The Millennium begins after Armageddon, when the beast (the Papacy) and false prophet (Islam) are gone, and the dragon (paganism/secularism) is bound. The first resurrection is seen not as a literal bodily one, as only "souls of those who had been beheaded for the testimony of Jesus" (Revelation 20:4, WEB) were seen, not their bodies. This resurrection is viewed as a revival of the principles and values of those martyrs, a long period of peace when the Church is united and leads the nations.

The strength of this view is that it is consistent with the heavy use of symbolism in Revelation, and is in line with the rest of Scripture's teaching on a single resurrection. A weakness of it might be its de-emphasis of the land promises to Israel in the Old Testament, and the lack of a visible, bodily reign of Christ over the nations (until after the Millennium, that is).

Modern Postmil - Just as premillennialism has shifted focus and changed definitions in modern history, the view of postmillennialism has also changed drastically. It is now tied to the framework of (partial) *preterism*, the view that most of Revelation was fulfilled in the first few centuries of the Church. Instead of there being a marked time when the Millennium begins (after Armageddon), it is now usually said to have already started, and that we are currently living in those times. This is why postmillennialism is labeled as an 'optimistic' eschatology. Things in the world are said to be slowly getting better and better as biblical principles take hold. As proof of this, modern postmillennialists point to statistics showing the reduction of global poverty, crimes, and deaths.

Another consequence of this major shift is the use of Christian nationalism as a theological tool- the Church is destined to reign, so it must 'rise up' and take hold of civil power in this time of the Millennium. Some would say that Mosaic laws such as the death penalty for blasphemy should become civil laws, ushering in a new theocratic rule. Again, this is far different than the classic postmil view, where there is a marked time that the Millennium begins- after Armageddon, when the enemies of the church are no more. This is not the Church's doing, but by the display of God's power and judgment. Many famous historicists were postmillennialists, and they would not recognize the version of it that is popular today.

Amillennialism - This view of the Millennium sees it as a synopsis or overview of the entire age of the Church, from when Jesus founded it to when he returns. Miller calls it "a panorama of the Gospel age."[7] Amillennialism means 'no' Millennium, and the events are viewed as symbolic of the realities of our new life in Christ until he returns. The binding of the dragon is a symbol of Christ binding Satan through the event of the crucifixion; the apostles sit on the thrones of judgment through their words in the Scripture; Christians are those who are resurrected into a new life through the power of God, reigning with Christ as kings and priests; the end of the Millennium is the releasing of Satan for one last battle, whom Christ slays at his second coming.

A strength of this view is that the symbols can easily be compared to our new life in Christ as described in the New Testament, and it is a beautiful picture summary of those realities. It keeps things simple, showing one final battle of Armageddon, the return of Christ, a single resurrection of all people, and then the last judgment. One issue that it brings up is the reality of Satan's work in the world today, some of which is described in the events from Revelation 1-19- so how can it be said that he is truly 'bound'?

Modern Amil - The framework of *idealism*- the view that sees Revelation as symbolic of spiritual realities instead of specific chronological events- is now heavily associated with amillennialism. If one were to be labeled as 'amil', it would be implied that they were idealist. Because of the similarities in their approach to interpretation of the symbols in Revelation, it is easy to see how these views can go hand-in-hand. However, this is not necessarily always the case, as some historicists and preterists hold to the amillennialist view of the Millennium.

Traditional Vs. Modern Interpretation

For most Christians today, the four major frameworks of interpreting the bulk of Revelation have been forgotten, or lumped in with the three views of the Millennium in chapter 20. It becomes even more confusing when the modern definitions of those Millennial views have changed radically.

But even if you disagree with the historicist framework, my hope is that you'll realize that there is more than just the currently popular futurist interpretation out there, and that you'll better understand how to define and navigate the historical views outlined in this chapter.

When I first became aware of the historicist interpretation, I was awestruck. My mind was blown when I realized that the view I had absorbed throughout my entire church life wasn't the one that the Church held from the beginning, but rather the opposite- it was a relatively recent innovation! In my zeal, before I had fully grasped the intricacies of this classic view, I started to share it with my friends and family. I found out quickly that for many of them, challenging the only view they had ever heard about their whole life was a sure way to be nearly branded a dangerous heretic!

Many of us consider our eschatological views to be issues of the utmost importance, and any disagreement with them rises to the level of a first-order issue, alongside the most fundamental doctrines of our faith. We consider them to be settled; not open for discussion.

It would benefit Christians immensely to reconsider the priority they place on their eschatological view. Dr. Mohler writes that "God's truth is to be defended at every point and in every detail, but responsible Christians must determine which issues deserve first-rank attention in a time of theological crisis."[8]

He suggests a sort of 'theological triage,' an ordering of doctrines according to their importance, in much the same way that the triage nurse at an emergency room ranks the seriousness of a medical emergency. He suggests the following order:

> First-level theological issues would include those doctrines most central and essential to the Christian faith. Included among these most crucial doctrines would be doctrines such as the Trinity, the full deity and humanity of Jesus Christ, justification by faith, and the authority of Scripture... These first-order doctrines represent the most fundamental truths of the Christian faith, and a denial of these doctrines represents nothing less than an eventual denial of Christianity itself...

> The set of second-order doctrines is distinguished from the first-order set by the fact that believing Christians may disagree on the second-order issues, though this disagreement will create significant boundaries between believers. When Christians organize themselves into congregations and denominational forms, these boundaries become evident... Second-order issues would include the meaning and mode of baptism... In recent years, the issue of women serving as pastors has emerged as another second-order issue...

> Third-order issues are doctrines over which Christians may disagree and remain in close fellowship, even within local congregations. *I would put most of the debates over eschatology, for example, in this category.* Christians who affirm the bodily, historical, and victorious return of the Lord Jesus Christ may differ over timetable and sequence without rupturing the fellowship of the church. Christians may find themselves in disagreement over any number of issues related to the interpretation of diffi-

cult texts or the understanding of matters of common disagreement. Nevertheless, standing together on issues of more urgent importance, believers are able to accept one another without compromise when third-order issues are in question.[9]

Christians should be able to stay in close fellowship with one another, even when their eschatological frameworks or millennial views are different. We should have no reserve in studying or discussing these views constructively, sharpening one another.

If nothing else, please do not lose sight of God's faithfulness in the past, even as our culture fixates on the details of the future. Do not forget the amazing fulfilments of God's promises in Daniel: the prediction of world empires before they appeared; the precise timeline given for the coming of the Messiah; the exact number of days that the Temple would be defiled under the terror of Antiochus Epiphanes before he met his end; the warning Christ gave to the disciples of the destruction of Jerusalem and the Temple. Only our God knows the future, and as the Bible shows us, he does not leave his people without a prophetic word of what is to come.

---

1. Albert Barnes, "Notes, Critical, Illustrative, and Practical", Revelation 20 introduction.
   Available online at https://www.sacred-texts.com/bib/cmt/barnes/rev0 20.htm

2. Steve Gregg, "Revelation: Four Views, Revised & Updated", 13.

3. See Gregg, ibid, 48-55. Gregg points out the earliest interpretations (also in chapter 6 of this book) of a future apostate Antichrist coming from within the Church, appearing after Rome falls and claiming 3 of the 10 kingdoms that appear from its ruins- these are the foundations of a historicist framework. "Events, which later historicists would view as ancient

history, were, in those days, present and future realities. This means that the fathers would have spoken futuristically, even if they were identifying the prophetic events with the same phenomena that historicists, and some preterists, now associate with past fulfillments."
A more developed historicism is seen in the 12th century, while futurism and preterism are developed during the Counter-Reformation in the 16th century. The idealist view is developed during the 18th century.

4. Gregg, ibid, 52-53: "Coming to the defense of the papacy, Spanish Jesuits presented two alternative approaches to the historicism of the Reformers. One response was that of Francisco Ribera (1537–1591), a professor at Salmanca, who taught that John, in Revelation, only foresaw events of the near future and of the final things at the end of the world, but had none of the intervening history in view... This was the beginning of many of the ideas that later developed into features of the modern futurist approach to Revelation. Another Jesuit scholar, Luiz de Alcazar (1554–1613), introduced a preterist approach to Revelation, in which chapters 4 through 11 were interpreted as depicting the church's struggle against Judaism, culminating in the fall of Jerusalem in AD 70; while chapters 12 through 19 reflect the church's struggle with paganism, ending in the fall of Rome in 476; and chapters 20 through 22 as the triumph of the church in papal Rome."

5. Gregg, ibid, 53.

6. Three historicist authors quoted extensively in this book each have different views of the Millennium: Albert Barnes was postmillennial, Oral Collins was premillennial, and Fred Miller was amillennial.

7. Fred Miller, "Revelation: A Panorama of the Gospel Age", 169.

8. Albert Mohler, "A Call for Theological Triage and Christian Maturity." Available online at https://albertmohler.com/2005/07/12/a-call-for-theological-triage-and-christian-maturity

9. Mohler. ibid.

Chapter Thirteen

Appendix A

Resources for Further Study

I t is well worth diving deeper into the historicist interpretation of many Bible passages not covered in this book, which was only meant to be an accessible introduction. Many free resources are available online, but they are often older books.

Albert Barnes, *Notes, Critical, Illustrative, and Practical*

Albert Barnes (Dec. 1, 1798 - Dec. 24, 1870) "was an American theologian, clergyman, abolitionist, temperance advocate, and author. Barnes is best known for his extensive Bible commentary and notes on the Old and New Testaments, published in a total of 14 volumes in the 1830s."[1] Historicist author Fred Miller (who I've quoted in this book and recommend below) calls Barnes "the master of historical interpretation, bar none!"[2] The best part is his *Notes* can be found for free online in many places and formats- I have used the site *sacred-texts.com* in this book, but they are also on *studylight.org*, *biblehub.com*, *Google Play Books*, and many more. Old physical copies (separated into many volumes or specific books) of his *Notes* can also be found for purchase.

Because they cover the entire Bible, they are a great resource for any particular passage one is curious about, but for a beginner to the historicist interpretation I recommend starting with Barnes' *Notes* on Daniel 7.

https://www.sacred-texts.com/bib/cmt/barnes/dan007.htm

Fred Miller, *Revelation: A Panorama of the Gospel Age*

Fred Miller (May 8, 1931 - Feb. 9, 2018) was an American scholar of ancient Greek and Hebrew, as well as an author, preacher, and teacher who planted churches in New England and founded a school for ministry in Vermont.[3] He created the website *moellerhaus.com* that his family maintains, which is full of his writings and other resources. His book on the historicist interpretation, *Revelation: A Panorama of the Gospel Age*, is no longer in print, but it is available to read for free from his website. His approach to prophecies he believes are related to Russia and Ukraine seems novel to me, and I don't entirely agree with all of his views, but he is a rigorous scholar that deserves a look.

http://moellerhaus.com/revdir.htm

Oral Edmond Collins, *The Final Prophecy of Jesus: An Introduction, Analysis, and Commentary on the Book of Revelation*

Dr. Oral Collins (May 9, 1928 – Jan. 14, 2013) is a serious scholar, archaeologist, and educator with an impressive academic career at Gordon-Conwell and Brandeis. He wrote the best modern academic treatment of historicism, *The Final Prophecy of Jesus*. It's a great book, but it's only available in a physical format for no less than $40-$70. It's also a very dense tome, and not geared to beginners in the subject. Collins actually has an Adventist background, but his approach to the historicist interpretation rejects all of the errors from that system. It can be purchased from Amazon:

https://www.amazon.com/Final-Prophecy-Jesus-Introduction-Commentary/dp/1556352603

Steve Gregg, *Revelation: Four Views, Revised and Updated*

Steve Gregg is a Bible teacher, author, and radio talk show host. His book *Revelation: Four Views* is a parallel commentary of the futurist, preterist, historicist, and idealist views of Revelation, all side by side. It's not the best way to learn about historicism in particular, but the book is a good tool to get an overview of the four major views. Gregg does a good job of giving a neutral perspective of each view. It can be found on Amazon in multiple formats:

https://www.amazon.com/Revelation-Parallel-Commentary-Revised-Updated/dp/1401676219

Other Authors to Check Out...

Many other classic books on the historicist perspective are available for free online. Some of them are easier to read than others, but each of the authors are scholars in their own right:

Thomas Newton, *Dissertations on the Prophecies*

Edward Bishop Elliott, *Horae Apocalypticae*

Henry Grattan Guinness, *History unveiling prophecy*

Robert Fleming, *Apocalyptical Key*

Isaac Newton, *Observations Upon the Prophecies of Daniel and the Apocalypse of St. John*

Thomas Rawson Birks, *First Elements of Sacred Prophecy*

...And Some to Avoid

Sadly, there are some authors associated with what they would call 'historicism', which is usually bundled with problematic or even heretical ideas such as Seventh-Day Adventism, Nontrinitarianism, Anglo/British-Israelism, Christian Identity, and Neo-Confederacy:

Ellen G. White

Le Roy Edwin Froom

Robert Caringola

Charles Jennings

Roger Rusk

Truth In History, truthinhistory.org

---

1. Wikipedia, "Albert Barnes (theologian)."
Available online at https://en.wikipedia.org/wiki/Albert_Barnes_(theol
ogian)

2. Fred Miller, "Revelation: A Panorama of the Gospel Age", 137.
Available online at http://moellerhaus.com/7bowls.htm

3. From his obituary, available online at https://www.almonfuneralhome.c
om/obituaries/Frederick-Peter-Miller?obId=2958685#/obituaryInfo